A Summer in Tuscany

By

Sandra J. Swanson

ISBN 1-58500-416-2

1stBooks - rev. 06/20/00

About the Book

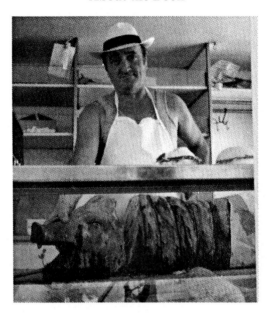

The porchetta and the porchetta man

A Summer in Tuscany is read with a warm smile. Funny, informative, thoughtful, the book takes you to the heart of the Italian countryside and into the lives of Tuscany's most charming characters.

Readers who harbor a dream to "live Italian" for a few weeks or for a few months will find the book invaluable. Go on an odyssey with a budding American opera star and her "entourage," (her family) to rent a villa in Tuscany and a palace in Spoleto. Pack light; you'll travel in a stick shift Fiat (a.k.a. Fix It Again, Tony).

Sit back on the terrace of a Tuscan villa overlooking the vineyards, olive trees, and medieval town. Go along to the Prada outlet and to an accidental dinner dance given by the local

Communist party. Visit a famous Antinori vineyard and meet the vineyard owner. Wander through streets made for handcarts, wind your way through the white roads of Chianti, experience the world's most luxurious spa and Lucca's famous market, where an entire shop sells only horse meat; steaks, ground, chops.

Pack drip-dry clothes. Italy hangs its wash out to dry. Struggle with buying Italian detergent and then wrestle with the Italian washing machine. Watch a Perugina prostitute pose. Shop Deruta, home of the famous Italian majolica. Learn how to make a truffled omelet and how to sauté squash blossoms so that the flowers open on your plate. Encounter a shadowy band of gypsies, a ring of pickpockets. Go to the young Diva's first night opera performance, a dinner with Tony Blair, lunch at Maria de' Medici's.

Along the way, the reader will learn enough Italian to bargain in the local open air markets where English is not spoken, to order in a ristorante where no English translations are available, to taste the best wine at the degustatione where the winemaker will give you a special deal on a case of Chianti merely because you know how to say "degustatione" (day-goo-staht-see-OH-nay). Make yourself clearly understood by the gimlet-eyed Italian barber as he sharpens his strop! The Italian language and pronunciations are inserted seamlessly in the text.

Summer in Italy, from the comfort of your chair. Once you've finished the last page, you'll want to start reading again from the first page. Travelers will want to take many of the pages of *A Summer in Tuscany* along to Italy. Many excellent photographs.

-- ML Ford

R e a d y ...

*T*he 747 swooped through the Swiss Alps at day break. Through the scratched windows, I glimpsed the first land features I had seen since our San Francisco connector flight left the shimmering summer heat of Dulles Airport at dusk. It was snowing. A rainbow ribboned past the window. The plane dipped. The first light caught the Matterhorn. I hadn't expected the Matterhorn. I was dazzled.

The previous dawn, my husband, our two daughters, ages 21 and 24, and I were driving across the Golden Gate Bridge to the airport, our headlights poking holes in San Francisco's July fog. The two impressions of fog and snow whited out my mind, numbed by a dozen hours of sitting in airplanes. The details of the previous months of planning unraveled. I was glad I had written everything down.

*T*he first thread of our family Italian summer was spun the day after Christmas, nearly six months before the Matterhorn sighting. Six months of planning for one summer in Italy.

Shuffling through the Christmas cards that chilly day, my oldest daughter, Cristina, found the letter she had been thinking about since it came in the mail weeks before. It was from Yann, a 25 year-old Parisian friend; a budding opera singer. He had sent her the name and phone number of a voice coach in Italy with whom he had studied. He highly recommended the voice coach for Cristina, who was also studying opera.

We trusted Yann. He and Cristina had performed a joint recital in October. Cristina is a soprano. Yann is a tenor, with *attitude* or "color." He's also rather tall, with romantic, wavy, long blonde hair, great bones, and Danube blue eyes; although I understand that the Danube is no longer as blue as Yann's eyes. Yann said the Italian coach would be perfect for Cristina, to add some "coloratura;" color, to her voice.

After listening to Yann, whose performance the audience described as "highly dramatic," Cristina felt that by contrast, her singing was umm ... flat. She attached herself immediately to the idea of studying in Italy (though I sensed a nostalgic pull to see Yann in Paris). Fortuitously, Cristina had studied Italian for two years in high school and one in college. She spoke some Italian, she sang some. At 24, caught in the after-college-before-career doldrums, she was also ready for an adventure, a trip anywhere away from home.

Ignoring the rubble of Christmas past, we found the globe and learned that nine hours separated California from Italy. It was 9:00 a.m. on the day after Christmas in California. It would be 6:00 p.m. in Italy. Yann's note gave us the voice coach's number -- a local Italian area code and seven digits -- but no indication of how to dial into Italy. Cristina looked in the phone book. She handed me the phone and read, "Press 011, then the country number -- 39 -- then the area code and the local number and the pound sign to make the call go through faster."

Juggling Yann's note, the globe, and the phone, I pressed the number sequence, wondering if the Italians have buttons on their phones and if the voice coach spoke English.

"Pronto!" a woman's voice answered immediately, startling me out of my pondering.

"Kate? Um. Hello? Is Kate there, please?" I yammered uncertainly, as the globe crashed to the floor.

"Yes, my dear, this is Kate." A voice of music lilted across the Atlantic and drifted over the North American continent.

I stammered. Cristina looked at me quizzically. I nodded to her and mouthed, "She speaks English!" I introduced myself to Kate and told her that Yann had given me her phone number. She remembered Yann. How was he, she asked in her lyrical voice. I told her about the joint recital, a good segue into the real subject. I told her that Yann thought my daughter Cristina should study with her. There. In Italy, that is, this summer? That Cristina is a soprano, that she has perfect pitch, that she graduated from college with honors as a music major, that she reads music the way most people read books ... that ... that ... I rattled on, as mothers do. When I looked up, I saw Cristina standing there, shaking her head, laughing. She left the room.

Kate Gamberucci told me she was originally from Scotland, a fact that explained her first name and her endearing brogue. She was now Profes-soressa of Canto; Professor of Singing, at the Florence Conservatory of Music. She took private students during the summer, at her home in San Gimignano. When she pronounced the name of this town, I wrote it phonetically, for future reference: Sahn-Jim-ee-NYAH-noh. Kate said she would be pleased to work with Cristina. Yann's recommendation was all she needed to accept her as a student. They could begin working together any time after July 10, the date Kate would finish teaching her classes at the Florence Conservatory. Cristina could come to her house for lessons three or four times a week.

Friends of a friend, we chatted as confidants. She was married but currently separated from her husband and they had a teenage daughter. I wondered to myself if the two facts were causally related. Kate rarely had American students. Mostly, her students were from Italy. She had never had a student from California. She suggested that since Cristina was making such a long trip, she should study with her five or six weeks.

"Also, dear," she intoned, "I'm taking a small company of singers to study and perform near Spoleto at the end of summer. We'd be pleased to have Cristina come along." Flabbergasted at our success, I thanked her profusely and said I'd talk it over with Cristina and we'd call her again in a few days if that was OK.

She said "ciao." I repeated the word back to her. It sounded good. So -- the Italians really did say "ciao."

It took me a while to read the notes I had scrawled and to relay the info to Cristina, and a nano second for her to jump on board. We were both breathless. Crist said she'd better write to Yann to thank him and to tell him the good news.

I got out the cumbersome World Atlas. The large book taught us how to spell San Gimignano (Sahn-Jim-ee-NYAH-noh) and located the town in the heart of Tuscany and in the center of Chianti, a bit southwest of Florence and a smidge northeast of Siena. A coffee table book of Italy that I'd never opened before described San Gimignano as Tuscany's most

3

impressive medieval walled town. The book likened the town of towers to "a mini Manhattan." Thirteen of the town's 76 original twelfth and thirteenth century towers still stood. The others had been destroyed over centuries of family feuds.

Sahn-Jim-ee-NYAH-noh

Cristina and I stared at the photo of the picturesque town. "How colorful," we agreed excitedly, referring to the medieval family feuds. The local San Gimignano wine was Vernaccia, a crisp white wine, and the town was surrounded by Vernaccia vineyards.

We found Spoleto in the Atlas, also a medieval walled town, south of Tuscany in the province of Umbria, a bit north of Rome and a whisker south of Assisi. We knew it to be a famous art and music center. A photograph in the book showed a magnificent opera house. Cristina and I quickly committed ourselves to at least eight weeks in Italy.

Over the next few days, we talked over our project with Robert, my husband, and Jensen, our younger daughter. We showed them the Atlas and the book with the photographs, trying to entice them to come along on our adventure, if only for

4

part of the time. There would be plenty for us to do while Crist was getting "colored," I explained. I didn't want to spend eight weeks away from them.

Robert said he could join us for a little while. Jensen had to be back at her university in late August. She'd come until then, IF she could bring a friend. She looked at me slyly. "Maybe Laura?" she asked. Laura Granucci is Italian. She and Jensen met in high school and became attached at the hip. They went to different colleges and now they saw each other only on vacation, but they had remained close friends. I thought of Laura as my third daughter. Jensen went off to phone her.

Over the holidays, I had mentioned the possibility of an Italian sojourn to Robert's aunt and uncle, who were then visiting from New York. They said they had no summer plans. In fact, they planned to retire in May and had made no summer plans beyond planting a garden. They said, "We could plant a smaller garden. Italy sounds good!" When I phoned to tell them our news, I asked again if they would like to join us. They said, "Si!" They had already bought Italian tapes.

We had an enthusiastic group. We needed accommodations; a place to stay near San Gimignano (Sahn-Jim-ee-NYAH-noh) for at least six weeks, then another place for a few weeks in Spoleto, and places to stay on our way there and back. We needed a tour guide. I volunteered to fill the position.

I had been to Italy years ago on a sort of college survey tour. I had seen the familiar Italian landmarks with my group: Rome, Florence, Venice, Pisa, Siena, Orvieto, and Assisi. Our group had visited dozens of churches and taken slide photos of each other with the most famous sights. We took guided tours of the major museums.

On a typical day, our bus would arrive in say Pisa, in the morning, and unload us for a few hours. Our guide would walk us through the high points of the town, leaving an hour or so free for us to do some souvenir shopping and photo snapping. Then he'd load us back into the bus and we'd proceed to our next destination. Every minute of our time was planned, including most of the meals. I remembered that we had "done" Assisi and Orvieto in one day. I couldn't remember which town was which.

This time, I envisioned living in a sprawling, private villa, surrounded by vineyards. We'd have a cook. A huge swimming pool. I'd take long naps after superb alfresco lunches. This wouldn't be a sightseeing tour of Italy. It would be a real vacation, as close to a native experience as possible; Italian summering. We'd have a car, too. No packing into busses for us. On days when Crist didn't have singing lessons, we'd explore. We'd take the back roads. We'd wander through towns we had never heard of, poke through the outdoor markets, taste wine, buy olive oil. Some days, we'd simply bask in the summer heat by our pool. Cristina's performance with the opera company would be the summer's crescendo. The family agreed on three of my visions: No forced marches through museums. A car. A swimming pool. They were engaged.

I eagerly responded to all ads offering "Villas in Tuscany" or "Italian Villas." I found them in *The New York Times,* in our local papers, and in the back pages of upscale magazines. I paid as much as $15.00 for some brochures, while others were free. The brochures; many of them heavy, glossy, color magazines really, began to arrive the first week of January.

Paging through them was frustrating. The villas were located in unfamiliar, unpronounceable towns. I didn't know the Italian geography. I didn't know the Italian language. Robert ordered some Italian language tapes. We all listened to them from time to time. I bought three Michelin road maps of Italy from a local travel shop -- the map of all of Italy, of Central Italy, and the map of North Eastern Italy. I carefully unfolded the maps, knowing I would have to refold them to take with us to use on the road. I taped them to the dining room windows. The large road maps blocked out the sun, forcing me to turn on the dining room lights during the day.

I spread out the many villa books on the dining room table. We ate in the kitchen until July. I studied the confusing maps as if they were the Rosetta Stone.

The regional Italian maps were measured in kilometers, another subject I knew nothing about. Three-inch Post-It's were the same width as 18.6 miles, a fairly easy "yardstick" for measuring approximate distances. For example, Florence, which I now called "Firenze," (fee-REN-say) was about one and a half Post-It's from San Gimignano; under 30 miles. I wrote on a Post-It: "Firenze to S. G. -- 30 miles" and attached it to the map of cental Italy, where Tuscany is located.

Most of the rental villas, I soon learned, were originally large houses, now broken into apartments with mysterious names such as Francesca and Marco. (Many of the names turned out to be those of the villa owners' children.) The apartments shared the villa's common facilities; perhaps a swimming pool, a garden, or a terrazza (tair-AHT-sah); an outdoor terrace.

An apartment that "slept seven" averaged between $1200 and $2100 a week. The larger villas, the ones of my dreams, were not divided into apartments, but they were far more expensive: $10,000 a week was not an uncommon rental price. We didn't particularly want to share a pool or a terrazza with strangers, but we weren't prepared to spend $10,000 a week for exclusivity.

An alternative was the agrivillas; apartment rentals on working farms. The idea of living and helping out on a farm appealed to us. We imagined getting up early to feed adorable farm animals and to pick armloads of sunflowers and lavender. But the fine print described the typical agrivilla apartment as having one bathroom for every three double bedrooms and the locations were remote from even the smallest towns.

Sitting at the kitchen table after breakfast one day, Cristina said, "Listen to this!" She read to me from one of the farm brochures: "The Tuscan countryside is full of vipers. If you are bitten, you have a half hour to take the serum." What the serum was and where to get it, the book did not say. Cristina furrowed her brows at me. I furrowed back. We decided against life on the farm or anywhere more than 20 minutes from a good pharmacy or, as we had learned from our Italian tapes, a farmacia (farm-ah-CHEE-ah.) The project was becoming more complicated than we had expected. That a single -c in a word was pronounced as "ch" was something I had to repeat to myself many times a day. "Just think of 'ciao,'" Cristina said helpfully.

I read through the villa books, turning down the corners of the pages that showed the most appealing homes. I bought sticky red dots and attached these to the tiny towns on the map where my first-pick villas were located. I jotted distances between the red-dotted towns and San Gimignano on Post-It's and stuck them to the map, too. Robert began referring to our dimly-lighted dining room as "The War Room," and to my efforts as "Mom's March on Tuscany."

By mid-January I had narrowed the villa choices from many hundreds to the few dozen that met our requirements. Each had a swimming pool, one modern bath for each double bedroom, and they were all within a Post-It or two of San Gimignano (Sahn-Jim-ee-NYAH-noh), a name I could now say without hesitating too much.

Books in hand, I phoned the agents who represented the villas. The villas I liked were either already booked or not "up to standard," meaning the agents had not actually seen them and so they could not, "in good faith," recommend them. In any event, they informed me in a business-like way, I was several months too late to get anything "decent." Most people, they advised, notably the British, booked a year in advance. I hadn't fully realized that I was competing for reservations with a world-wide community. The agents chuckled at my naïveté and alluded to Tuscany as "Chiantishire."

I put aside the brochures I had pored over for so many hours until only one remained. It was from a villa agent right here in San Francisco. I phoned. Yes, the villa I liked was available. The agent had been there. He had slides. He'd send them. Phone when you get them, he said.

The slides came. We were elated. The villa was magnificent. A terrace framed by an elegant archway looked out over vineyards. The ceilings were high, the floors were polished terra-cotta. The many windows were trained on views of the

Tuscan countryside. The baths were modern. The swimming pool was large and crystal clear. I had found the ideal Tuscan home for us, just two Post-Its from San Gimignano. It was a bit more than we wanted to spend, but I knew that we had run out of options. Jubilant, I phoned the agent to reserve the villa for six weeks.

As we chatted about the final details of the reservation, he paused and mused, "You know, you don't want this place. It's too far from San Gimignano. You have to be in San Gim (San-JIM) several times a week. If you got behind a tractor, it could take you an hour each way. For your purposes, you should be within walking distance of town." He said there was a San Gim villa rental specialist in London. He gave me the fax number. Deflated, I faxed off to London a request for info on a villa for six or seven people, within walking distance of San Gim, with a swimming pool and modern bathrooms, for six weeks or so sometime after July 10.

The next morning, January 21, several pages of the now-familiar villa data were waiting in my fax tray. The London agent had taken the liberty of forwarding my request to the local San Gim agent, whose cover letter politely explained that only one "suitable" villa remained. It was a 20 minute walk to San Gimignano, and about 100 meters from a wonderful, local ristorante, ri-store-AHN-tay; restaurant. There was a swimming pool, a modern bathroom for each bedroom, a terrace, a view of San Gim. The villa was surrounded by vineyards and olive orchards. The agent, who was also British, would give us a substantial discount if we reserved for six weeks. Did I care to book the villa? I faxed a Yes, also asking her about a cook. I phoned for airline reservations. When they were confirmed, I contacted Kate to confirm our arrangement. She would be expecting us. "Phone when you arrive," she said cheerily.

By the second week of February, we had our plane tickets, reservations for all accommodations except our last week, and confirmation of a mid-size rental car. Having a fax makes it simple. You fax the hotel or rental agent, writing in English, and they fax you back a confirmation that is almost English, all within 24 hours.

Some hotels ask that you fax your credit card number as a deposit. Others require checks, in lire, LEE-ray; (plural of lira, LEE-rah). I set up an account with Ruesch International, in Los Angeles, to get these checks. When I needed one, I'd look at the dollar-to-lire rate on the Internet. The rate varied by time of day and day of week. When it was the most favorable, I'd phone my contact and ask him to cut and send me a check in lire. I'd send my personal check to Ruesch, plus a $3.00 service charge. Ruesch mailed a lire check to me, payable to whichever party I specified, and I mailed it to the party in Italy.

ASIDE: If you have to wire lire instead of sending a check, you must pay a service charge to your bank. Additionally, the Italian bank removes their "carrying charge" of at least 30,000 lire.

We were to pay for the villa in three stages: a third in March, a third in May, and the final payment on July 1. Between sending checks and charging down payments on a credit card, we had paid for most of the trip before we left. With the framework in place: villa, hotels, and car, I filled in a few spaces. I made a reservation by fax for the Uffizi Gallery in Firenze. I booked a few lunches. After a slow start, I learned a key Italian word: prenotazione, pray-no-taht-see-OH-nay; reservations. And the Italian word for summer: estate, ess-TAH-tay. When my pronunciation faltered, Cristina patiently helped me out.

Then I moved to the texture of the trip. I read older books (e.g.,*Death in Venice*) and newer (i.e.,*Under the Tuscan Sun.*) I read travel guides, scrutinized maps, and memorized recipes from Tuscan cookbooks. I rented *Il Postino* several times, to hear the language (easiest Italian movie to understand) -- to look at the clothes (wrinkled, but still attractive. There are few clothes' dryers in Italy -- the country hangs its wash outside to dry) -- and to look at the countryside (it's not Tuscany, but still -- it's Italian). I saw the film *The English Patient* and vowed to find the dim dome where the frescoes resided for Hana's rope-lift by torchlight. I surfed the Net as late as the day before we left, gleaning tidbits of what purported to be "insiders' tips." These included the location of Hana's frescoes -- the Tuscan town of Arezzo.

S e t ...

As we prepared for our summer in Italy, we listened to Italian tapes and often had rudimentary Italian practice conversations. Our dialogue was impressive to our non Italian speaking friends, but silly if you knew Italian. We had only one rule: KEEP TALKING. The English translation of one of our typical discourses was:

"Good day.
Fruits of the woods!
How are you?
I am thirsty.
Are you British?
I am hungry.
Can you repeat that please?
The bank is closed.
Would you like something to drink?
Fill it with gasoline.
How much do I pay?
Lire is the plural of lira.
I would like Antipasto, please.
What's your name?
I don't know, I am a foreigner."

Learning a bit of the local language allows the traveler to dine better, to shop more wisely, to locate and blend into the local life off the beaten path, and best of all, to make Italian friends. Read it, say it, then say it with *attitude*: Estate. Ess-TAH-tay. Italian for summer.

I read that you should spend one hour of planning for every day you are on vacation. It seemed that I spent an hour of planning for every minute we would be in Italy. I pronounced us ready: we had pages of information, we knew some Italian, we had £1.000.000, a tidy stack of Italian money secured at a very good rate through International Currency Express, sent via Federal Express.

We had individual ATM cards to four individual ATM accounts and our own individual four-digit access codes; a necessity. We each had a couple hundred dollars in Traveler's Cheques. We had two separate Visa cards, Visa being the card most accepted in Italy. We'd carry only one card and keep the other hidden away for an emergency.

We had some American currency, just in case. We had Xeroxes of our credit cards, of our ATM cards, and of our passports. We had airline tickets and Xeroxes of our airline tickets. We had our International Driving Licenses, easily acquired through AAA. We each had a copy of our itinerary. We had all our confirmations and copies of them. We had comfortable shoes and drip-dry clothes. We had an in-house cat-sitter. The dog would live with good friends. I stopped the newspapers, had the mail held, and pre-paid the major household bills through September.

We'd travel light, just the four of us. Jensen's friend Laura would arrive after Robert left. Robert's aunt and uncle would arrive on their own from New York, and meet us in San Gimignano.

Only our day by day living would be unstructured; terra incognita; tabula rasa. We planned to do whatever we wanted whenever we felt like it, secure in the knowledge that we had a roof over our heads and a car and that we could order antipasto, ask for gasoline, and otherwise plead ignorance by dint of being "foreigners."

Andiamo! Let's go.

Now that my ears were popping down through the Italian clouds I had stage fright. We landed in Milano, mee-LAH-noh; Milan, at Malpensa Airport at 8:30 a.m. It is a 45 minute drive from this airport to downtown Milano. Studying the Michelin road map of Northern Italy from the dining room in California, I had decided that going into Milano in the morning rush hour would be an unpleasantly abrupt introduction to our Italian summer. We would arrive tired. We'd be on the road in an unfamiliar, stick shift rental car. We would have to mix it up on the Super Strada with crazy Italian drivers bumper to bumpering in their Ferrari's at over 100 k. The cultural road shock of Italy would outweigh its culture.

Instead of Milano, we chose "The Lake Country." Using hotel info sent from the Italian consulate, I had booked us into a hotel with spa on Lago Maggiore; Lah-go Mah-gee-Oh-ray, "The Bigger Lake," a half hour's drive north of Malpensa Airport, the opposite direction from Milano. We would miss rush hour traffic. We would sun and swim through our jet lag.

At Malpensa Airport, an efficient facility, we gathered our bags and picked up our rental car, a Fiat that Jensen referred to, constantly, as our "**F**ix **I**t **A**gain, **T**ony." Following the directions I printed out weeks before (in large type for blearly eyes) we drove north, skirting Lake Maggiore, racing up to the lakefront town of Stresa on swervy, two-lane roads banked with flowers and lined with stone villas that the new sun blushed apricot. White chairs dotted green lawns fronting the lake. Uniformed workers crisply wiped dew from chaise lounges, preparing for the day. The only car on the road at that hour, we drove straight to our hotel and checked in. Drawing back the elaborate gold and red drapes, we stepped onto our tair-RAHT-sah; terrazza, for our first *real* view of Italy. In the distance rose the snowy crags of the Alps. The lake glistened below, the three elegant Borromean Islands, famous for their grand renaissance gardens, graced the lake's center. Only distant church bells and crowing roosters interrupted the sweet morning tranquillity. I sighed.

Our first *real* view of Italy

At this point, I should say that the second largest expenditure for this trip was the installation of an automatic watering system for my garden at home. Without it, we couldn't have made the trip. I spend the first hours of every day in my garden and most of the time used to be with hose in hand. The expensive watering system changed all that. As I fingered the magenta bougainvillea that clung to our Italian terrazza and stared at the postcard scenery, I imagined my system squirting away in California, the garden oblivious to my absence. To leave my roses at their peak, to miss a season of butterflies, to not see the hydrangea trees in full blossom was the dearest price.

The staff finished turning down our beds and placing our luggage on folding stools. I fumbled with the language and the lire and they left, we thought, happily. We sat silently for several minutes, disoriented, the memory of the plane's engines droning in our ears. The beds tempted us.

"Let's swim?" I offered awkwardly. In a daze, we got out our swimsuits, which we had packed on top, and put them on. We slipped on cover-ups and sandals, also packed on top. We filed down to the front desk to ask about towels, a word that even Cristina couldn't come up with in Italian. We asked in English. The woman told us, in English, that the pool man had the towels. Of course. We walked to the lake front pool. We swam. The water was cool, refreshing. The air was warm, not hot. I sat in a lounge chair between the pool and lake, watching fish swim around in the clear lake water to one side, and my family in the clear blue water on the other side. Again, I was dazzled.

For the three days before leaving California, we had all taken half a gram of Melatonin at what would be 11:00 p.m. Italian time. That, perhaps, and the peaceful surroundings, the sweet air, and sleeping on the plane, were helping me get over the dreaded jet lag. The details of planning and packing began to slip from my thoughts. We were here. None of that mattered anymore.

I fell into the pool to test the reality. I swam, then floated, immersed in the blue above. When was the last time I had smiled? I promised myself that my term as tour director had expired. We lazily toweled off and chaised in the light sunshine.

Hemingway slept here

In the late morning, we found our way to the rooftop spa, to look out at the Alps, the islands, and a sand-colored palace, the Grand Hôtel des Iles Borromées; the hotel where Hemingway stayed when he was in his late teens and where his hero from *The Sun Also Rises* rested. It was like watching a movie. Cristina and I lolled in the Jacuzzi, giving ourselves up to the bubbles and jets. When we were limp as cooked pasta, we showered and pulled on some comfy clothing and headed to town to get some real Italian food.

We walked the Lungolago; the broad, lakefront promenade, to Stresa's main street. It was rare for us to be out together as a family. When was the last time we had all walked down a street together? Probably when Robert and I had to hold the girls' hands for safety. We started out four abreast, then repositioned ourselves to walk two by two. We kept repositioning ourselves and we stumbled some. Only a few others shared the promenade with us; women with babies in strollers, a few young couples. We turned onto the narrow, brick lane lined with enoteca, eenoh-TAY-cah; wine stores, and food shops, boutiques, and caffès (cafés.)

We chose to dine at the Pappagallo (parrot) Caffè. We liked the painted parrot sign out front. The owner handed us menus and guided us to his outdoor patio. The ceiling dripped with real grape vines, heavy with clusters of ripening fruit. The grapes grew from a central vine that was a few feet thick. A plastic roof half-covered the ceiling. Hearing thunder, we chose a table under the plastic. Before we had our napkins in our laps, the rain began. The enormous, eponymous parrot sat in a cage on the restaurant's uncovered terrace. He began to squawk and preen in the downpour.

We alternately worried about the parrot and about how to order from the menu. When the waiter came, we first pointed to the drenched parrot and asked, "Va bene?" (vah-BEN-ay) Is he OK? The man laughed, "Si, si, si." We read the Italian script as best we could and said our Italian lines: "Please, the house antipasto and four orders of gnocchi Piemontese, plus a pizza, and a carafe of house red wine, thank you very much." "Va bene," the waiter replied; vah-BEN-ay. We were very hungry.

The rain turned to hail big as marbles, and we learned our first new Italian noun: la grandine -- hail; lah gran-DEE-nay. Then, "Grandina!" It's hailing; our first new Italian verb. We hoped we wouldn't have much use for this new vocabulary. The parrot quieted. When the hail turned to heavy rain and the rain began to run onto our table and all four of our wine glasses were full of water, the owner moved us to another table. When rain poured onto that table, we moved to yet another table. I again asked about the parrot. The waiter laughed and moved him under the overhang. "Va bene?" he asked. "Va bene," I replied, thinking that speaking Italian here was going to be easier than I thought. We finished our lunch of fresh gnocchi with a white sauce and ordered more wine, profiteroles, and cappuccino. The rain continued. This seemed the perfect way to spend our first Italian afternoon -- the four of us sitting cozily, drowsily together, listening to the rain, slowly eating excellent food; living in the moment, a family. Va bene.

It was now after 3:00 p.m., or 6:00 a.m. California time, as Jensen pointed out; a scant 24 hours since we had closed our front door at home. My mind drifted to our dog, Romeo, and to the cats, Bitz and Norman, and to my garden. Reading my thoughts, Jensen hugged me and said, "I'm sure everything at home is fine, mom." That we were happily together was what mattered.

The lunch service over, the owner and the waiters gathered at an indoor table near the kitchen to dine. The cook brought them a platter a couple feet long, piled high with piping hot, whole, fried anchovies. Our wondering eyes followed him. He stopped at our table, and offered one to Robert. "Molto grazie!" Robert said enthusiastically. He bit it in half, his eyes opening wide, and he said, "Amazing." The cook laughed, brought him a plate, and dumped a half-dozen fish onto it. As full as we were, we all ate the fish. They were very hot, crisp, perfectly cooked, without a hint of a fishy or oily taste; amazing.

When the rain let up, we walked back to the hotel; full, relaxed, drowsy. We dozed, then took another stroll together on the Lungolago, in a more comfortable two by two, and had a simple dinner at the hotel.

To reserve a hotel in Italy and in most places in Europe for more than two nights, the management requires confirmation of "half board," meaning that you commit to eating breakfast and dinner at the hotel. For a week, you usually have to pledge "full board" -- all three meals. A British couple who dined at the table next to ours told us that if you are a "full board" guest, as they were, you could ask for a box lunch, so you could day-trip and not miss what you had paid for; a good tip. We were pleased to take half-board: the price amounted to less than $20.00 per person for a large breakfast and a multi-course dinner each day.

We took a half-gram of Melatonin at 10:00 p.m., fell asleep watching *Gunsmoke* in Italian, and slept through a rainstorm that lasted all night. We took the Melatonin for the next three nights. We slept very well.

The Captain, the Islands, the Peacocks

The sun was brilliant on our first Italian morning. We felt we were over our jet lag. We breakfasted on the hotel's lakefront terrazza. The guests were an international set; Swiss, British, a few French. We were the only Americans, as we would continue to be through most of the summer at the places where we stayed. I hadn't planned it that way, it just happened. Our breakfast was cross-cultural: a generous buffet of cold cuts, breads, cereals, boiled eggs, fruit juices, yogurt, fruit, coffee, and tea. There was something each of us liked.

We went to the boat dock at 9:00 a.m., to the sign that read "bigliette;" tickets. We planned to buy ferry tickets to go visit the three Borromean Islands. The guide book said that the ferry tickets cost around £13.000 a person, about $30.00 for the four of us. The ferry would take us to all three islands in a period of three hours.

As we stood at the ticket booth, a man wearing a Captain's hat asked where we wanted to go -- Isola Madre? Isola Bella? Isola dei Pescatori? All three, we told him. "Va bene," he said; fine. He would take us in his private boat, he explained. We could stay at each island as long as we wanted, and what's more, he'd give us a special rate for four for the day, £88.000. I pulled out my pocket solar calculator. "Fifty something dollars," I informed Robert. The man turned his back to me. He would deal only with Robert. "Capitano: Va bene?" he asked Robert, who repeated back the man's words, "Va bene," gleefully, just as he had in our Italian language tape practices. He paid the man. They both grinned idiotically and shook hands. Using Italian-English and sign language, the boat driver told us to meet him at the dock just up the promenade, under the palm trees, and then walked away, pocketing our lire. Va bene. Robert was pleased with himself.

We females looked at each other, dubious, then we all dutifully walked to our rendezvous point. We had time to do a "lire review," a drill we hadn't made time for before we left. The major denominations were £1.000, 2.000, 5.000, 10.000, 50.000 and 100.000. Periods were used instead of commas, and what looked like the British pound sterling symbol (£) was used as the symbol for lire instead of an ordinary L. The £ preceded the amount, as the dollar sign precedes the dollar amount. To find the lire equivalence, divide the lire by the current rate.

At the day's currently favorable exchange rate of £1.700 to a dollar, £1.000 (divided by 1700) was worth 58 cents. So £10.000 was worth $5.88, and £100.000 was worth $58.23, and our £1.000.000 was worth $588. As the summer continued, the rate would increase to £1.820 per dollar, or about $5.50 for £10.000. We would gain about 40 cents for each $5.88 we spent. The previous year, the exchange was £1.530 per dollar, or $6.53 for £10.000. We would gain more than a dollar over last year's rate for each £10.000 we spent. Italy was 18% off for Americans right now.

The bills were all roughly the same size, the £1.000 smaller than the dollar and the larger bills slightly larger than the dollar. The most interesting bill was the £100.000, with an engraving of the artist Caravaggio's face as well as a detail from one of his paintings. The latter appears to be a gypsy fortune teller reading a young man's palm. Actually, she is slipping the ring from his finger, a dramatic foreshadowing of what was to come for us later in the summer.

The £10.000 notes were the most useful for outings. The Bankomats; Italian ATM's, which offered the option of reading their instructions in English, spit out £50.000 notes and occasionally £100.000 notes. When coins piled up, local merchants were pleased to exchange them for bills. We read that a £500.000 note would soon be issued, though we didn't see any, and that the Eurodollar would prevail at the millennium, though the Italians we met were against it. When (and as some Italians scoffed, "IF") the Eurodollar became the standard, all currency rates would be the same, and the charm of European exchange rate bargains would be over. The value of the "Euro" would float, however, providing a possibility of a good exchange rate.

Twenty-foot long, private power boats came and went from the dock, dropping off passengers, picking up others. Our man arrived. He waved, we waved. He docked, we boarded, watching the overcrowded ferry boat lumber across the wake. We agreed with the Captain that the private boat was a good choice. He took off fast and the wind blew fresh sea smells to us.

Isola Bella

Our Capitano first sped us to the largest island, Isola Madre; the Mother Island, in the Borromeo family since the 1500's. He said he'd be back at the dock in two hours, "Va bene?" He asked Robert. "Va bene," Robert proudly parroted to his new compadre.

There were few visitors on the island. We walked through the eight-acre maze of English style gardens, first planted at the beginning of the 19th century. The famous camellias and azaleas had long since lost their spring bloom. The rhodies were setting buds for next spring. Only the geraniums, all of them red, were in blossom. We strolled more easily, more comfortable together, as if we were the royal family itself. We inspected the peacocks, remnants from a time when the island was stocked with hunting game. The birds obligingly preened their plumes for us. We toured through the Loggia del Cashmir; Kashmir Lodge, home to the Borromeo's, a palace whose construction began at the beginning of the 16th century.

Napoleon Bonaparte (né Nabulio Buonaparte; buona parte being Italian for "a good place") had stayed in the palace on a hunting trip. Napoleon's father was born in Tuscany, certainly a good place. We decided the palace was a comfortable, gracious home where we could live happily ever after. My family wanted to know if our villa in San Gim would be as grand as this house. I didn't think so.

The girls loved the 18th century marionette theater, a display of dozens of marionettes and many backdrops and costumes, many macabre, all in perfect condition. I snapped a photo of one of Countess Borromeo's 18th century French dolls, another well preserved collection. We stood at a balcony to watch frogs plop into a pond whose centerpiece was papyrus reeds from the Nile River. We rested on a bench to stare at the immense, drooping blue-green needles of a 200 year-old Kashmir cypress, the oldest and largest of its kind in Europe; so large, I could not photograph it.

The pond grew papyrus from the Nile River

When we returned to the dock after our eclectic tour, our Capitano was waiting. He rooster-tailed us over to Isola dei Pescatori; Fisherman's Island, and said he'd be back at the dock in two hours. Va bene. This island was the "people's island," previously an active fishing village, now supported by tourism. Picturesque cottages lined the narrow, cobblestone streets and colorful laundry waved a greeting from the fishermens' cottage eaves. We found an outdoor, waterfront ristorante where we ate a simple pasta dish, ziti with bits of fresh vegetables and olive oil, and drank house red wine, played with the dogs who accompanied other diners, and looked out at the water until it was time to meet il Capitano.

Our last stop was Isola Bella; beautiful island, named for the Countess, and by far the most elaborate of the three islands. We could see this island clearly from our hotel terrazza. From there, it appeared to be a spectacular layer cake. Now we could see that the layers of the cake were tiers of gardens that stepped down from the island's peak all the way to the plate of water. White peacocks were the icing. Peacock moms ran in circles trying to round up their fluffy, white chicks. The exuberant chicks ran between their moms' legs and hid under their elegant wings, then dashed off onto the lawn. Jensen dubbed them "chick-peas."

A white peacock and one of her chickpeas

I sat on the clipped lawn and took pictures of the peacock play while my family toured the Grand Borromeo Palazzo; palace. I felt aloof from all of this splendor. It didn't seem real. I daydreamed that I was in my own garden, deadheading annuals, cutting roses, squishing aphids, checking the lilies for moisture, reprimanding Romeo for digging up the dahlias. How could I be there and also here in a renaissance garden?

Our Capitano returned us to Stresa in the late afternoon. We walked to the center of town for lemon granita and cones of gelati. Back at the hotel, we swam and soaked.

As I write, I sit on our terrazza in my swimsuit at 6:30 p.m., Italian time. The sun is hot on my back. I listen to the birds and the evening vespers' bells, looking up every so often to see the calm of Isola Bella and Isola Madre. What was a blur of green this morning I now see as a carefully architected landscape. Fuschia colored, scented geraniums sprout from a huge flower box at my feet, up and over the balcony. Stems and petals litter the floor from last night's storm. I won't pick them up. I'll sit here sunning like a well-fed, Italian cat and try not to think about my own cats

Dinner reminded us all of the film, *A Room with a View.* Our waiter -- we learned that we had our own waiter -- showed us to the corner table nearest the lawn. We looked out to the manicured slope and lake. Our name was written on a table card, along with "No. 1." I hadn't noticed it last night. We recognized several of the people who sat near us from the previous evening. We all nodded to each other. The menu was "continental." Headliners were Parisienne Soupe, Consommé Madrileno, Breast of Chicken, Sautéed Fillet of Sole, Calves' Liver and Bacon "Inglese;" English style, and Roast Beef. The waiters spoke perfect English. It was a comfortable segue into Italy. I promised my daughters we'd have plenty of pasta dinners later in the summer.

After dinner, we walked onto the lawn that spread to the Lungolago and sat in chaises to serenely sip espresso and look out at the water. I felt like a patient at an elegant Swiss sanitarium. At any moment, Charles Boyer might appear from the shadows to withdraw a silver cigarette case from his tuxedo pocket and to ask me for a light, or for a dance, perhaps. The girls fidgeted. I unfolded myself from the lawn chair and we walked into town. The shops were open and the sidewalk restaurants were crowded with diners. The bars were boisterous. The streets were crammed with vacationing revelers, none of them Monsieur Boyer.

The next few days blurred by as recuperative hospital days. After breakfast on our last Stresa morning, Robert thanked our waiter for his service. Unsure of half-board tipping etiquette, I put a few thousand lire into an envelope, marked it with our waiter's name, and left it on our table. The waiter caught me at the door, bowed, and thanked me. I guess we did the right thing.

Verona & Venezia

We drove to Venezia; Venice, stopping first in Verona. When I had made our Veronese lunch reservation six weeks before, the person I spoke to on the phone advised, "Park at the Duomo and take a taxi." We preferred to find our way to the ristorante by following the map in the Michelin Red Guide, which located the Duomo on the opposite side of town from the ristorante. We drove through the double arches of the medieval town wall, and grazed for a while, by car. We had plenty of time before our 1:00 rez. We drove through miles of impossibly beautiful and harrowingly narrow streets.

"There's the Duomo!"

"There's the amphitheater!"

"There's 'Juliet's Balcony!'"

We reminded ourselves of the movie family, the Griswold's.

Shakespeare chose Verona sight-unseen as the setting for *Romeo and Juliet*. The locals later constructed "Juliet's balcony," easily the most popular sight in town. This first experience of driving on streets designed for handcarts was a good physical demonstration of why Italian cars are small. To pass an oncoming car meant keeping all fingers and hands inside the windows on both sides. You clamped them together and prayed for safe passage. Even Jensen agreed that "smaller was better," as long as there was enough trunk space. Our compact car was described as a "mid-size." The "small size" was similar to an American Geo or a Neon.

We started to look for Michelin's streets around 12:45 p.m. We found them without much trouble, enjoying every mis-turn. We got into the vicinity of the restaurant, but we couldn't find the actual ristorante. We decided to continue our search on foot. Robert shoe-horned the Fiat into a parking space on the street, demonstrating another reason why smaller is better in Italy. I asked a passerby if he knew the Ristorante Re Teodorica. He laughed and said, "Certo," of course. He pointed up the hill and said, "Cen' metri." (Chen-MET-tree); 100 meters, a bit longer than a football field. We looked up. We were at the foot of the stone steps that led to the ristorante–standing in front of the ristorante's sign.

This was the first of several similar incidents that illustrated to the Italians how ignorant or blind -- or both -- Americans could be, and probably why the restaurant manager had suggested that we take a taxi.

The Italians walked in their towns. They drove only between towns. They quantified any walking distance in town, no matter how short, long, or steep, as "cen' metri."

This was the *longer* and very steep "cen' metri." Imagine turning a football field on end, replacing its smooth surface with irregularly shaped stone steps, and climbing its height. In addition, Robert, whom we were now calling "Roberto," had his suitcase with him. It didn't fit in the trunk. We had been warned, "Never leave anything visible in the car." His two-suiter draped over his back, he hunchbacked up the steep stairs, glaring at me only once, earning his lunch.

The climb was worth it. The ristorante overlooked the red tiled rooftops of all of Verona. Only three towers were taller than our perch. The outdoor terrazza was closed because of morning rain. The waiter showed us to a table indoors. Two other tables were occupied. Three French people sat at one, a man about 50, a man about 40, a woman about 30. They were well dressed and looked like familiar French film stars whose names we couldn't quite recall; maybe they were. Speaking fluent Italian to the waiter, they ordered several courses and ate quickly. They spoke French to each other. When they finished dining, the older man took a small cigar humidor from his chic leather attaché case, and offered Cohibas to his companions. The waiter snipped the ends of their cigars with a flourish. He lighted them and then brought coffee. We were impressed to see Cuban cigars smoked in the open and surprised to see cigars not only accepted in a restaurant, but graciously so. To hear these people switch from French to Italian with such facility also fascinated us. The gulf between the Americans and the Europeans widens.

The local Lion's Club (literally) occupied the third table. Eight elderly Italian men were turning lunch into a long, memorable afternoon. The waiter knew each of them. They bantered back and forth in Italian, as he brought them platter after platter of food and many bottles of wine. We wished we knew what they ordered, and we hoped we could order as smoothly as the French trio had.

When the waiter came to our table, Roberto said authoritatively, "C'i porta una bottiglia di acqua minerale naturale, e una bottiglia di Valpolicella, per favore." The girls and I feigned boredom, pretending that Roberto always spoke in long, complete Italian sentences without pausing. This was a perfect, verbatim memorization from the language tapes. Roberto had studied to the end of the tapes. If you get that far, you learn long, complete sentences. This one was: Please bring a bottle of natural mineral water -- that would be without the bubbles -- and a bottle of Valpolicella wine -- the local wine. The waiter bowed respectfully, and went off to do Roberto's bidding. Roberto beamed. He was fitting into this trip just fine.

We surreptitiously looked up the names of the menu dishes in my "Complete Pocket Italian Menu Book." Some of the dishes were in the book. Most were not. We eased into lunch by ordering a simple insalata mista; mixed salad, and the pasta special recommended by the waiter, tagliatellini with zucchini blossoms and scampi. It turned out to be an almost orange pasta, colored by saffron. The tagliatellini was fresh, the dish was simple and excellent. Roberto's choice of the local wine was the "perfetto" pair-FET-toh; perfect, accompaniment.

As we were finishing, around 3:00 p.m., the ristorante began to fill up. To dine "early," in Italy, i.e. at 1:00 p.m. doesn't require a rez, much less a rez made six weeks in advance.

After lunch, we drove to Venezia, arriving at 5:00 p.m. We stopped at the San Marco Garage to ask where to catch a Vaporetti; ferryboat, to take us to our hotel. A tall, portly man with a deeply authoritative voice told Roberto, "I will take you," in a way that made us feel we had no choice. We meekly got the bags out of the car. The man put them on a cart. Roberto parked the car in the garage and then joined us. The man wheeled the cart about cen' metri down an alley to a canal. We followed.

At the end of the alley waited a private speedboat, allegedly a water taxi, with two attendants. They said it would cost £100,000 to go to our hotel. I tried to bargain, but they ignored me. They would deal only with "il padrone," Boss Roberto. They gestured for The Women to get into the boat. The Men would stay on deck. As we boarded, Roberto gave the big man what he thought was a generous tip -- £10.000. The man guffawed, and said he owed him £18.000. We scrounged in our pockets and came up with the extra £8.000. The boat ride to our hotel, undertaken silently, was under five minutes; not bad wages.

The view from our Calcina room

We stayed at the Pensione Calcina, John Ruskin's home toward the end of his life. He had previously lived at both the famously elegant Danieli and Gritti Hotels, where he wrote the 450,000 words of *The Stones of Venice*. Yet, the Calcina features the only Ruskin memorial in Venice. I had a hunch that if John Ruskin chose to end his days at the Calcina, he had good reason. We did not, however, have a propitious start. We lugged our bags from the "piano"; the ground floor, to the first floor, which in Italy was really the second floor, where we had two rooms not far from each other. There was no elevator. The porter was out.

While I was explaining about how the "piano" is the first floor and that the first floor was actually the second floor, Roberto dumped our bags on the floor and flopped onto the bed to snooze. As I was unpacking, Jensen and Cristina burst into our room. They told us how delighted they were with *their* room. They had twin mahogany beds, carved headboards, matching bedstands and armoires. Freshly-ironed antimacassars trimmed all their table tops and Victorian lamps cast a romantic light on real oil paintings, as good as Canaletto, they said. Their double windows looked out to the Giudecca Canal. Their bath was marble with mahogany cabinets, another view window, a good shower and tub, plus a towel warmer, hairdryer, and a half dozen large Turkish towels.

Our room was similar, but the addition of a 12' x 15' terrazza facing the Canal made it seem expansive. I cheered up Boss Roberto by reminding him that when we got to our villa, there would be no more luggage-lugging. He put another pillow under his head and slept.

I had not over-sold the Calcina to my family. I had promised them nothing. I hadn't filled them with expectations that might not be met. "It's just a place to stay. We won't be in the room much, we'll be running around Venice." They expected the worst, so it was a thrill to have such lovely rooms. Unpacking was quick; we had placed the clothing we planned to wear while traveling on top of "the villa clothes." I sent a few things down to be cleaned and pressed. We were still overly organized, very civilized American tourists.

Crist and Jens and I sat on our terrazza and watched the vaporetti; the passenger ferry boats, churn up and down the canal, and planned our evening. We had a dinner rez on San Marco Square. We knew that each ristorante on the square had live music at night. When Roberto woke up, we wandered around our part of town, the Dorsoduro (meaning "hard back") Venice's version of Greenwich Village. The ever-dwindling local population and most of the students lived in the Dorsoduro. There were few tourists, and we didn't see (or hear) any other Americans. We lost ourselves in the back alleys, then followed the signs toward "S. Marco" to find our ristorante. Wherever you are in Venice, regardless how lost, you have only to look for "S. Marco" signs to find your way to San Marco Square.

We had waited too long. The rain started. It turned cold. We couldn't see farther than a few yards. We grabbed a table under an umbrella at the nearest caffè, near the Accademia Museum, and drank wine and ate pizza in the company of Gen-X men and women who spoke French and Italian. We could understand only that they spoke of the Accademia.

The Accademia housed a collection that read like a menu: Carpaccio and Bellini figured prominently. It was more famous for the Titians and Tintorettos. I hoped we could stop in. We walked home in the rain. Canal water washed over the sidewalk, but our feet were already wet, what did it matter? There were worse things than sloshing along Venetian canals in the rain, the streaky street lights dissolving in rainwater pools.

Harry's Bar in 1931

The weekend in Venice centered on the Festa della Redentore, the Feast of the Redeemer, celebrating the end of the plague of 1575. The festivities annually took place on this weekend, at the Redentore Church, designed by Palladio, on the island known as La Giudecca, obliquely across the Canal from our terrace. We were told that the tourists would watch tomorrow night's festivities from San Marco Square, opposite the church, or else from a cruise boat, while the locals would participate over on La Giudecca. We decided we'd join the locals.

At 7:00 a.m., under soggy gray skies, an impressive procession of dark, flat, army boats began to maneuver through the water in front of our terrazza, heading up the Canal toward the church. We watched from the terrace as the army unloaded long sections of metal and began construction of the bridge that would span the Giudecca Canal. At sunset on Saturday, canal traffic would stop. The army would complete the bridge. Thousands of Venetians and four Americans would cross the bridge to the Festa -- we hoped, to feast. Fireworks would follow, from San Marco Square, across the way. We locals would have front row seats.

After a good breakfast and delicious coffee, Jens and I left for San Marco Square. Roberto and Cristina opted to sleep late. The rain had stopped. The morning was chilly, but turning bright. We wanted to beat the lines for the sights and also to avoid the 9:00 a.m. drop of pigeon food into the Square. In front of our hotel, the produce barge was making deliveries. Chefs from various restaurants lined up to collect what they had ordered. The bargeman handed off cases of radicchio, peaches, arugula, eggplant, and tomatoes. The chefs examined each case, prodding the peaches for ripeness, polishing the eggplants on their sleeves searching for defects, all the while nodding seriously, and checked the foods off their order sheets. I took a few photos. The bargeman and the chefs were pleased to pose for me.

We got to the Duomo as it opened. We went first to view what the Venetians purport to be the remains of St. Mark, swiped by the Venetians from Alexandria around 830 B.C. to give the city religious credibility and to attract pilgrims; a.k.a., tourists like us. We saw the original quadriga on display inside, the four horses that were created in Greece, once mounted Trajan's Arch, then pranced to Constantinople, from where the Crusaders hobbled them off to Venice so that Napoleon could trot them up to Paris to straddle the Arc du Carousel, a construct Jensen had fallen in love with on a previous trip, and the reason she wanted to see the originals. The Austrians later corralled the quadriga and returned it to Venice so she could.

We went to the top of the Campanile to take pictures. There was no line at the early hour. We shopped our way around San Marco. I bought several linen tablecloths and napkins with gardenias hand sewn into them, a Venetian lion tie for Robert; gold lions on navy silk, and a silver ring for Jensen. Venice is a Disneyland for shoppers, supported entirely by tourists. There is little other commerce. The workers from the hotels and shops can no longer afford to live in Venice. Most have moved over to Maestre, near the train station.

A few minutes before 12:00 p.m., we positioned ourselves where we could watch the two Moors strike the hour on top of the Clock Tower.   There was some scaffolding around the structure, but the Moors and the bell were unencumbered, heightening our expectations.   However, the Moors were apparently on Feria, Fair-EE'ah; holiday, and though we heard a dozen bells, none clanged from the Clock Tower.

Before we left California, I had picked up an assignment to take some photos for an upcoming book on Papa Hemingway. Happily, all the shots assigned to me were of bars and food. I had taken a photo in Stresa of the Hemingway Bar at the luxurious Grand Ile des Borromées.   The hotel's "Hemingway Bar" is really a small service bar plunked in the lobby, indistinguishable from any other service bar anywhere in the world. Several men, attractive, sophisticated 50-ish Hemingway types were drinking martinis when I arrived for the shoot, so I simply took photos of them drinking their martinis.   The next shoot was Harry's Bar, here in Venice.

Jensen and I walked over, and sidled up to the bar. Fashionably dressed Venetians sat at tables drinking coffees and Bloody Mary's. We were the only women at Harry's and the only people at the bar. The head bartender, Nevio, was a tall, lithe, darkly handsome man of the James Bond genre and generation, with just a touch of white creeping above his ears into his clipped, dark hair. He wore a perfectly tailored white shirt and jacket with a black bow tie and moved like Cary Grant. He smiled engagingly, and asked what we would like.

"Due Belline, per favore."   Two Bellinis, please.

He whipped up a pitcher of the peach mixture and filled two glasses for us, leaving the extra in the pitcher. We toasted: "Cen' anni!"   (chen-AH-nee) A hundred years.   "Squisito!" (SKEE-see-toh) said Jensen. Exquisite.

Another bartender, Lorenzo, joined Nevio to make up the luncheon martinis. Lorenzo was cut from the same cloth as Nevio, but closer to Jensen's age, and more flirtatious. Nevio placed a tall glass pitcher on the bar. He took a bottle of Noilly Prat dry vermouth and, freestyle, poured an exacting amount into the pitcher. At the same time, Lorenzo poured in Gilby's Gin -- the British Gilby's, Britain's finest. Their concoction reached precisely to the lip of the pitcher. Nevio stirred his masterpiece to blend. With a wink, Lorenzo returned to the kitchen. Nevio poured the martinis into a dozen or so glasses that looked like double shot glasses, and put them into the refrigeration unit to chill for the lunch crush. Then he poured the remaining Bellini mixture into our glasses. All of this took less time it did to read this paragraph -- too fast to take a photograph. Lorenzo returned briefly, and I asked if I could take a photo of him and Nevio.

"Si, certo!" Yes, of course. It is a good photo, but it doesn't capture the duo's savoir-faire.

We sat enjoying our Bellinis and drinking in the aromas from the foods the chefs were preparing for lunch. A small window opened from the bar to the kitchen. We could view the masters creating carpaccio, cutting up chickens, putting roasts into huge pans, stirring sauces, and carving vegetables. Nevio gave me a postcard of the bar as it looked in 1931. It looked virtually the same. The chief new addition was the window behind the bar.

We left Harry's and walked through the public gardens close by; small, but well-kept, and populated by elderly Venetians who sat on benches reading their newspapers. Back at the hotel, we gathered up Roberto and Crist. The four of us returned to San Marco, to Florian's, on the south side of the Piazza. We sat outdoors, since it was warm, but we toured the interior first. It looked like a series of small jewel boxes painted by Fabergé.

Florian's opened in 1720 and became an instant landmark, same as Harry's did when it opened. Straight across the Piazza from Florian's was Quadri's. The outdoor portions of the caffès looked alike, with dozens of identical white tables and chairs. But philosophically, the two were different. During the Austrian rule of Italy, when they brought back Jensen's quadriga, the Austrians hung out at Quadri's. The wary Italians kept their distance, across the way at Florian's. We followed Italian custom. Florian's black tie orchestra played, and Roberto impeccably ordered a bottle of water and one of chilled Rosata.

We watched the hordes of pigeons and clutches of cats, wondering if the cats kept the pigeons in check, or if it was up to the many small boys who chased after the birds. The tourist groups gaped at us as if we were on their tour.

Florian's interior was a series of jewel box rooms

The heat and the wine, the noise and the stares, the pigeons and boys, cats and shutterbugs overwhelmed us. Hungry, we walked in the general direction of the Dorsoduro, looking for Pranzo; lunch. We had no rez, no plan. It was after 2:00 p.m. when we peered into the Ristorante Tre Leone; three lions. Boisterous laughter and great food perfumes drifted to us. We went in. The waiter seated us next to the table where a dozen gondoliers were lunching. We ordered some wine and an assortment of food. The girls and I took turns going to the bathroom, Jensen first. When she returned, she warned us that we shouldn't go "in there," but I had to. The facility, known in some circles as a "Turkish toilet," was barely six inches off the ground. I have not figured out how to approach a toilet that sits so low in a graceful or hygienic manner.

ASIDE: Italian law requires that bars allow public access to their rest rooms. We took advantage of this in Venice and elsewhere, choosing the most attractive bars. Usually,we'd buy something first -- a token -- say, a pastry or a postcard, and then ask permission to use the rest room.

Our three course Tre Leone lunch of salad, pasta, and veal was delicious. The portions were generous, the "conto;" the check for the four of us was under $50.00 with good wine. The gondoliers put on a show for Cristina and Jensen, making jokes and laughing, flexing their muscles, winking and flirting. When we left, we followed signs back to S. Marco square, to where the gondolas were lined up waiting for passengers. We doubted we could ever find the back alley ristorante again.

Roberto dealt with the gondoliers, playing one off against another to try to secure a better rate for an hour's ride. He could not get any of them to reduce their price below £100.000. We turned his back to the gondeliers, walked away from the launching area. One gondolier trailed us. He said to Roberto that he would take us for £80.000. "Va bene," said Roberto, lighting up. He confessed to us that he didn't care so much about the cost, he was more interested in his ability to communicate. We clambered aboard the gondola, rather hoping that our gondolier would be sober enough to negotiate the tricky turns.

Each gondola was black, it's the law. So each driver went to some trouble to customize his gondola to stand out from the others. Some had unique designs carved into the sides, some laid colorful oriental carpets, others plumped lavishly tasseled satin pillows for passengers to lounge on. Vases of fresh flowers sprouted from the bows. Our gondola had elaborate carving inside, above the seats. I wished for pillows, because it was too uncomfortable to sit back. We sat forward. Our gondolier took us from his station on the Grand Canal through the narrow, back "fondamenta," quays, a colorful tour possible only by boat. When our gondola met another at a blind corner, and they were all blind corners, our Capitano demonstrated his skill in manipulating his long pole to pass precariously close. As he did so, he got Crist and Jens to turn around a chat with him, staring deeply into Jensen's blue eyes, making the pass more perilous. Cristina, the only one who understood what he was saying in Italian, blushed and turned her back to him. Soon Jensen followed her lead.

The gondolier dropped the names of the famous people who had once lived in Venice, including John Ruskin, and among them, Robert Browning, who was a relative on my mother's side. He lived briefly in Venice with his son, Pen, a name that still makes me smile. Henry James wrote about the restoration and redecoration the Brownings accomplished on Pen's home, the Palazzo Rezzonico, that it " ... transcends description for beauty." My grand uncle was named Browning, after the famous relative. Robert Browning caught cold while visiting Pen and never recovered. He died in Venice at the age of 77. My grandfather was born the same year, and the gondolas were all painted white.

Roberto, Jens, and Crist on a perilous turn

We four toured the Doges' Palace next. We walked across the Bridge of Sighs, and through the musty prison, as good tourists must. Nobody protested the bow to culture. My family found the prison fascinating.

On the way back to the hotel in the early evening, we stopped to listen to street musicians -- a chamber quartet -- playing near the Accademia Museum. I wondered if my family would consider a brief visit to the museum. Across the way, I spied several interesting pieces displayed outside a shop; small tables, mirrors, and large masks unique from the others we had seen in shops closer to San Marco. Roberto and I left Crist and Jensen to the music and crossed over to have a look. An older man who reminded me of the carpenter Geppetto came from the shop to enthusiastically tell me the life story of a picture frame I liked. He had got it in disrepair from a museum and restored it himself. It was black, with gold leaf pressed into the bas-relief. Under my arm, I carried a watercolor of a fondamenta. I had bought it from a street artist near Harry's. We compared its size to the frame's. It was a perfect fit.

"Gianni Cavalier," the man smiled, crinkling his eyes. I wasn't sure if this was a statement or his name. I opted for the latter, and Roberto and I introduced ourselves. Gianni told us it was his shop, that he restored all the antiques himself. Each piece had a history. He also crafted all the masks. They were one of a kind; art, or at least exceptional craft, not meant to be worn. He showed me a sizable order from Gump's, the elegant San Francisco emporium where his masks were sold at prices histrionically marked up from Gianni's originals. We chatted, in Englitalian. I told him I was a giornalista; journalist, specializing in stories and photos on gardens, food, and fashion. He showed me an article about his shop that *The New York Times* published a few years ago, and asked for my card.

Now that we were friends, he invited us to leisurely browse the myriad treasures hidden within the shop that was also his workroom. I fell in love with a gold lion mask that looked as if Gianni had made it for a giant. Sig. Cavalier was pleased with my choices. He said he would give me a very good price. When

I signed the credit card slip, I paused, thinking he had forgot to charge me for the frame. "No, no, no," he said. He autographed the back of the mask, then wrapped it carefully for me, along with the picture frame, creating a package several times larger than both. We continued chatting as he walked us out. "Write to me!" he called. Si, certo. I'd take a photo of the mask hanging on our dining room wall, and another of the framed picture and I would send them to him. I couldn't forget Gianni (pronounced "Johnny") Cavalier.

Back at the hotel, we all went to our terrazza to check on bridge progress. The army was building the bridge across the canal from the church and also from the opposite shore, the Zattere, the promenade that ran in front of our hotel. They left the middle of the canal open to traffic. Glittering cruise ships were coming in for the festa. The traffic on the canal was getting heavier. The locals were out picnicking and careening in their speedboats. A parade of gondolas passed. The noise and the excitement were building.

The air turned cold and even colder rain began to pour down. We again canceled our plans to walk to dinner at San Marco Square. I had packed no warm clothes. The guide books concurred that summer in Venezia would be hot. Roberto lent me a pair of his khaki pants and a crew neck sweater. I gratefully put them on. I pulled up the waist band and belted it so that it puckered around my waist. I rolled up the pant legs. I rolled up the sweater sleeves. Crist said I looked sort of like Charlie Chaplin. We ran to a nearby pasta place and sat under the dripping sun umbrellas, the only diners outdoors. The tables inside were full. I still couldn't get warm. I went to bed early, while my family strolled the canals in the rain, stopped to hear a late night concert at a Dorsoduro church, and walked some more -- an experience they would treasure.

A Venetian Festa

At 7:00 p.m. the army stopped all traffic on the canal and put the final sections of bridge into place. At 7:30 p.m. the bridge opened. We joined the crowds of Venetians who walked across eight abreast, hoping that the temporary structure would hold under our collective weight.

When we got to the other side, we began to look for a place to feast, or at least to have dinner. Many tables were set up, but we didn't see any caffès or ristoranti or bars. The savvy locals had brought picnic dinners and their own bottles of wine and water. We continued to walk along the canal, searching. Hundreds of tables were set up, end to end, with tablecloths even, but we still saw no restaurant service.

Many minutes late, we came to some tables where waitresses were serving food. I asked one of the waitresses if we could have dinner there. I couldn't understand her long answer, but it didn't sound encouraging. She turned her back to us and went into the kitchen, a building across from the tables. She returned with a man who wore a full-body white apron and a toque. We took him to be the Padrone. I asked him the same question. He looked at the tables where people sat eating and conferred with the waitress. She nodded.

"Va bene," he told us. He said they were serving a festa dinner of six courses and that the dinner, which included a half liter of wine per person, would cost us £50.000 a person, cash. "About $30," Jensen said under her breath. My hungry family nodded agreement. "Va bene," I said, forking over the £200.000 with a smile, thinking, It's Saturday night, we're in Venice, and it's the Festa -- let's feast! The waitress showed us to four plastic chairs, two of us on each side at the center of a long table for 12. We sat across from each other, surrounded by Venetians. The elegantly dressed couples stopped talking and started smoking when we sat down, not a good sign.

Soon, the waitress handed flatware rolled in napkins, four paper place mats, and a bowl of bread to the people nearest the kitchen. They hand over handed it to us. Glasses followed, then our first carafe of wine, a Chianti, we guessed, and the first of the six courses: an oversized tray with eight square, metal containers filled with hors d'oeuvres: grilled squid, octopus, deep-fried potatoes, sautéed zucchini, stuffed tomatoes, grilled pork, shrimp skewers, and chicken in a dark garlic sauce. None of the foods tasted familiar to us. We tried them all, sensing that the Venetians watched sidelong to see our reaction.

"Molto bene!" We exclaimed dramatically, as if we were performers on stage.

Our second course was a generously-sized bowl of several dozen plump, perfect, steamed mussels. The third was a family-sized platter of spaghetti with piquant anchovy sauce. The dish was not attractive. We each took a small portion. It was exceptional. We ate it all. By then it was dark. The waitress lighted the many votive candles on our table.

Overhead, the hundreds of tiny lights that were strung along the canal earlier in the day twinkled on. Next we were served a gargantuan salad of fresh greens with a fishy-luscious vinaigrette. We had lost count of courses. We thought the salad was our last course. Didn't the Europeans always serve the salad last? The waitress took away the salad bowl and presented the main course: a whole, grilled fish for the four of us. On both sides of us, the Venetians dug into their fish. So did we. The fish was succulently fresh with a crisp crust. We savored every morsel. Soon, it was gone. There was a satisfying pause before the dessert, an equally satisfying, smooth crème caramel.

None of the Venetians had ever met an American, much less four Americans from California. At first, they treated us as imported exotics, like the white peacocks in Stresa. To us, the Venetians were the exotics.

As we ate our way through the courses and sipped through our four carafes of wine, we each made individual conversational inroads with the people who sat next to us. They spoke no English. We had to listen carefully and compose our grammar even more carefully. I couldn't tell if the effects of the wine made the speaking easier or more difficult. It certainly made us all gregarious. Long "digestive" pauses separated our halting sentences, as if we were waiting for a simultaneous interpreter to step in and help us out. The Venetians spoke slowly and patiently; far more kindly than the Italian teachers on our tapes.

Our dinner companions were all native Venetians. They enlightened us about the food. It was catered, they told us, explaining why we couldn't simply drop in for dinner. They said that there was no ristorante here. Normally, the "kitchen" was a warehouse. The people we sat with had reserved together for this party months before, and had meant it to be a private party, explaining why they were piqued to see strangers dropping in, and tourists, too. Four of their friends were no-shows. We had taken their place. They led us to believe that the two missing couples were young and in love and had different plans. We told them how pleased we were to be included in their special party.

They warmed to us. The conversation became more fluid. The man sitting next to me was a wine aficionado who traveled to Tuscany regularly. I told him that we would be in Tuscany for six weeks, and that any advice would be much appreciated, especially about wine. By the time the evening was over, he had filled his paper place mat with a carefully drawn map of his favorite places to taste wine in Tuscany. He signed the map with a flourish and presented it to me and also produced a bottle of Prosecco, the popular Italian sparkling wine, to share with us; his new American friends.

It was almost midnight when we finished dessert. My new friend said that the Venetians stayed up all night for the festa. The tradition was to stroll the Zatterre (the promenade in front of our hotel) after the fireworks, and then go to the fabled Lido beach to watch the sun come up, then return to the Zattere for the gondola races in the morning. After consulting the rest of the party, he graciously invited us to join his group. We were flattered. I took a poll.

Crist said she was too tired to stay, too tired even to wait for the fireworks. I confessed that I was tired, too, probably from overeating. Jensen and Robert said thank you very much, but they, too, were tired. I offered to walk back to the hotel with Crist. Robert and Jensen wanted to stay to watch the fireworks.

Crist and I thanked our new friends, said extended goodnights to our group, and started back together toward the bridge, a distance of at least half a mile. The festa was in full swing. To our left, along the canal, tables were filled with cliques of revelers, laughing, talking, singing. The tiny lights danced the length of the canal. There were distinct groups, separate parties. As we walked farther, we dodged accordion players, guitar players, groups of singing inebriates, and passed hotly embracing couples -- among them, possibly, the two missing couples from our table. When we reached the bridge, two policemen closed the gate.

"Chiuso" (kee-YOU-zoh); closed, they told us, matter-of-factly. We heard some shouts and noise across the canal, at San Marco Square. The fireworks were beginning. Crist and I had no choice. We walked to the edge of the canal, to a front row view. The fireworks lighted the famous buildings in the square, rose to a dizzying height, and filled the sky. They were more spectacular than any Fourth of July show that we had seen. We rallied and joined the crowds as they cheered and shouted at both the pyrotechnics' rise and then their glittery reflection in the Grand Canal -- the Italian version of "Oooh, Aaaah!" The show lasted until after 2:00 a.m.

When the officers opened the gate to the bridge, Crist and I were the first across. We felt we were leading a parade. The participants sang, wrapped their arms around each other, and we all laughed and danced across the bridge. At the hotel, Crist and I went to the terrazza to watch the continuing party. The Venetians partied past us, a city-wide snake dance with the Lido beach as their destination. There seemed to be thousands of revelers. The procession was still going on when I woke and peered at the clock at 4:00 a.m. In a few hours, they would be watching the sunrise. I fell back asleep, wishing.

The kind of shouting and cheering you hear at a football game woke us around 9:00 a.m. Roberto and I rolled out of bed and went to the terrazza in our pajamas. The gondola races were starting; Venice's mini-version of Siena's Palio. There was a light chop on the canal. The gondoliers' friends and relatives paced the gondolas in their speedboats, strategically creating wake to slow the opposition's progress. The gondoliers concentrated fiercely to keep their tippy craft afloat, not to mention competitive. We watched for a while, took a few photos, then had to pack our bags. We grabbed a quick breakfast at the hotel. I had two large cups of the wonderful coffee, and drank it as if it were rich cream, slowly savoring every sip. I looked forward to mornings of exceptional Italian coffee at our villa in San Gim. We'd soon be there. We ordered a water taxi. It arrived immediately. We handed over £100.000 and sped off, weaving our way through the gondola races, wondering if last night really happened or if we dreamed it all.

On the road again, we drove to Ferrara for lunch, a reservation I had also made six weeks before. The town was deserted. Presumably, everyone was at lunch. It is the custom for Italian families to dine out for lunch on Sundays and our ristorante was full of local families. It was good that we had a rez. I had read that the ristorante was famous for its antipasto. The display inside the door was formidable. A buffet table was crowded with platters. After seating us, the waiter invited us to help ourselves. When we had eaten our antipasto, he would take our order for pasta and for the main course.

I was surprised that I was hungry again after last night's feast. What the eye sees, the stomach responds to. We ordered some wine and ate leisurely, sampling almost every kind of sliced meat, stuffed vegetable and hot and cold and marinated and fresh seafood and vegetable. The foods were entirely different from the previous evening's fare, and equally delicious. When the waiter came to take our order, we had to tell him that we could eat no more. No main course? No. Dolci? (DOL-chee) dessert, he asked? No thank you very much, we replied. "Va bene," he said, with a puzzled look that said, "Americans are strange folk."

We returned to the Autostrada, the toll way, as opposed to the Super Strada, the free way, to drive to our home for the next six weeks. Roberto was becoming a competent Italian driver. Like the Italians, he was impatient with a driver who stayed at the legal speed limit, and began passing these "slowpokes" frequently. It is illegal to drive in the left lane in Italy, except to pass. Using the turn signal is imperative. Roberto would signal, pass, then quickly get back into the right lane. Speeding cars zoomed by. The cars moved up so quickly we couldn't see them until they were a few feet behind us.

Moving to our Villa

We raced in a rainstorm past Florence, through many tunnels, and into the heart of Tuscany. The rain stopped there. The gentle hills were emerald green with vineyards, blending with the bluish silver green of the olive orchards. We rounded a curve and saw the towers of San Gimignano. It was like seeing the Matterhorn out the window, unexpected. San Gim looked just like its photo.

Again, I had stage fright. Making the transition from the theoretical to the real was stressful. I had written this script, but I hadn't cast it, I hadn't scouted the locations in person.

Following the written instructions, we found the rental agent's office easily. I asked Gaynor, the British rental agent, if Annie and Rolf, Robert's aunt and uncle, had arrived. Oh yes, she told us, they came in yesterday, they are fine. I gave her our passports, the breakage deposit for the villa, and money for laundry service. I had arranged to have fresh linens delivered weekly: sheets, bath and pool towels, tea towels, and tablecloths. I had also negotiated to have the villa cleaned once a week, to include making up the beds. While these requests seemed simple, making the arrangements took considerable effort. Rental agents do not like to work out "extras" for the clientele. We later learned that the renters of other villas did not have such "luxuries" as cleaning people and bed-makers. Nobody had a cook. The Brits brought their own linens in their cars. The services I was able to procure turned out to be very reasonable. I paid Gaynor for all the linens for all six of us for the next six weeks, amounting to about $130.00. I was to pay the cleaning people directly at the end of our stay. They charged £25.000 an hour per person, about $14.00, and Gaynor thought that a couple hours a week would be enough time for two people to clean the villa and put fresh sheets on our beds.

Gaynor told me there was a problem with the box I had sent from San Francisco on July 10. DHL had promised three-day delivery. Now Italian Customs wanted a copy of my passport. I gave my permission, and Gaynor Xeroxed my passport, wrote a note on the copy, in Italian, and faxed it off. She gave us keys to the villa, two clickers that would open the villa gates, and two pages of typewritten instructions for finding them.

"The Box," as we would refer to it all summer, held the items I believed essential to our stay and objects we didn't want to carry: at the top of the list was a pound of Cristina's sheet music. Kate expected her to perform some American show tunes in San Gim, which would now be impossible. Next on the list were binoculars, for taking a closer look at the Italian birds I expected to watch. There were disposable cameras for taking snapshots, Kodak film for more serious shooting, plus toilet tissue and "American" gifts for people we'd no doubt make friends with. I had sent Saran Wrap, disinfectant soap, Tide, scented candles in case the old villa smelled "funny," and insecticides and sunscreens. I had tucked in the Tuscan and Umbrian travel books and cookbooks, including the Green Michelins, plus photographs of my garden to share with the gardeners I hoped to meet, and some good journal-writing paper and reliable pens. My down pillow completed The Box. The cost to ship The Box was $210.00, maybe more than the value of the goods inside.

We drove to the villa, veering off the paved road onto an unpaved, narrow, twisty, dusty country lane that was no more than a deer trail. As per the instructions, we turned left at the ristorante called Il Refugio, and continued bumping along what looked and felt like a footpath until we saw the gates that were described. There were no street names, no house numbers. Roberto stopped the car in front of the gates. Jensen clicked the clicker. The ornate, heavy portals majestically swung open. Roberto slowly drove through them, tantamount to carrying the bride through the door of the new house. Two rows of the characteristic, stately, Tuscan cypresses flanked the long, paved driveway. We drove between the tall trees, up and up. The ideal travelogue rolled before us, lacking only a music track.

Annie and Rolf, dressed in swimsuits, came to the car to greet us. We all talked at once. We carried our bags into the villa, a simple stone house. Annie and Rolf had "opened it up" for us, flinging wide the doors and windows and they had also made up our beds. I hadn't thought to ask if the beds would be made up for our arrival. The Italians do not offer information. I thanked them for their thoughtfulness. We put our bags in our bedrooms, and we all sat together at the big table on the sprawling terrazza, nestled between vineyards and olive groves, looking out at the San Gim skyline, as we would for dozens of hours spreading out over the summer. We listened and laughed while Annie and Rolf told us about their trip, and I smiled at the promise of Italian summering.

Annie and Rolf's Adventure

Following instructions I had taken from the Internet and sent to them, Annie and Rolf took the train from Milano's Malpensa Airport to Florence. At the Florence train station, they switched trains for Poggibonsi (Poh-Jee-BONE-see), the nearest town to San Gim. On the train, a British woman told them that the train stops only briefly at Poggibonsi (Poh-Jee-BONE-see.) They must be ready to toss their luggage off the train and to quickly jump off themselves.

As the train slowed, Rolf readied their four large, heavy suitcases for the toss. Before the train stopped, he began pushing the suitcases out the door onto the platform. The conductor told him, "No, no! No è Poggibonsi." It's not -- (you know) -- Poh-Jee-BONE-see. Rolf jumped off the train when it stopped, wrangled the bags back onto the train, and threw himself back onto the train just as it left the station. When they got to Poggibonsi, they had plenty of time to get their luggage and themselves off the train. They found a taxi to take them to Gaynor's, and on to the villa. The trip was almost seamless. Annie and Rolf interrupted themselves with laughter every time they had to say "Poggibonsi." Every time they said it they pronounced it differently, and we all laughed harder.

Once at the villa, they continued, they had no food. They had no car. They had eaten no breakfast or lunch. I had made a reservation for them at Il Refugio, the ristorante cen' metri from the villa. They headed up there at 5:00 p.m., a reasonable time for a 60 something couple to dine on a Sunday in New York. A wedding was in progress at the ristorante. The manager told them, No, no, no! They couldn't come in. It was a private party. Annie and Rolf persisted, telling the manager that they had a reservation for dinner. The man checked. Yes, they did. But even so, he said, even if the ristorante was open, it didn't open until 7:30 p.m. "Wait there," he commanded.

They waited to the side of the festivities, watching the wedding party. At 7:30 p.m., the party was still in full swing. The manager showed Annie and Rolf to a table, and they dined well. They were the only people besides the wedding party to have dinner there that night. Annie said many people dropped in for dinner but were turned away. They glared toward Annie and Rolf's table, but Annie and Rolf sat and ate and enjoyed watching the dancing for hours.

"A real swimming pool"

After the recount, Annie and Rolf took us on a tour: the swimming pool was crystal clear and enormous. "A real swimming pool," Roberto said, "instead of the kind you can only dip your toes in." Terra-cotta rimmed the pool, a smooth lawn surrounded it. The head of the outdoor pool shower was big as a sunflower. Steps led to an olive grove and a plum orchard where a hammock lazed between two fruit trees. Lying down and reaching up, you could pick the plums, Rolf told us. They showed us a small terrazza in the olive grove with a barbecue and a table and chairs. Looking out, we saw the San Gim skyline. We could have dinner in the grove one evening, Annie suggested.

All of the property looked straight to San Gimignano. Rolf pointed out the path that led to town and told us that the walk would take about 20 minutes. Crist caught my eye and we smiled as we remembered the advice about the vipers and the pharmacy. Annie explained that we would pack up our garbage in the car, and take it to bins on the road below. So much information to sort out, but we knew we had weeks to do it.

Annie and Rolf had their own separate apartment. We shared a common stone wall. They had a kitchen and a bath with a shower and bidet, but no tub, plus a bedroom and a sitting room with a double daybed. Their windows opened to the pool and framed the vineyards like a pretty painting. They loved their place. They were already wondering why they had such a large home in New York when all they needed was this. They also had a capacious storeroom, where they offered to stash our suitcases.

On the other side of the stone wall, we had two double bedrooms, two bathrooms the same as theirs, a full kitchen furnished with a table that could seat eight, a living room with two leather sofas; one a double sofa bed. Another table, not much more than a card table, with four chairs completed the furnishings. We could "sleep six" on our side of the wall, if the occasion arose. Annie and Rolf could "sleep four." In all, our villa "slept 10."

Our covered terrazza extended the length of the kitchen and living room, and looked out on both sides to vineyards. There was a lawn to the left, and a square brick patio in full sun for hanging laundry. The terrazza looked to the towers of San Gimignano. The villa was not enormous and not lavish, but it was large enough for our needs, and it was immaculate. Paintings of Italian landscapes not as good as Canaletto hung on the stone walls and several homey pieces of majolica, the Italian ceramic tableware, decorated various tables and bookshelves. There were a few paperbacks in a bookshelf, Italian best sellers and what turned out to be unspeakably trashy British romance novels; not the sort of thing one would take back home to England.

Roberto and Rolfo, first night on the terrazza

As the summer moved forward, we came to love our villa and to appreciate everything about it. We spent most of our time on the terrazza.

Our hosts, who owned the villa, Maria and her husband, whom I shall call Max, since none of us could understand what his real name was, showed us the wine cellar cum laundry room, and gave us wine from their vineyard, a bottle of red and a bottle of white, neither with labels. They said the bottles were their gift to us. They would sell us more, if we liked, for £5.000 a bottle; $2.85. We thought it a fair price. They spoke no English, which I saw as a Conversational Italian 101 opportunity. Gaynor had told us that the villa owners would be there only occasionally, but it soon became apparent that they lived there full time and would be there, if not necessarily in full view, all the time. Their home was the second floor of the villa.

We swam and sunned away the late afternoon of our first day in San Gimignano. While the Women unpacked, the Men sat on the terrazza. We had another dinner rez for the local ristorante, Il Refugio, (eel ref-OO-gee-oh) that evening. The Italian -g is pronounced as the -g in "gee-whiz" or "gelato." The women went in the Fix It Again Tony, the men walked. The ristorante had a large terrazza with about 20 umbrella tables. Most of the tables were already full. When we arrived, the manager told us that reservations were always necessary. Annie and Rolf nodded their understanding. I ordered pasta with fresh porcini mushrooms and understood, too.

Around dessert time, not the most delicious part of the Italian meal for those of us whose tastes run to deep dish, fresh berry desserts in the summer, I realized that we had nothing to eat for breakfast the next day. Our fridges were empty. Our cupboards were bare. We had done no shopping. I explained the situation to our waiter and asked if we might take some of the bread and butter home. He returned with a large bag filled with bread, butter, ground coffee, milk, and pears. He wouldn't accept any money.

I walked home with Roberto and Rolf and my breakfast bag, a beautiful summer evening stroll, and all downhill going home. It was a 10 minute walk. We stretched it to more. We were amazed to be in Italy, and more amazed that we were confidently strolling in the dark to our very own Tuscan villa. We pressed the gate clicker and our gates obligingly swung open. A few steps later, we were home.

The dusty road to San Gim

Settling in

We devoted our first day in San Gim to the delight of shopping for villa provisions. Our first stop, two kilometers (k) away, was the Pietrafitta degustazione (tasting room) that we had noticed on our drive to the villa. The better degustazioni (plural of tasting rooms) offered their own products, a range that could encompass wine, grappa, olive oil, honey, and other singular goods, as well as tastings of each. Roberto was familiar with Pietrafitta.

ASIDE: To quickly figure out approximate kilometers to miles, halve the kilometers and add 10% -- 10 k is about 6 miles.)

We bought a few bottles of the Pietrafitta DOCG Chianti, some Pietrafitta Rosata; a lightly delicious rosé wine that went well with Tuscan sunshine, and a liter of their own extra virgin olive oil, wildflower honey, a liter fiasco of Chianti, and the Pietrafitta grappa.

The SuperAll, a huge grocery store in Poggibonsi (PO-Jee-BONE-see, try it, you may like saying it) was the next stop. We picked up a few bottles of the famous San Gimignano Vernaccia (£5.000), along with Saran Wrap, dish detergent, bathroom soap, Kleenex, candles, Sambuca (also £5.000), and a fifth of Johnny Walker Red Scotch because it was only $8.00 a bottle here in Chiantishire. We bought salt, pepper, sugar, all the other staples, plus fruit, croissants stuffed with apricot, the only kind sold, juices, milk, butter, fresh pasta, tomatoes, basil, parsley, garlic, bread, steaks, and fresh, homemade sausages. We filled the trunk for $75.00. (The day after I returned to San Francisco, I bought far fewer groceries and paid exactly $175.00).

We put away our goods, unpacked our clothes, and settled in for a long summer's sojourn. We swam, wandered the property, and chatted the afternoon away, remembering Henry James famous opinion about the two best words in the English language: Summer afternoon.

I offered to prepare dinner. I was secretly excited about working with real Italian materials, stove, pots and pans, knives, and serving pieces. I kept it simple. I simmered a tomato sauce with garlic and basil and the superb olive oil, and folded the sauce into fresh fettuccine. Roberto barbecued steaks and opened the fiasco, Annie tossed a salad. The food was wonderful. I used a Tuscan recipe I had read at home and tried at home. There was no comparison. A Tuscan recipe relies on Tuscan ingredients. It is axiomatic and absolute. We ate on the terrazza. After dinner, we sipped Sambuca until late. It tasted smooth and perfect, though I had never cared for it at home.

I had no writing paper. My writing paper and my favorite pens were in The Box. I made these notes on the side of the "English" Il Refugio menu. The translations were not as good as the preparations. For example, the bruschetta (brew-SKET-ah) was a round of grilled bread, rubbed with a garlic clove and topped with fresh, ripe, chopped tomatoes, drizzled with extra virgin Tuscan olive oil. A single order of bruschetta was composed of three pieces, ample for three people as a starter course. I copied the menu exactly:

Antipasto Toscano
Ham, Tuscan Salame, small pieces of toast

Affettato misto - Mixed delicatessen
Sliced ham, Tuscan salame, mortadella

Bruschetta
Olive oil, salt and garlic on toasts

Bruschetta al pomodoro
Tomato, olive oil, salt and garlic on toasts

Crostini di mare -- big sea toasts
Crustaceans on toasts

Crostini toscani -- Tuscan toasts
Meat sauce on toasts

Crostini misti -- Mixed toasts
A choice of Tuscan meat sauce, mushrooms and tomato sauces on toasts

Insalata di mare -- Seafood salad
crustaceans salad

Cozze al limone -- Mussels with lemon
Cozze alla livornese -- Mussels with tomato

Misto mare freddo
Cold mixed sea food

Misto mare caldo
Mixed cold and warm sea food

I wrote my notes using a pen decorated with a reproduction of Botticelli's Venus on the Half Shell. I paid £5.000 for the pen, and it sk ip pe d. Tomorrow, perhaps I'd turn the page and make my notes on the Primi Piatti; first courses. To think that by the end of the summer we might have sampled all these foods ... !

Firenze, Dante, and DOCG

Two days went somewhere without me. On a stay in France last year, my hosts, whose château was equidistant from Giverny and Versailles, a felicitous location only a half hour by train from Paris, the Express, complained to me, "Why are you always scribbling in that notebook?"

When I sent them the results of the scribbling months later, they were enchantés. I had noted the sauces that Suzanne prepared, the way Daniel cut up the duckling before barbecuing it, the unique matches he used to light his endless cigarettes, the decor of their master bath, similar to a chic parfumier, and their dinner attire. Suzanne was particularly taken with the remembrance of a dinner party on her terrasse one evening. Our table sat under an enormous umbrella she had lighted without revealing the light source. It began to rain. A baby porcupine ran from the lawn under our table for cover. We dined for rainy hours with the tiny creature dodging between our legs.

Day before yesterday, I walked Cristina to Kate's house for her first working session. We had a small conversation when we arrived -- introductions, mainly, and then Kate showed me to the door. When I arrived to pick up Crist, we chatted briefly. She said it was all going to be "Fine, dear." She waved, "Ciao!" to us and we found ourselves in the street.

Yesterday was about the same. Crist has divulged only that it was all working out well. She seemed pleased, so I was pleased. Kate and Crist had come up with a schedule. Crist would go to Kate's house three days a week, Tuesday, Wednesday, and Thursday. The hours might vary. The days, too, might vary. Kate suggested a late afternoon time, to avoid the heat. Crist preferred an early morning schedule, to reserve the rest of the day for "hanging out" and swimming. They compromised. Some days they would get together in the late morning, other days in the mid-afternoon.

I have found something to write on. It is an 8-1/2" x 11" school-ruled notebook with a drawing of an American Indian on the cover. And so I continue scribbling with my ski p p ing Venus pen. Go figure.

Jensen said she didn't feel well today. She begged off going to Firenze, opting to stay home and rest, to have the place to herself. I rather envied her. Robert, Crist, Annie, Rolf, and I drove to Firenze, for our 11:00 prenotazione; reservation at the Uffizi Gallery. Had I not made the reservation, most likely we would not have visited the gallery. The group grumbled at my early morning insistence on promptness, preferring to lounge on the terrazza with their coffees. I decided that after the Uffizi, I'd retire as Tour Guide.

A hot day, a few raindrops cooled us off on our walk from the train station parking garage. We walked through the Piazza della Signoria first, to see Cellini's Perseus in the Loggia della Signoria. The Perseus was missing. It was "out;" being restored. We looked at the plaque imbedded into the Piazza commemorating Savonarola's hanging and auto-da-fé. It was also on this Piazza that the famous book burning took place, when Savonarola convinced his followers to throw away their worldly goods. Artists tossed their own work onto the fire, writers their own books. I read that the work the artists and writers selected to destroy was not among their best and possibly not even their own. We watched the Fountain of Neptune splashing behind the plaque, supposedly erected to assuage the collective Florentine conscience; to put out the fire they started all those years ago.

The line for the Uffizi snaked to the right of the entrance, as far as we could see. Following the instructions faxed by the museum's reservations people, we went to the front of the line, to the left of the entrance. I told a man with a clipboard that we had a prenotazione for 11:00 a.m. and I said the spelling of my name in Italian. The letters of my name were the only letters I had learned. I couldn't say the Italian alphabet. I was glad I had learned to spell my name, as I had to clarify my last name many times over the summer.

The man asked, "seis?" Six? No, I told him we had only cinque; five. One of our party was -- umm, sick. I imagined the party sitting by the pool, sunning and sipping something icy cold. Signore Clipboard motioned to follow him. He went to the Cassa, the cashier, and came back with a refund for the sixth person. He handed us our reserved tickets. I thanked him, sheepishly, surprised that the system had worked as planned and that we had an unexpected refund, too. I tried to tip him, to make recompense for my lie, but he refused. We took the elevator straight up to the third floor, to the Picture Gallery, where all the art was moved after the flood of 1966. The lower floors are uffizi; offices.

We walked through gallery after gallery. Irritatingly,*Pictures at an Exhibition* looped in my head. The quieter, legato parts of the piece were a good walking pace, the crescendos right for entering a gallery and running smack into say, the immense Botticelli's, the dramatic Caravaggio portrait, or Michaelangelo's Holy Family; then more quiet measures for rumination. We cinque went our five separate ways and somehow met up a few hours later.

We left the Uffizi, walking past even longer lines than before and crossed the Ponte Vecchio along with roughly 1/10th of everyone born in the modern world in the past seven decades. The shops sold only jewelry and fanciful pieces of hand-wrought silver. Shop after shop advertised .997 pure silver; more pure than sterling. The shops were small, with most of their stock displayed in the glass showcases fronting the street. Each shop had a window opposite the door. Looking in the door, you saw through the shop to the Arno River. The windows were like frames displaying trompe l'oeil seascapes. In the flood of 1966 all of the priceless goods washed into the river; the silversmith's careful hammerings, the goldsmith's intricate necklaces, the bracelets, rings, the watches, goblets, the silver services and precious stones -- thousands and thousands of pieces drifted into the river like so many gum wrappers.

During our brief chat yesterday, Kate suggested that we get something to eat at the food shops on the street that ran across the Ponte Vecchio. "There are good places on both sides of the bridge, and the food is far cheaper and much better than the ristoranti," she advised me. I trust local knowledge. But this group wanted to sit down at a serious restaurant. We went to Alfredo's for lunch, across the bridge and up a block toward the Uffizi. We sat looking out at the calmly flowing Arno, trying to fathom the treasure buried beneath. Crist and I ordered Fettuccine Alfredo, anticipating the cheesy creamy sauce served by American restaurants. This fettuccine arrived tossed with a sauce of butter, fresh peas, and prosciutto, no cream, fine. The ristorante was touristy and not inexpensive, and the food was not bad.

After lunch, we returned to the Piazza del Duomo to take in the Ghiberti doors, the Baptistery, the Duomo, and Campanile. Giotto, who history has it was brutto; a physically unattractive, even ugly man, was paid 100 gold florins to serve as Bell Tower architect. He died as soon as his marvelous accomplishment was completed, not terrible timing.

The afternoon turned warm and humid. Representatives from all over the world composed themselves in circles on the Piazza, like geometry drawn with a pencil compass on grid paper. Could Giotto have imagined such a drawing?

Walking away from the Duomo, we took an inviting, narrow street and came upon Dante's home. It was closed, but Japanese tourists took turns posing for each other's cameras in front of the locked doors. We continued on, to Dante's church. We entered, and sat in a pew until our eyes became accustomed to the darkness. We were the only people in the cool interior. A large painting of Beatrice's wedding -- not to Dante -- hung on a side wall. Dante is pictured creeping away from the ceremony, distraught. There was a mark on the same wall, and a plaque, taller than my head, at least seven feet up. The plaque said the waters of the flood of 1966 came to that level. The waters rose quickly, too fast to save all the precious art or to move artifacts, paintings, tapestries, and altars to higher ground; more drowned treasure.

On the way back to the car, we shopped the enormous San Lorenzo market. I had read that the merchandise was of good quality, the prices reasonable, and that bargaining was expected. The goods all looked similar, and were priced according to quality. A cheap handbag was inexpensive, a bag with better workmanship was the same price as in a store. I didn't see any interesting, unusual, or otherwise exquisite goods. The fun of it was bargaining with the merchants, something you couldn't do in the shops.

Back home, we stripped off our city clothes and put on swimsuits. In Florence, we wore simple clothing, mostly black, as the Florentine locals did, erring on the side of a "business look." The black clothing was practical, didn't show the wrinkles or gelato stains, and looked at once dressed up and casual. We had hoped to blend in with the locals so as not to attract attention from pickpockets and street merchants, but they spotted us as tourists immediately. Our black clothing also attracted the heat and we were all damp. Tourists who wore tank tops and shorts and sneakers were turned away from the churches, but they looked comfortable in their casual clothing.

One corner of the pool, my favorite corner, looked to the cityscape of San Gim. I lollygagged there. To swim amid olive groves and luxuriant vineyards in the shadow of a medieval walled town was an incongruous experience.

Osteria or Trattoria? Jens, Annie, and Rolf at il Refugio

We had another dinner rez at Il Refugio, our local Ristorante or Trattoria or Osteria, we weren't sure which. According to the guidebooks, there were three classes of restaurants. At the top, the finest and most expensive, was the Ristorante -- defined as a restaurant with white tablecloths. The mid-price range was the Trattoria -- defined as smaller than a ristorante, and often outdoors. At the low end was the dining establishment known as the Osteria, referred to as "the working man's restaurant;" similar, I guess, to the American diner. The osterias specialized in large portions of local products and low prices. Through the summer, I could discern no such clear-cut differences between eating places. For example, Il Refugio had outdoor tables covered with white tablecloths and specialized in large portions of local products at very reasonable prices. Books offered a smattering of knowledge, but there was no substitute for first hand experience.

At Il Refugio, I ordered fettuccine bathed in fresh, black truffle sauce. It was sublime. Crist ordered fettuccine with asparagus, a simple dish with a surprisingly rich undertaste that we decided was the product of a reduction of porcini mushrooms. The others ordered the famous Bisteka Florentine, sold the way fish was sold, by the "etto," or quarter pound. Later, we learned to be insistent about the size of the steak when ordering, telling the waiter that we wanted say, due etti; half a pound, or tre etti; three quarters of a pound. Otherwise, the chef or the waiter decided how many etti (ET-tee, plural of etto) to serve, and you paid for whatever the resulting weight was. We didn't know that. We didn't know what an etto was. Roberto, Jensen, and Rolf all ordered steak without specifying a weight. The staff was feeling generous, the steaks were over a pound each. The chef grilled them outdoors, and served the slabs solo, with only a lemon chunk. You were meant to squeeze the lemon over the steak, and it was delicious.

The hefty steaks looked like American T-Bones, and were about $8.00 each. The à la carte patate frite; French fries, and the salads and other contorni; vegetable side dishes, were $3.00 each. The superior DOCG house Chianti was $6.00 a bottle. At these prices, what matters an extra etto or so? Va bene. We took the leftovers home to squeeze into our tiny fridges. Unlike the French, the Italians were pleased to wrap up leftovers for you.

The seals DOC and DOCG were as common on wines we bought in Chianti as they are uncommon on the wine we bought at home.

DOC stands for denominazione di origine controllata. It's the Italian government's seal of authenticity, guaranteeing that the wine makers have met certain standards set down by the government. The quality standards a winery must meet include how the wine is produced and aged, which grapes and how much of each type are used, minimum alcohol levels, and the maximum yield of grapes per hectare (a hectare being the metric equivalent of about 2-1/2 acres.)

DOCG (the additional -g stands for garantita; guaranteed) is the mark that promises more stringent standards than DOC, including a tasting of the wine before the seal is granted. DOCG wines include Italy's finest: Barolo, Barbaresco, and Brunello di Montalcino. When we bought wine with the DOCG stamp, we were always a bit awed, even though the DOCG prices in Italy are reasonable to inexpensive. We thought about carrying home some of the DOCG, but dismissed the idea -- the bottles are too heavy, and we could buy, at a premium, of course, most of the same wines at home. We opted to enjoy them in Italy as often as possible, an integral part of our vacation.

An Italian Shave

San Gim, or "San Jimmy" as Rolf was now calling our new home town, was shrouded in fog at 7:45 this morning, just like San Fran. The bells from town rang crazily on the off-minutes, without telling us the time. The only other sound was a farmer's tractor. Each dawn, the farmer began to work up and down the vineyard rows below us. Sometimes he sprayed, sometimes he scuffled up weeds. He woke me up. I incorporated the creaky sound into my dream, which usually centered on speeding around curves in our small car, and slept a bit longer.

Roberto, Rolf, and Jensen went to San Gim to the Torture Museum, a comprehensive display of various fascinating "implements;" a cultural event advertised by bright red posters on virtually every lamp post throughout Tuscany, including the streets in Firenze that lead to San Gim. The signs left the impression that San Gim was the Torture Capitol of Italy.

Before viewing the medieval torture devices, Roberto stopped in one of the barber shops for a haircut and shave. There were many barber shops in Tuscany, as many as one per block in the small towns. We didn't know if an appointment would be necessary. It wasn't. Roberto had memorized the page in his Italian Phrase Book devoted to "At the Barber Shop."

He related his experience: it was similar to the movies, he said, the scenes set in Chicago during prohibition, complete with hot towel wrap, mug of foam, straight-edged razor, and Italian-speaking customers and barber. The barber smoked while he worked. Rolf waited outside. When the barber removed the hot towel, Roberto looked out the window. Rolf caught Roberto's eye. He was making the "he's going to slit your throat" gesture, sweeping his forefinger across his throat. Roberto laughed, but he confessed to being nervous, and not just about remembering the barbershop phrases. Afterwards, he said he felt great, and he looked to me like Giorgio Armani himself. He continued to get shaves every few days. The cut was £10.000, $5.70, the shave was £6.000, $3.40 at the constantly climbing, favorable exchange rate. Roberto said he tipped whatever change he had in his pocket. Next, he needed to read the page entitled "Italian Coins." Some are worth less than a penny, while others are worth around a dollar.

I drove Crist to her third lesson with Kate today. I had met Kate briefly at the first and second lessons. She and Crist worked behind closed doors, as conspirators. Today, Kate asked me to return early. When I did, she slyly asked Crist to sing Mozart's *Deh viene non tardar* from "Le Nozze di Figaro;" The Marriage of Figaro. I had heard Cristina sing the aria many times before, the first time at her college Senior Recital, but it was new this time, much more "colorful;" dramatic. Her voice had opened up. She sounded stronger in the higher registers; a demonstration of the "coloratura" in "soprano coloratura." The improvement, or change -- I wasn't sure which word was more accurate -- was impressive. Kate was a gem. She was the bow, Cristina the violin. As corny as it sounds, they made beautiful music together.

Kate was married to a native Italian and had a 17 year-old daughter. Kate was tall, slim, blonde, and beautiful. Her daughter was quite lovely, too, but very dark, taking after her father. The quintessential teenager, she contradicted her mother on every point. I was amused to see that teenagerness is a universal phenomenon. Kate was separated from her husband,

and living with her daughter in a rented apartment just cen' metri from the main archway into San Gim.

She told me that about 20 years ago, she became very ill with an unusually virulent virus that killed everyone in San Gimignano who caught it, except for Kate and one other. This might have been the Russian Flu. Kate had made a strong recovery, but in the last few years, she had developed unusual symptoms and problems that her doctors could not explain. They thought her problems might be related to the original virus. Her left foot drooped. She had to wear a leg contraption in order to walk. She was developing kidney problems. She had been to many specialists and was now pursuing nuclear medicine, but she still had no diagnosis or prognosis. The situation reminded me of the Polio virus. Those who previously had Polio, about 20 to 30 years ago, were now becoming ill again. I asked Kate if there was anything we could do, explaining that Robert was a doctor and knew people in many of the American clinics. She shook her head, thanked me, and said she planned to see a doctor in England.

On Monday, Kate and her daughter would leave for England to visit the boarding school her daughter planned to attend in the fall. I couldn't imagine Kate making this strenuous trip. She was strong, and strong-willed. Cristina would have a week off while Kate was gone. Kate gave her plenty to work on, a new aria and two new pieces for the "Music of Shakespeare" portion of the opera company performance next month, along with new colors to mix into the pieces.

After Crist's lesson, we treated ourselves to gelati. The sign "Proprio prodduti" hanging in a window meant that the gelati shop makes its own gelati, rather than buying bins from a manufacturer. Each shop that advertised proprio prodduti had a specialty. Today I tried the pistachio at one shop, taking tiny tastes to make it last, but eating quickly enough that it wouldn't melt, an art! Crist's favorite was the fragola (FRAH-goal-ah); strawberry, which tasted exactly like fresh-picked warm strawberries, but ice cold.

A stroll through the back steets of San Gim

We shopped through San Gim, and found a small shop near the Cistern with majolica patterns I hadn't seen before -- wonderful lemons worked into irresistible designs on delightfully shaped plates and bowls. I chatted with the artist, whose name is Silvano Mezzetti. He looked about 20, but must have been older, since he had his own shop and was featured in the brochure from the tourist office profiling the finest local artists. When we arrived, Silvano was removing a pitcher from the kiln: cream-colored background, pale lemons worked into a pattern with fanciful, dark blue trim. I asked if I could buy it. "Certo," he smiled; of course. When I got it home, I couldn't find his signature. Usually, the artisan signed the bottom of the piece. Then I noticed that Silvano had Hirschfelded his initials, "SM" into the dark blue trim -- delizioso -- charming!

We stopped at the rental agent's office on the way home to check on The Box, which had still not arrived. Gaynor told me that she traced the box to DHL in Livorno (known in English as the town, Leghorn). The woman she spoke to said it was "in customs," and hung up. I apologized to Gaynor, thanked her for her time and efforts, and asked her to please keep track of her expenses. I was truly sorry that I sent the thing in the first place. It was unnecessary. The Italian culture has flowered for centuries. Italy's products are equal to ours and in many cases, more sophisticated. You have only to recognize a few Italian nouns. It took Jensen and me many minutes at the grocery store to find Tampax, and I bought body lotion only to learn, the hard way, that what I bought was shampoo.

Annie bought me a pot of basil at the market today. It was root-bound and very dry. I loosened the roots, and planted it in one of the boxes of red geraniums on the terrazza, drenching it with acqua. I knew it would grow and prosper in its native conditions of hot sun and rich earth, and also keep the flies away. Many homes in Italy had a pot of basil sitting outside the kitchen door to repel flies.

In the late afternoon, we sat at the pool. The farmer continued to work his way through the rows of his vineyard until dark, stopping only briefly for lunch. From my "pool bed," actually a chaise lounge, I watched him move his machine slowly back and forth. His tiny figure made a reassuringly creaky progress, not unlike the giant black ants that constantly moved back and forth across the terra-cotta pool pavement.

Dinner in the olive grove: Crist, Annie, Rolf, Roberto, Jens

Annie prepared a feast for us this evening. We dined on the terrazza in the olive grove. We gathered at dusk to drink the crisp, chilled Pietrafitta Rosata and to snap pictures of us in the grove with San Gim in the background. It was a magical evening of warmth and happiness. I used two rolls of film; 48 frames to remember our evening by. We ate barbecued chicken, infant green beans, an arugula salad, garlic bread, and a fantastic pasta salad, followed by lemon cake. Annie cooked all day, Jensen chopped and carried and cleared and cleaned up. It was a highly memorable evening; great American cuisine made even better with Italian materiel, served on Tuscan soil in the shadow of a medieval walled town.

The Porchetta and the Porchetta man

This Saturday was our first clear morning. Church bells rang and clanged and a thousand hounds bayed in response as if the bells tolled for them. Fog floated in wisps under the San Gim skyline. The town looked like a fantasy; a castle in the sky.

Kate had recommended the Saturday morning market in Castellina in Chianti. Roberto stayed home to have his day off. His understudy, Jensen, moved up to the lead rôle of Italian driver. To go anywhere, we had to first drive through Poggibonsi. It is the hub. All roads led to Poggibonsi. Once there, we joked that there was a magnetic force that kept us there. Actually, it was a confounding roundabout. The road from Poggibonsi to Castellina was narrow and twisty and steep, similar to California's Highway, U.S. 1, the famous Pacific Ocean coastal road, and also reminiscent of Paradise Drive, the road behind our house, which we drove every day.

Jensen had learned to drive on roads like this, and her own car, an ancient Volvo sedan, had a stick shift. She was used to downshifting around blind curves that dropped off precipitously. She got us to Castellina quickly and effortlessly. There were no other cars on the road until we neared town -- where a large Jaguar loomed in front of us, speeding toward us in our lane. Instinctively, Jens drove out of the situation and then easily found the market. We were all impressed.

ASIDE: Rarely do Italian drivers stay within the confines of their narrow lanes, adopting the "your lane è my lane" attitude. They almost always cross into the opposite lane on the curves, as the Jaguar had. We hugged the right side of the road, especially on the curves.

Castellina in Chianti's market wove all the way through the main street of the medieval walled town. Clothing for sale billowed on lines like laundry -- pretty, printed, long, cotton dresses, shirts, shorts, pants, undergarments, shoes, bags -- we could have bought our entire traveling wardrobe here in a few minutes instead of packing and lugging our American clothes thousands of miles. After the waves of clothing and bins of underwear, there were displays of household items -- linens, dishes, aprons, flatware, pots and pans, and kitchen gadgets. Then came the van offering paper towels, plastic wrap, toilet cleaners -- all the household necessities. The main event lay ahead -- the food vendors.

First, the Porchetta van (por-KET-tah). Every market had one or two Porchetta vans -- motorized, white vans filled with meats. One side opened to reveal a glass display case, similar to the sandwich vendors in the States -- the vans that service construction sites and manufacturing plants. In the countryside, Porchetta vans stopped along the roadside to dispense food for hungry travelers. The butcher also sold prosciutto crudo (raw) and prosciutto secco (cooked), but his raison d'être was the Porchetta, the whole, roasted pig. The pig was stuffed with coarse salt and spices, including rosemary, and spit-roasted so that the skin was crisp and stiff as a fresh saltine cracker. The pig was over a meter long, plus the head. The head was cleanly severed, and displayed to the side of the body. The pig's girth was a good 14-15 inches.

I walked up to the van and gaped. The tall, well-fed, good-looking Porchetta man smiled and challenged, "Dica!" Tell me. I said, "Porchetta, per favore." He began to slice off pieces until I said, "Basta!" enough, and then he sliced off a few more. He handed me a generous taste of the meat and another of the crispy crust. As I tasted, he wrapped up the Porchetta slices in smooth butcher's paper, making a clever paper pocket on top. He filled the pocket with several tablespoons of the stuffing. I found Annie and Rolf and Jensen and shared my find with them. The stuffing was too salty for our increasingly salt-free American palates. But the crust was delicious. We ate it all, even the fatty layer under the crust. I took a few photos of the porchetta, of the porchetta and the porchetta man, and of Rolf and the porchetta man. Rolf was grinning like a little leaguer who just hit a homer. It would be our favorite photo of the summer.

For £1.300, I bought six porcini mushrooms, whose heads were the size of beefsteak tomatoes, and three warm, fragrant tomatoes of the same size, for the same price. We were now in the heart of town, in front of the main enoteca, La Castellina, a 14th century palace with a 500 year history of making wine and olive oil. The wine was still produced on the lower floors and the ground or "Piano" floor (piano means "level) was a tasting and buying room. We entered.

In addition to their wines and olive oils, they sold woven shopping bags with interior compartments to accommodate six bottles. Generous side pockets could store other foods. I bought a bag and filled it with their olive oil, two bottles of their Chianti Classico Riserva 1990, and then moved on to the bakery across the street, where I added homemade apricot tarts and bread to my new basket. At the produce store next to the bakery, I chose peaches and grapes so sweet they made my teethe ache. My bag was full, my cup ran over. Annie and I sat on a bench to wait for the others, who had remained in the enoteca to taste some wines. I showed Annie the bottle of olive oil. The label was handwritten. The translation is to the right:

"olio extravergine di oliva (extra virgin olive oil) contenuto netto 0, 750 litre (net contents 750 liters) scadenza: GIU" (expiration date: July)

The oil was the color of gold, lighted with pale, olive green. It was corked, but once uncorked, I doubted it would last us more than two weeks, much less until next July.

When the other three had finished their tasting, and bought a few bottles, we continued on through the narrow streets. We noticed a fancy blue bow affixed to one of the doors. Across from the door sat a white-haired woman, on a bench. She was looking at me looking at the bow, grinning toothlessly, and rocking back and forth like an excited two year-old. I laughed and pointed to the bow, and before I could formulate my question, she explained that her first grandson was just born. His name was Paolo, the blue bow was his birth announcement. She wore a cheerful blue print Sunday dress and a black cardigan sweater. She would sit there all day, or maybe all week, proudly rocking back and forth until she had told all the neighbors her good news. Annie sat to rest next to her on the bench. I took their picture. We wished the "nonna;" grandmother, congratulations. Annie, who had six grandchildren, told me "I know just how she feels." We squeezed the nonna's hand. We saw inside her eyes and shared her pride.

We walked back to the car through the meandering market. I wanted to buy some flowers. But the flower stands had only a few plants and fewer flowers. The shops' large pails were filled with silk flowers. This would be standard throughout the summer. Tuscany grows grapes and olives, vegetables and fruits, not fancy flowers to decorate the tourists' villas. I didn't buy anything. We drove back home around lunch time. Just before our turn-off to the villa, we saw a sign, "San Donato 2 k."

"Let's see if there's a ristorante there?" We all chimed.

Jensen drove past our driveway for 2 k. On the right, we saw a ristorante and a sign: Osteria Antiche Terre Rosse (Old Red Earths.) We drove into the small parking lot and parked. The manager showed us to an outdoor table. The Osteria's tables were set with white linens, under umbrellas. The waiter brought us a large basket of bread. I asked if we could have some olive oil, to dip the bread in. He didn't understand the California custom. He brought us a serving bowl full of fine oil, probably half a liter. We dipped in. We all had the easy to pronounce and translate special, pasta with pesto made from basil and noci (NO-chee); hazelnuts, and salads, mineral water, and chilled San Gim Vernaccia. The heat from the food and the sun peaked when we had finished eating. The cicadas piped up. The day slowed down. We didn't want to move a dito; a finger.

We were glad we weren't tourists who had to get back on a bus and move on to a new town, to yet another hotel, to lug baggage and to unpack and re-pack. We were glad we weren't with the bicycle tour that slowly made its way past the Osteria up the steep hill. The sweaty riders stared at us. I didn't feel a bit of guilt when I ordered dessert for us: cantuccini with Vin Santo. Cantuccini are the locally made, small biscotti. "Vin Santo," holy wine, is also a local specialty. The wine was served in a sort of double shot glass. The biscotti came in a large bowl. You dipped the biscotti into the Vin Santo to soften both, and slowly made your way through the wine and cookies until both were gone. Vin Santo was an acquired taste. We acquired it about half-way through the biscotti. It tasted like a combination of sherry and Madeira. It is the same color, a light caramel.

Vin Santo is badly mistreated in its making, as compared to making say, Chianti. The wine maker, or the vineyard owner, picks his best white grapes at harvest time, and puts them onto cane mats. He puts the mats onto racks in his attic until the autumn heat dries them, which could be months later. The white grapes turn into sweet, tan raisins. The raisins are crushed and pressed and put into wooden barrels where the farmer has left a judicious slosh of leftovers from the previous year. The dregs are called the "madre;" the mother, and it is the madre that gives birth to the unusual taste of the off-springing Vin Santo.

The barrels are then put back into the attic for several years to season through the cold of the winters and the rising heat of the summers. The fermentation stops and starts, according to the weather, and when the Padrone thinks his wine is ready, usually in spring, around Easter, accounting for the name; Holy Wine, he brings the barrels down from the attic and bottles the wine. I had bought a bottle of Vin Santo in San Gim and some cantuccini from our favorite bakery, Lucia e Maria. Now we knew how to serve the two. I thought that rather than a dessert, the combination of wine and cookies would be a lovely late-afternoon treat, maybe a 5:00 p.m. snack -- as was zabaione. Zabaione was served to children in the afternoon, after school.

Back home, we napped first, then swam in the early evening. Still wearing our swimsuits, we ate Annie's wonderful leftovers at 8:30 p.m. Jensen and I contributed some eggplant slices, sautéed in our new olive oil and splashed with Balsamic. We poured the luscious olive oil over everything. It wouldn't last the week.

The Olive Freeze and The Rustic Path

Blue, blue sky this morning, much more colorful than any previous day. High stratus clouds streaked the sky, and it was warm even at 7:00 a.m., as I sat at the terrazza table in my white cotton pajamas, barefoot. I rose early to pick my own fresh flowers, dewy snippings from our garden: pink hydrangea blossoms, Queen Anne's lace, pale pink roses, and sprigs of lavender and rosemary. I arranged them in a signature San Gim mottled green and white ceramic (majolica) pitcher and put the pitcher on the outdoor table.

I also cut some long, dried artichoke stems from the olive grove above. The purply prickly flowers looked good with the rose-colored gladioli Annie bought me at the market. Each of the stems was four feet long. I arranged them in a tall terra-cotta urn in our kitchen and thought we were becoming very homey. Only for a moment did I wonder if my fragrant rose, "Just Joey" was opening its immense, ruffly apricot colored blooms back at home.

The sun cast stubby shadows next to the short olive trees in the grove. In 1988, a devastating freeze killed all the Tuscan olive trees. A few farmers cut their trees to new wood right after the freeze. In the spring, new shoots appeared. They didn't have to replant. Those farmers who didn't prune -- they were the majority -- had to first remove their old, dead trees, and then replant their groves, losing a growing season in the process.

Then, in December of 1996, there was a severe one-day freeze, which damaged many trees again. The farmers had learned by then to quickly cut back the frozen branches to new wood. So the olive trees throughout Tuscany are new and short, shorter than the groves in the Napa Valley. The blunt-cut branches look as if vandals took up the pruning clippers, but the trees are healthy. Baby green olives are beginning to weigh down the junior branches. The olive harvest takes place in November and December. By then, the olives could hang to the ground.

Crist and Robert and I walked the "rustic" path to Kate's this morning. It took them exactly 20 minutes, me a rough 30. I kept jumping in place when I heard the bushes rustle with what I took to be vipere, vipers, so it took longer than it would to fearlessly stride straight up the path as they did. I was very hungry when we arrived. While Crist had her lesson, Roberto and I window-shopped. The first thing to catch my eye was a golden Belgian waffle displayed in a bar's window. We went into the tiny bar to see what else looked good. A glass case offered apricot-stuffed croissants, apricot tarts, custard-stuffed donuts, biscotti, and an interesting torta: a round loaf of bread cut lengthwise and filled with layers of sliced tomato, salami, cheese, and hard boiled eggs. The man behind the counter was cutting the loaf in wedges and serving it to the locals at the bar, along with cups of espresso. A long line waited. Some patrons drank coffee, some drank red wine, others asked for beverages that were orange and green and came from the line of liqueur bottles behind the bar.

When it was my turn, using the menu written on the blackboard as my cue card, I asked for a hot waffle with marmalade. In a very deep voice and with a pretty good accent,

Roberto commanded "un caffè." We examined the liqueur bottles. The green was artichoke liqueur. After spending several minutes in the back kitchen, the counterman brought out my hot waffle, smothered in butter and orange marmalade. When it was gone and I was gooey, we went into a majolica shop, where we saw a magnificent table that would be perfect for our Italianate patio at home. The shopkeeper told us he could custom make a table like it in any design we wished. He quoted a good price that included shipping. He would ship by boat, to the Port of Oakland, he explained. It would take eight weeks to make the table, another eight for the shipping. I told him we would think about it. We picked up some food for lunch. Roberto chose some Chianti and a large chunk of aged Reggiano.

We returned a few minutes early to pick up Crist and to hear one of her new songs. We could hear her singing when we were still a block from Kate's. She was working very hard and sounded better each day, if such a thing was possible. Together, we three retraced our steps and jumps on the path back home. We all sat on the terrazza and dined on roasted peppers, olives, artichoke hearts, mortadella, salami, bread, melon, and grapes. The Chianti and slivers of Reggiano made a delicious coupling. We sat until the mid-afternoon landscape became totally still, and then we dozed here and there.

In the early evening, we swam, tanning ourselves in the late sun, and gazing at the changing shadows in the groves and vineyards. Soon, we were hungry again. I finely sliced two of the grand porcini mushrooms lengthwise for hors d'oeuvres, dipped them in a light mixture of flour and water whisked together, and fried them in olive oil, a dish we had enjoyed in the ristorante in Ferrara. Then I sautéed the rest of the porcinis in oil and butter, splashed them with Vernaccia and put them aside. I whisked together an Alfredo sauce, American style, simple cream and the complex local Romano cheese, and added the mushroom sauce and mushrooms to it. Crist cooked pasta. We tossed it all together, and grated some of Roberto's Reggiano to pass.

I served the pasta with a tomato salad (quarter clove of garlic crushed onto a platter, tomatoes sliced on top, drizzled with olive oil, freshly ground pepper and snippets of our basil). We dipped the dense bread into the juices. At home, I would use a medium clove of garlic for a tomato salad, but Tuscan garlic is very potent.

At home, I would pop the bread into the oven to crisp it up. There was no oven, so I couldn't heat the bread. As I had read, Tuscan electricity is minimal. We had a lamp or two in each room, a bright but inadequate light in each bathroom, and the outdoor lights that we couldn't use. Maria and Max requested, Please turn off lights when not using or when not here. Don't turn outside lights on at night. We presumed that we shouldn't turn them on in the daytime either. We used lots of candles.

The Tuscan houses were like American cabins in the countryside. Each had a septic tank, and the stoves were fueled by propane. We had no small electrical appliances. We made toast over the stove's open flame, turning the bread on the tines of a fork. Sometimes, we didn't drop it into the fire. We usually burned both the toast and our fingers. The Tuscans toasted their bread on a grill, rubbed it with garlic and a dab of olive oil and served it as an antipasto; bruschetta. They didn't serve toast for breakfast. Our refrigerator was below the counter, a bar refrigerator, really, not much larger than a hotel room mini-bar. After a week, we stopped hoping it would make ice. We filled our little fridge with white wine, milk for our coffee, the rich butter, and a few leftovers. Annie and Rolf defrosted their refrigerator, and it never worked again. They stored their perishables in our fridge.

I couldn't find any coffee I like. Each day I bought a new kind and it all tasted bland -- strong, bitter, but bland.

Hot Dogs and Il Trovatore

NO HUNTING

The farmer began his tractor work before 7:00 a.m. this morning. The San Gim dogs seemed to bark all night long. They were hunting dogs, owned by every countryside resident. In my wanderings, I had seen the dog pens where the hounds were kept. Two to four dogs were penned inside a fenced enclosure of perhaps eight feet by 10 feet. The roof was tin. The sun beat down on the roof all day and by late afternoon there were hot dogs cooking all over Tuscany.

Tuscan property was all posted "vietato cacciare" -- no hunting. The hunters had killed everything that flies, walks, and crawls for miles and miles around. There was a moratorium on all hunting until the countryside was "repopulated." The dogs had nothing to do but wait and bake and bark.

At home, one of my greatest pleasures after finishing my daily gardening work would be to sit on the patio and watch my birds. Finches filled the shrubbery, waiting their turn for thistle seed at the bird feeder. Doves nested under the eaves, cooing back and forth. Hummingbirds bathed in the fountain, then flitted from abutilon to fuschia to salvia to sip their fill of the nectars. Robins hopped on the lawn, listening for their next meal. The mockingbirds showed off their repertoire. Jays fought over the birdbath, quails whistled along the patio wall, and above it all, turkey vultures and red tailed hawks soared, looking for lunch.

Here, a sighting of a half-dozen birds in an entire day was my best count. I saw only swallows and pigeons on the villa grounds. The swallows swooped to the pool, swallowing a mouthful of water on each skimming pass. I saw my first hummingbird moth though, a creature I had only read about. They were exciting to see, and plentiful. They were the size of hummingbirds, but they were -- well, huge moths. They had survived because they are not birds. They hovered on our terrazza, often brushing my shoulder. I didn't need the binoculars packed in The Box.

Robert, Jensen, Annie and Rolf went to Siena for the day. Crist and I went to Kate's " real house" this morning, the house where she would normally live with her husband. Kate insisted that Cristina practice at her real house while Kate took her daughter to England. She thought Crist might get sidetracked at the villa. She didn't know her well yet. We were to meet Kate's maid at the house at 10:00 a.m. sharp. We left early. We arrived too early, a happy happenstance that allowed time for a stop at Lucia e Maria. We chose warm, sugary donuts stuffed with fresh custard to eat while we walked to Kate's real house. The house was on the perimeter wall to the left of the main town entrance. Kate's maid let us in at exactly 10:00 a.m. We brushed the sugar off our clothing and walked smiling into the dark, sun-heated house.

There was an outdoor terrace that looked over to the town wall, then a sun room, with a 4' x 6' painting of Kate when she was maybe 25. She was still as beautiful as then. The artist had scrawled a complimentary note to her on the painting. The music room had a Steinway grand and stiff, formal Victorian furnishings. I left Crist there to work, and returned to the sunroom. While Crist practiced, I picked up a coffee table book about the Etruscans, dedicated to Kate by its author, and went out to the terrace to read, to listen, to wait. While Crist's voice was soaring, I was learning that the Etruscans believed that their destiny was determined by what happened in the skies. Not much has changed, I thought, as I sat there on the terrace watching the distant clouds as they began to gather and swell.

Crist worked for over an hour. She is a dedicated musician. She has innate talent but also works very hard at the technical aspects of her singing, repeating a phrase over and over until she thinks it is perfetto; perfect. She came from the hot, dark room, blinking at the sharp sun. She was sweating, her voice was thick from singing. But she smiled beautifully.

We wandered through the San Gim streets and alleyways in search of good coffee and an outdoor ristorante for a future dinner. We entered a crowded bar where locals stood drinking espresso, and asked for an etto of ground coffee, "a portare," to go. The counterwoman gave us an odd look, but scooped coffee into a bag for us. We browsed on, into an enoteca off the Cistern. We noted a ristorante in the back. Stairs led to the outside. We climbed them. More stairs led to a rooftop ristorante that looked out on the countryside. I jotted down the name and phone number, not that we have a phone, and made a tentative rez for my birthday, August 7. We got gelati, pesca; peach for me, fragola for Crist. I kept asking for fish, pesce, instead of peach, pesca, same as I do in French. The counter-people alternately laughed and gave me disparaging looks. I shrugged and explained, "Sono straniera;" I'm a foreigner. I hadn't thought of myself as a foreigner before.

We took our gelati over to the stage in front of the Duomo, to watch the rehearsal for tonight's performance of *Il Trovatore*. We couldn't get tickets. We had no idea which opera or concert was being performed when. We knew only that there was a program almost every night, as there was in every small town in Tuscany all summer long. When we saw the odd poster advertising an entertainment, we inquired about tickets, but except for the plays that were performed in Italian, all performances were always sold out.

We sat in the shade to watch the rehearsal -- on the usual white, plastic chairs, at the edge of a group of old men; locals, who sat there most of the day whether or not there was a performance. They chatted and laughed loudly together, paying no attention to the rehearsal. In front of us sat a row of slim, tanned, bejeweled, chic Italian men and women who appeared to be affiliated with the opera. Their conversation was as softly musical as singing. I felt we were accidentally sandwiched into a Fellini film about the production of an opera; miscast extras.

The acoustics were such that we thought the performers were merely mouthing their words, not singing; saving their voices. We walked to the center of the stage, and it was the same. But when we walked to stage right, we could hear every word. We stood in the sun and listened through the first act.

The cast took a lunch break, and so did we. We climbed a steep side street to a trattoria we had seen the day before. This trattoria was indoors and had white tablecloths. We sat sandwiched again, this time between Germans, Italians, and two Japanese women who inexplicably spoke only Spanish. Our lunch was luscious, tagliatelli with basil pesto for Crist, crespelle stuffed with homemade ricotta and spinach with a Bolognese sauce for me. Crespelle are pancakes, stuffed and rolled up, similar to Cannelloni. We split a green salad and a half carafe of the delightful local Vernaccia, a light, white, perfectly chilled foil for the rich, hot food.

So far, we had made our own dressing to go with our salads. With the bowl of greens; insalata verde, or the bowl of mixed greens; insalata mista, the waiter brought a compartmentalized stainless steel container holding vessels of olive oil, vinegar, salt, and pepper. We poured and shook and tossed and served ourselves. We poured some of the olive oil on our bread, too. The Tuscan bread was unsalted and tasteless, with a consistency more like cake than the crusty, chewy "Italian" bread we were used to at home. The locals dipped the bread in their sauces and soup, and used the bread to make the hearty bread salad known as panzanella, and the bread and tomato soup commonly offered on Tuscan menus. Tuscan bread was a vehicle. I began to put a few small chunks into pasta sauce, a nice textural addition.

Grated cheese did not automatically come with a serving of pasta as it does at home. We usually had to ask for it. It came in the same kind of glass container cum spoon as American restaurants, but it was quite substantial and tasty. In San Gim, the grated cheese served was the aged Reggiano. It was the color of dark toast.

Because of the heat, the heavy food, and probably the wine, and most definitely the fear of rustling snakes on the rustic path, we decided to taxi home instead of walk. We lay in the coolness of our bedrooms to rest and read for a while, and then we swam.

I watered my "garden" before dinner. I had been watering the basil twice a day and it was growing like Jack's Beanstalk. It was crowding out the hardy geraniums. I didn't allow myself to wonder about my garden at home. I would miss the entire life cycle of some of my plants and hundreds of rose blossoms. My own basil would grow tall, blossom, and die.

I had read several Tuscan cookbooks before we left California and tried a number of recipes in my kitchen at home. I began at the first page and worked my way through, following the pattern I used when I learned to cook in the first year of our marriage. I had cooked page by page through Julia Child's *Mastering the Art of French Cooking*.

With the Tuscan cookbooks, what sounded scrumptious turned out boring. It was because I didn't have Tuscan ingredients. I made another simple sauce for our pasta tonight, following a Tuscan recipe I had tried at home: Pour a generous amount of luscious local olive oil into a saucepan, heat it, then slice three small red onions and let them simmer in the oil. When they softened, add a generous dollop of Balsamic vinegar, and let the mixture get caramelly. Add a medium sized clove of garlic, minced, and several fresh tomatoes and a few chunks of bread.

I snipped a generous handful of our own pungent basil into the sauce, and simmered the mixture for about 15 minutes. I moved the pot off the fire to stew in its own juices while I boiled water, adding to it a spoonful of olive oil and a pinch of salt. Crist cooked fresh tagliatelli al dente. We tossed the pasta and sauce together and called it "Toscana." I minced a handful of green olives to serve on the side, to mix into the pasta; an exceptional combination. Roberto grilled sausages on the barbecue. Each butcher shop and Alimentari; grocery store, offered several varieties of sausages concocted by the butcher. The sausages were about six inches long and as thick as three thumbs. We didn't know their contents, whether beef, pork, or "other." We assumed that the butcher made the sausages from meats that had not sold; random leftovers. We had selected sausages, one of each kind, pointing and saying, "un di questi, per favore" (oon dee QUEST-ee); one of these, please.

We had bought five sausages. Roberto pricked them with a sharp knife before putting them on the outdoor grill. Fat oozed and sizzled from the sausages, splashing the coals and the terracotta. We moved the grill to the brick walk to spare our lovely tile. When the sausages were ready, their size had diminished to two crisp thumbs each. The taste was beefy and slightly spicy; very hearty. Annie mixed up insalata mista. We put the bowls and platters on our outdoor table, to serve family style. We also nibbled on store-bought side dishes: peppers and eggplant marinated in olive oil. We agreed it was "the best dinner we ever ate." Every night we say the same thing, and every night it is true.

Individually, Tuscan ingredients are richer than those at home. By comparison, the Tuscan flavors are extreme; neon to California's Technicolor.

We left for Italy 16 days ago. Any reticence is gone; both my feet are here. I could use some Italian shoes to put them in.

Fattoria Bosco and Montalcino

I got up early to try the new coffee. I made two pots, using the stove top espresso makers that make one cup each, and quickly making several pots so we could all sit and have coffee together. The coffee tasted old, even when we added the rich, warm milk and a small amount of sugar.

What would take the listless taste away? Crist and I described the decadent sugared donuts stuffed with custard that we had tasted at Lucia e Maria yesterday. Rolf grabbed the car keys and we were off. We parked at the back gate to San Jimmy, where the locals park, and walked the length of the twisty strada to Lucia e Maria. Lucia was tending the cash register and the bar while Maria waited on customers at the pastry counter. The display case was full. I asked for six custard donuts by pointing to them and saying, "Seis;" say, six. I chose three apricot-stuffed croissants; pointing and saying "tre;" tray, three. I'd developed a taste for the croissants, as I hoped to for Italian coffee. A few apple tarts and turnovers filled with a smidgen of custard rounded out the breakfast selection. Maria arranged them on a paper tray and wrapped it in tissue paper.

If I could write a sonata, or an aria to be inserted into an operetta, I would call it "Lucia e Maria." A plump, dimpled woman would sing it. We retraced our footsteps and stopped at the other San Jim bakery in hopes of securing some of the crusty pane di olive; olive bread, but it was still in the oven. There was only pane di noci, hazelnut bread. As I was deciding if the group would like it, a Signora bought it all.

We dashed home with our treasures. I strip-teased the tissue wrappings off the tray. The audience was receptive. Jensen wondered how much custard might be in one of these donuts. She cut it in half, and squeezed out the custard into a measuring cup. The custard filled the cup. (Gulp.)

Roberto is on short time, leaving soon for home. The group decided he and I should spend the day together. "Take your car," they offered generously. I picked Montalcino as our destination because it was one of Italy's greatest wine towns, because Roberto loved the local wine, Brunello di Montalcino, and because it wasn't far. We wound south on the Chianti Road and then onto a confusion of single-lane, gravel back roads known as the "white roads" of Chianti. We were alone on the trail and glad of it. The Fiat kicked up a wake of chalk white dust that choked the air as far as we could see.

Seeing open gates, we veered off the road and made an unscheduled stop at Fattoria Bosco, a grand medieval castle set on acres of renaissance-landscaped grounds. We hoped for a wine tasting. We explored the estate, walking up cobblestone pathways, peering into the windows of deserted out-buildings, scrambling up the stone walls to the top of the crumbling fortezza; the lookout point of the medieval fiefdom. A black squirrel scurried up an ancient oak with her baby in her mouth -- my first black squirrel sighting, and a double at that. We had seen little wildlife, though Tuscany appeared to have more of what we Californians refer to as "open space" than California does.

We could find no one to ask about a tasting. We gave up and walked back to the entrance where a chain barred the road and supported a "privato" sign. We stepped over the chain and knocked on a door. A tall, dark young satrap opened it.

We asked, "Degustazione?" Tasting?

"Si," he said deeply and darkly. He solemnly led us to the tasting room, unlocked the door, and invited us to proceed ahead of him. Reluctant to enter the forbidding looking room with our sinister host, Roberto and I did our "After you Alfonse" soft shoe. I stepped in first. The room was dank and dark and acutely reminiscent of Poe's cellar in *The Cask of Amontillado*. The dour young man closed the door. My scalp tingled. He poured us a 1990 Brunello with a '95 chaser without meeting our eyes. He spoke no English. He spoke not at all. A cut-off shotgun casually slung over his shoulder would not have looked out of place.

For lack of anything else to say, I lamely asked the young man how many bottles Bosco produced last year. He brightened somewhat, and replied, I think, a million bottles. The wine was divine. As we praised it, he warmed to us and poured more. We wanted to buy some, but we didn't have much cash. This was an unscheduled stop, I tried to explain. He said he could accept only cash or Eurochecks. We had no Eurochecks -- I reckoned that only Europeans carried them. We had £100.000 that we had earmarked for lunch money. We didn't want to spend it all. We didn't know if we'd find a Bankomat in Montalcino. The young man told us a bottle of the '90 would be £35.000, about $20.00. Without conferring, we dug deep in our pockets to buy three, leaving us liraless.

We drove on to Montalcino with a few mis-turns, all of them dusty, white hairpins. We enjoyed unplanned visits to towns cen' metri long, towns that are not even specks on the Michelin map.

ASIDE: For the average tourist who doesn't go off piste, the Michelin maps are excellent. For the more adventurous, local tourist offices had maps that pinpointed the tiniest country towns. Many of the pin-dot towns had the same name. We counted six San Donatos.

In January, I ordered our Michelin road maps through a bookstore in Marin County. They arrived a week later. In the meantime, I gathered info from the current Michelin Red Guide of Italy and some Green Guides. I sent the Green Guides ahead to Italy in The Box; a big mistake.

The symbols and other markings in the Red Guide at first appeared to be indecipherable code. Once you have mastered the code, the Red Guide was invaluable. I quit trying to gestalt the mysterious hieroglyphics after several false starts, and began at Page One, as I had with Julia Child's book, reading carefully to learn how the Red Guide works. Town entrances and exits were keyed to the Michelin maps. You matched up the symbols and you knew where you were entering the town. Distances between towns were listed. The Guide located the main streets and squares of each town and the town's chief attractions. It recommended and ranked hotels and restaurants in each town, placed their locations and, among other niceties, provided data on their amenities, including prices, phone, and fax numbers.

The Guide pointed to parking and also indicated which streets were one way, and which way. Like everything that is brilliantly thought out, the symbols were practical, and simple to use.

I had thought perhaps the restaurants and hotels recommended by the Red Guide would be the most expensive and/or elaborate. Instead, the Guide led us to restaurants that offered an extra something -- a lovely view, a stunning setting, a special dessert, unusually presented appetizers -- an uncommon feature that set the restaurant apart from others in the town. In all cases, restaurant suggestions from the Red Guide were at minimum clean, the service very good, and the food well-prepared.

The Guide listed the restaurant prices, giving a range, of say, £40/65.000 per person for dinner. Traveling around, we learned that the range cited was for a full-course dinner without wine. Normally, we ate as we did at home, ordering a salad and entrée, plus house wine and bottled water. Our dinner check, with cover charge and tip, was often half what the Red Guide quoted as the low-end price. We made a habit of ordering the house wine, which generally came from small, local vineyards that did not sell to the public. Except for once, the vino di casa was very good. We sent the bottle back that once without a problem.

When we asked a waiter for a wine recommendation, we were rewarded with respect that bordered on worshipfulness and a bottle to remember for days, at a price that was only a few lire more than the house wine. A waiter's selection was often occasion for careful uncorkage and decanting plus as much verbal "informazione" as we could understand.

All restaurants included "service" Sair-VEE-chay; the tip. We started our trip tipping our waiter about 10% above the check. We noticed that nobody else tipped at all, since the service was always included, so we stopped tipping quite so much, leaving the equivalent of about a dollar and a half on the table, less than 40 cents per person. Some restaurants, usually in the cities, also had "coperti," a cover charge. The charge was clearly printed on the menu, and sometimes on the menu outside the ristorante. The coperti; coh-PAIR-tee, ranged from £1.000

to £5.000 per person -- the latter would be for music or for a particularly special outdoor setting. The average coperti was £2.500 per person; $1.40.

We used the Red Guide mostly in the cities, taking potluck in the countryside where, if you chose a full course dinner with antipasti, primi, secondi, contorni, wine, water, dolci e caffè you would pay about £32.000 or $18.00 per person. A simpler dinner was about $12.00 with house wine. All the ristorante post their menus outside, even the smallest country osterias.

ASIDE: The Red Guide doesn't give area codes for the cities. Other guides, such as Cadogans' and Fromer's supply area codes. For convenience, I jotted the area codes into the Red Guide.

In Montalcino, Roberto and I followed our noses and ears to a bustling pizzeria/ristorante on a side street where the VISA symbol was displayed on the door. The large, round tables were filled with locals, except one where, surprisingly to us, six or seven American children were celebrating a birthday.

As we entered, we passed the antipasto table. Large, oval platters held stuffed artichokes and peppers, slices of grilled eggplant, tomatoes and buffalo mozzarella, and tiny green beans glistening with olive oil. The chef was placing a heaping bowl of fresh Tiramisu next to the antipasto. It all looked promising.

Roberto ordered our usual to start: "una bottiglia di acqua minerale naturale grande e una bottiglia grande di vino rosso della casa." He asked for antipasto di casa; house antipasto, the waiter would please choose for us. We savored the vegetables and vino locale; local wine, the Brunello. We ordered pizza (Roberto: tomato sauce, mozzarella, sausage, sautéed red onions. Me: mozzarella, fresh tomato and basil.) By the time it arrived, fresh from the wood oven, we were already full. We sipped wine and waited for the antipasto to settle. Pizza was always served whole, with a self-service serrated knife. We sliced off small pieces and shared, eating as much as we could. It was the best pizza we had ever tasted. With food like this, one's stomach made accommodations.

I ordered Tiramisu, along with due caffès; un caffè is always espresso. Taking our time, we managed to eat the entire rich, generous serving of dolce. Then we walked to the 14th century Rocca and on up to the top of the fortezza to walk off our lunch. The area was deserted, except for a theater troop setting up in the center of the 13th century Palazzo Communale; the town square. The Rocca was the last stronghold of the Sienese Republic, constantly under siege by its enemies, which included the Florentines, the French, and the Spanish. Finally, when the Montalcino population of Sienese had dwindled to a couple thousand, the Medici family attacked. And won.

Roberto, who was a history major, looked out contemplatively, the Sienese Lord surveying his kingdom, keeping a look-out for enemies, strategizing a counter to the next attack, mentally boiling oil for his serfs to pour over any foolhardy invaders. While he was thus engaged, I slipped away to the fortezza's terrace, lay down on a bench, and slept for 20 minutes. When I awoke, the effects of wine and food had evaporated and Roberto had also vanished. This was not unusual behavior on his part, so I didn't immediately panic that I was alone in a strange town thousands of miles from home.

I looked for him in Enoteca La Fortezza, Italy's second most famous enoteca (he had visited the first, Enoteca Permanente, in Siena.) He was happily browsing the Brunellos, as he would history books. The shelves were filled with fine cantuccini and cheeses and olive oils identical to those in San Gim, but twice as expensive. Roberto ordered a glass of 1983 Brunello, paid with plastic (an enoteca charges to taste wine, but the barman fills a large glass nearly to the brim), and we sat in the courtyard, slowly savoring the brownish wine that can age comfortably for 50 years. We watched the "show people" set up lights in the piazza, half-wishing we could stay for the evening's performance and wholeheartedly wishing that we could afford to take home a case of this extraordinary wine. Before leaving, Roberto bought a few bottles of Rosso di Montalcino, the "second" Montalcino wine, and one of Grappa di Brunello, in a tall, delicate, hand-blown glass vessel.

The Sienese Lord drove us back to the villa, fast. We sped through the vineyards and back through the tiny towns and past more vineyards and kicked up a Kansas dust storm. We shared some wine with the group, and told them about our day. Rolf reported they had rain in San Jimmy -- huge, hard drops. They were happy to have stayed home.

Annie had hamburgers ready to grill. She served up homemade French fries, a bean salad, and a tossed salad. We had been away from "American" food for only 17 days, yet after the first bite it seemed like an entire summer. She sliced bakery bread and served chopped onions and tomatoes and A & P brand Ketchup; almost like home. Afterwards, Roberto and Rolfo had their usual grappa and the Italian cigars they fondly referred to as "Guinea twisters."

Risky Business

I sat on the terrazza in the early morning, watching the chameleons play at my feet. They were used to me now. The sky was a clear blue, and a constant, cool breeze blew. Annie and Rolf had gone grocery shopping, as they did almost every morning. Annie had become our "store." We dropped in for a chunk of cheese, some bread, a biscotti. When our shopkeepers returned, Roberto and Jens planned to drive to Bientina, Robert's grandfather's ancestral home near Pisa, and then to Lucca for the day.

I washed last night's dishes and started a load of wash in the machine, both seemingly mundane chores, but each with a baffling Italian twist. The kitchen faucet excreted arbitrarily, aiming sometimes into the sink, pointing sometimes at me, often at the walls, occasionally to the ceiling.

The washing machine wasn't automatic. It wanted to be re-set for each cycle: wash, spin, rinse, spin again. I went to the wine cellar, where the washing machine lived, and put dirty clothing inside the round, glass door on the front of the machine -- a few T-shirts and a couple pairs of shorts were all that would fit into the small compartment. I poured some powdery detergent, an Italian brand, into the slot on top. I pushed several buttons and the device began to fill with water. The water moved about a quarter of the way up the window and stopped. After a few minutes, the machine sluggishly slopped the clothing over several times and stopped. I waited. The contraption flopped over the clothing several more times and stopped again. This appeared to be the normal pattern, so I returned to the kitchen to see if the faucet had any new tricks. When I checked the wash a half hour later, the "cycle" continued. I left again. An hour later, the flopping stopped. I set the dial for "spin." A half hour later, I set for "risciosqui," a risky rinse cycle that sent water rushing out the door onto the floor. I wiped it up with the remaining dirty clothing. Still later, I set it to "spin" again. From then on, I decided, we would hand-wash. We would each hand-wash our own clothing.

Fortunately, perhaps, there was no dryer. We hung our wash in the sun, over a plastic rack that Maria thoughtfully provided for us. The clothing dried within an hour. It was pleasant, taking it off the rack; I liked the smooth smell and the wrinkled look. We were grateful to have an immaculate house with modern bathrooms and good showers and a bidet to use for various purposes; rinsing out swimsuits, for example, and soaking our feet after a long day of walking on cobblestones, for another. Jensen and I ended up converting our bidets into vanity tables, covering them with flowered serving trays that we garnished with vases of roses and snippets of rosemary.

<u>Primary Italian Villa Requirements:</u>

1. Walking distance to a town.
2. A shower for every two people.
3. A large swimming pool.
4. An outdoor terrace for dining.

<u>Secondary Requirements:</u>

1. Quiet; off the main road.
2. No traffic, particularly no mopeds.
3. Clean, bordering on antiseptic.

The numerical order was unimportant. All requirements would have to be met. I wouldn't want to have to drive a half hour to get say, milk for coffee. I wouldn't want to be stranded while someone else drove off. The shower requirement was obvious if you were American and/or had long-haired daughters. The pool was a necessity because Tuscany can get very hot, and I had heard that sometimes villas "run out" of water. One could always go jump in one's pool.

I didn't particularly care about our villa's curb appeal. I was expecting something drab and dark. We were pleasantly surprised on all counts. The extras -- a shower at the pool, the vineyards and olive groves, a covered terrazza with a view and a barbecue, a private terrace just for Annie and Rolf, terra-cotta floors, comfortable furniture, paintings, good armoires and dressers, and reasonable lighting -- were truly appreciated only after a few weeks.

If we had fewer people or less time, my requirements might not be so stringent. The weather was another pleasant surprise. All data I read before leaving was unanimous: Tuscany would be unbearably hot in July and August. Not true: outside of town, in the hills, the breeze is steady and evenings can be chilly. Very cool. Downright cold.

Crist and Annie and I roamed San Gim today. We went to the Etruscan Museum. A flautist played the *Ave Maria* in the courtyard outside. It was hauntingly lovely, echoing the mysterious beauty of the museum's pieces.

I puzzled that the Romans could have erased an entire cultural identity and I wondered about the music, art, and literature that a modern day Etruscan culture would produce.

The food shops too, were filled with history and art, and among Tuscany's most fascinating sights. Where we went, nobody spoke English. Each experience was an Italian lesson. Today, we went first to the bakery that baked the crusty olive bread. My teeth needed crusty. The bread was "finito." We formulated a plan: the olive bread was still in the oven at 8:00 a.m. yesterday, sold out by 10:00 a.m. today. Our next attempt would be at 9:00 a.m. Being a tourist was not all play.

We continued our culinary tour to Lucia e Maria, where the breakfast pastries were also "finito." Lucia was filling the cases with panini; foccaccia sandwiches of tomato and cheese, tuna and tomato, and tuna and sliced eggs and tomato. Annie saw Maria slide a last rack of breakfast pastries into the case. A piece was broken. Maria popped the morsel into her mouth. A dreamy look washed over her face. We bought three of Maria's twisty crispy dreamy warm confections and an etto of the house espresso to sample.

Another store offering stuffed peppers, stuffed zucchinis, and stuffed tomatoes from deep coffers deserved at least as much attention as an Etruscan urn. The cases in the next shop brimmed with sliced grilled eggplant, a dozen kinds of olives, tiny braised onions, mushrooms, red peppers, and artichokes. One case sparkled with jars of fresh white and black truffles. We gathered, as stone-agers.

Local women, doing their last minute shopping before preparing lunch, bargained at the butcher shop. They swapped recipes and gossip, touted tripe, ogled octopi, selected squid, squabbled over breasts of veal, specified many etti of the fine Florentine steak, of the pale pink veal scallops, and the roughly-chopped meat. We felt a part of it. The women smiled at us, said a few words to us. What we lacked in Italian vocabulary, we made up in body language. We understood more Italian every day, and undertook to speak more. I found that Spanish was more useful for speaking Italian than was French. The Spanish vocabulary and pronunciation are very close to Italian. I could usually use a Spanish word with an Italian pronunciation to make myself understood. When in doubt, Crist was our walking Italian dictionary, pronouncing gazetteer, and our final word on grammar.

We found the trattoria where Crist and I had lunched so nicely on Monday, but it was chiuso; closed. Later in the day, we drove to our local Osteria to get a dinner reservation. It, too, was closed that day.

ASIDE: It's necessary to reserve at least a day in advance and to note which days a restaurant is closed, as they each close on different days -- the info is usually posted on the menu outside the restaurant, even in the country.

Along the medieval wall of San Gim, we found what Annie characterized as a "real" Italian ristorante. We were the only non-Italian diners. We ordered water, house red, a starter of braised artichokes, then pastas and risotto with zucchini blossoms. I ordered profiteroles for dessert; a dolce Annie was not familiar with. The owner, a trim, short man of about 50, wearing a spotless white shirt, suspenders, with a pleasing twitch to his mustache and a twinkle in his eye, brought us a plate of the fresh cream puffs drenched in warm chocolate sauce, and three soup spoons. Annie decided the dish was a fancy version of a hot fudge sundae.

On the wall hung a series of drawings and paintings of the owner, all affectionately crafted. As we dipped into the profiteroles, he flirted with all three of us. We were disappointed when he graciously excused himself to see about a commotion at the door. Two German families argued with the staff. They wanted to sit together at one table. The owner interrupted the argument. He apologized. He was sorry, but all the large tables were taken. He seated the two families at separate tables across the room from each other, the last two vacant tables. Immediately, the families began to shout back and forth to each other. The owner went to one table and asked the people to please talk quietly. Then he went to the other table and did the same. As he turned his back, the tables erupted into even louder talk. I asked for the conto; the check. The staff went from table to table, apologizing to the diners for these boisterous stranieri. The Italian family next to us rolled their eyes. We shrugged and rolled ours back. The owner brought our check and apologized to us. Only a veneer of his magnanimity remained. When I paid, I noticed he had written under the total, "sconto," discount, and had deducted the cover charge and service charge. I put the amount of the sconto plus the equivalent of $2.00 on our table and we thanked him again for our superbo lunch. When we left, the staff individually apologized again, smiled, and said, "Sera."

ASIDE: "Buona sera" means literally, "good evening." But at the stroke of 12:00 noon, the Italians begin to say "sera," (which sounds like the name, Sara) as a greeting and as a good-bye. They do *not* say "*buona* sera."

We shopped through town on our way out, discovering an alabaster store we hadn't seen before. We admired the exquisite handmade fruits, giant green grapes linked together with a real grape stem, pears, and peaches; rocks that I couldn't heft back to California. The cherries, gold tinged with crimson, were my favorite of the fruits.

We decided to take a taxi home. I had described to Annie how to call a taxi but clearly, she didn't believe me. I was tickled pink to demonstrate. Near the main arch into the walled city, apartments rose above the frutta store. A small panel of buttons, one for each apartment, was imbedded next to the door to the apartments on the street level. The names of the people who lived there were inscribed next to the buttons. One button said TAXI. You pressed the button, and above, the shutters flew open. Giuseppe poked his head out the window and shouted down, "Si?" You'd call, "Giuseppe! Vorrei un taxi, per favore;" I'd like a taxi, please. Giuseppe would excuse himself to phone the taxi driver. When he returned to the window, he'd tell you when the taxi would arrive, and where to wait. Soon a silver Mercedes pulled to the curb, a silver-haired man opened the door, and drove you to your destination.

We walked to the panel of buttons. Giggling, Annie pressed TAXI. Giuseppe poked his head out of the window. "Un taxi!" Annie squeaked out, in hysterics. Giuseppe retreated inside, came back, and said to wait next to the wall for five minutes. We thanked him. We walked to the wall, the silver Mercedes pulled up, the silver-haired man ushered Annie and us into the taxi and drove us to the villa. Annie laughed all the way home.

We swam and napped away the late afternoon. Jensen and Roberto returned in the early evening. Disappointed in their day, they told us that Bientina was a prosperous burg, and clean, too, but there was nothing to see or do -- just block after block of antique stores. They were the only tourists. Further, Lucca was deserted, crumbling; they couldn't even find the famous Lucca olive oil to buy.

We barbecued steak, Jensen mashed potatoes, I bit my tongue and sliced up a tomato salad and served a side dish of the San Gim marinated mushrooms and peppers. Jensen made our first scorpion sighting while she was washing the dishes; about the size of a dime, black, and hiding on the wall near the ceiling.

I think that when traveling, it's best to go without expectations, to be open for what might be there, not for what you expected to be there. To be the only non-tourist in a prosperous town composed exclusively of antique shops happens only in my dreams. Rolf maintained that his best experience so far was listening to an impromptu a cappella chorus -- a group of tourists -- in the Siena Duomo.

"Vorrai Reggiano!"

The scorpion was gone this morning when I cautiously ventured into the kitchen. Wonder where? It was another beautiful early morning of clear skies and a light breeze. I had been planning to go to the San Gim market this morning because we were having lunch guests: Sylvia, a neighbor from home, was staying at a villa nearby for her sons, ages eight and 10, and her sister, a documentary film maker from Milano, and the sister's daughter, eight years old.

I drove to town. At the San Gim market, the local women elbowed their way to the front of the lines. I didn't feel local. I didn't know the rules. I hung back to observe. A woman would successfully reach the counter, and begin to gossip: "Hello, how are you, nice day, is the wife better? good looking fish, but expensive? too much! how are the children? yes it's warmer today, give me one small piece and some of that, thank you, good day." From the first hello until a purchase was complete took a solid 10 minutes.

At the cheese booth, I watched a woman negotiate a deal for Reggiano. The vendor gave her a taste and sliced off a chunk for her. She liked it, she said, but she preferred a piece from a new round, not from a round he had already cut. The cheese man obliged with a hefty, uncut round of Reggiano, from which he carved her a piece and sliced her a taste. She said it was good, but the piece he cut for her was too big. He cut a smaller piece. It was too small. Now she insisted on a new round. He trimmed a taste for her. She liked it. He cut a pie-shaped wedge and offered it to her. They talked about the price. A deal was struck. As he wrapped the cheese, she counted her money, paying with many small coins and much small talk.

I got the man's attention. "Vorrai Reggiano!" I shouted -- too loudly. The other women stepped aside ... respectfully? I blushed and pointed to the first piece the previous shopper had rejected. The man cut off a generous taste for me, then pulled out an uncut round of cheese that was much darker than all the leftover pieces. He gave me a taste. Both were delicious. I gathered that the darker cheese was more aged and also more expensive. I told him I'd take due etti of each kind. He weighed the pieces, half a pound each. He said the aged Reggiano would be £3.500, a bit over $2.00. He insisted that I buy two more pieces, pieces that the woman had rejected. I was firm. "No, no!" I insisted. Soltanto questi! (Only these.) I loved playing this role. I had the rhythm of the speech, I thought; insistent, argumentative. Italian!

I had a stack of Marias, so I asked him for due etti of provolone cheese and some bite-sized, pillow-shaped buffalo mozzarella which he fished from a container of water. "Si, signora." I couldn't chitchat with him like a local, but I could communicate.

ASIDE: Maria Montessori is pictured on the £1.000 bill. We called a thousand lire a "Maria," for short.

At the roast van, I chose an entire roasted pork loin and two pounds of the homemade lasagne Bolognese, the latter for the children's lunch. When the roast man told me the price, I didn't understand. "Come dici?;" COH-may DEE-chee?; what did you say? He smiled, and showed me the receipt. Only a few Marias. Recognizing that we were "foreigners," most merchants automatically showed us the receipt so we could read how many lire we owed.

Frutte di Bosco, fruits of the forest, at the open air market

I bought tomatoes, kiwis, plums, peaches, grapes, bread, and wine and returned home to transform the foods into a feast and our table into my version of *The Wine Spectator* -does-Tuscany. I prepared the usual tomato salad, heated the lasagne in the ubiquitous Tuscan Teflon frying pan, sliced bread and pork, arranged a basket of bread, and bowls of fruit. About every week, I bought another small majolica bowl. By now I had four to fill with olives, olive oil, salt, and small chunks of Reggiano.

My neighbor, Sylvia, who is Italian, arrived with her entourage and a large package of the kind of salami only an Italian knows how to choose. I spread her treat with the rest of our picnic. The children ran to the pool. The adults sipped cold Rosata. Sylvia's sister was an Italian Intellectual, as it turned out, who specialized in award winning, uncompromising documentaries. I sensed a political agenda that I didn't clearly understand. I gathered only that her agenda did not include speaking English or having much to do with Americans. We spoke French and talked about French movies. Sometimes Sylvia translated my English to Italian for her sister. We opened Vernaccia for lunch. The three children inhaled the two pounds of lasagne. I had a taste and understood. Paper thin fresh pasta and Bolognese sauce prepared with the rich, local milk and Florentine beef is a non pareil. I would be spoiled forever.

We all swam later on, Roberto's last Italian swim. Our guests stayed until 6:00 p.m. Much later, it must have been after ten o'clock, we six assembled on the terrazza to lazily eat the leftovers and sip some Chianti. Summertime in Toscana!

Roberto parta
(Robert leaves)

The group all somehow managed to awake early, to bid their farewells to Roberto. Jensen would drive him to Firenze to catch his train to Milano. I would go along to drive back with her. He was our first departure, our first reminder that our Italian summer would have an ending. After he had closed his luggage and while he was saying his good-byes, I removed about half my clothes from the closet and stuffed them into his big suitcase to make room in my suitcase for Italian purchases yet to come. I also crammed in all the shoes I had packed except a pair of sandals, a pair of flats, and some Keds. He didn't know. I didn't ask him if it was OK. I didn't tell him. In time, I hoped he would understand. My clothing would spend the night with Roberto at a four star hotel near Malpensa Airport, and leave for home the next day. I imagined his surprise when he opened his suitcase.

While I was in the shower in the early morning, Maria arrived at the door with her cell phone and insisted to Crist, who answered the door, that I take the call. Dripping wet and wondering if it was OK to talk on the phone in such a state, I took the phone from her and listened to the clipped British words of Gaynor, our rental agent. The package I sent from California on July 10 was to be delivered today. I needed to bring £289,000 (about $168) to pay the custom's fees. Using my newly-acquired Italian "attitude," I told her I didn't know anything about custom's fees. I had already paid a large sum for shipping, I would pay no more. Please tell them to return the package to California, I said, waving my hands around. I no longer had any use for its contents, and in any case, the contents weren't worth $168.

Gaynor said, "Please stop by, and we'll phone customs together." Fine, said I. This conversation took some time, and I no longer had time to finish showering. I had shampoo on my head. I dried off, ran a brush through my soapy hair and dressed quickly. Roberto had promised Sylvia that we'd meet her at the Monteriggioni wall at exactly 10:00 a.m., to see her Agrivilla; farm. Jensen would come, too. We three were interested in seeing "agriturismo" first hand.

We drove first to Gaynor's. She sat us down and phoned the customs' woman and put the phone on speaker. After half an hour of communicating in Italian to English to Italian to English, mostly at the same time, the customs woman agreed to send the box back to California. I doubted I'd ever see it again.

(Postscript: I didn't.)

The medieval town of Monteriggioni was about 15 minutes away. Postcards of this highly photogenic town pop from the racks of tourist stores throughout Tuscany and usually turn up on Tuscan calendars, in a winter month, since the chief attaction is the town's stone walls. We were late to meet Sylvia. She was leaning against the stone wall glaring at her watch when we arrived. No time to see the town. I got into Sylvia's car. She motioned for Jensen and Roberto to follow us in the Fiat. Before I had my seatbelt fastened, we were roaring away from town. We drove up and down and around the tight curves of unpaved, dusty roads for many miles before arriving at what Sylvia referred to as the "compound;" several acres of vineyards with outbuildings, stables, a vegetable garden, and a swimming pool scattered throughout the property. The swimming pool was nearly a mile from the living quarters. It was all very rustic and cut off from the rest of the world; a self-contained, working farm. Each step we took produced a small cloud of dust. The silence was profound.

The compound was founded by what Sylvia described as "some intellectual hippies" in the 70's. Each participant bought a share, and owned an apartment in the complex. Her sister was an original participant. We walked into the main house, a rather Spartan 18th century edifice furnished with four sofas, then on through the outdoor dining area and to the stables, passing the garden on the way. Compound members were hard at work wherever we looked. A beekeeper gathered honey. A woman with a pitchfork worked at the compost heap. Another planted seedlings. Two men groomed horses. Sylvia paused and spoke to each person.

I asked, How is that she knew everyone? She explained that in the evening, the 35 participants gathered for a communal dinner. They were assigned seats away from their families so they could meet all the others.

She went on to tell us that the food was -- of course, it was organic, vegetarian, and all grown on the premises. Breakfast was do-it-yourself, lunch was on your own. They had a cook in the evening, but they all pitched in to clean up. When I asked, she replied that the nearest store was a 20 minute drive on "the white roads." There was no reason, however, to go to the store, she said. Everything they needed was here.

Sylvia showed us her sister's one room apartment. It was in a charmingly crumbly stucco building but was very modern inside. The room was small. A table for four, a free-standing fireplace, and two chairs filled the space. A ladder led to a loft that "slept six." They were a party of five. They had one bathroom. As we stood chatting with her, our stomachs began to rumble. We apologized, thanked her for showing us around, and reminded her that Roberto had a train to catch.

We left for Firenze. As we turned onto the smooth, speedy Super Strada, Jensen spoke first. "It's so unnecessary," was all that she said. We were cherishing our privacy, our bathrooms, and our proximity to San Gim. We considered ourselves gardeners, but not farmers; chefs, but not cooks. Maybe we were ugly Americans.

We parked in the train station garage and took the elevator. Roberto joined the long line of backpackers, French tourists, middle eastern tourists, and a soccer team, all waiting at the ticket booths. He bought himself a first class seat on the Eurostar train to Milano, leaving at 3:15 p.m., to arrive around 6:15 p.m. When he had finished his purchase, he realized that he hadn't made a seat reservation. He returned to the line.

It was 1:30 p.m. We took a quick lunch at a crowded Tavola Calda across from the Stazione. The Tavola Calda is the equivalent of a cafeteria. We each took a tray and chose from enormous platters of lasagne, several kinds of pasta, pizzas, several vegetable preparations, chicken, veal, beef, and fish. The food was hot, tasted good, and the price was about $4.00 per person. We ate quickly and returned to wait for the train.

Roberto hadn't taken a train in Europe before, so Jensen and I, who had taken the Eurostar in France, explained how the Eurostar works -- when it comes into the station, it doesn't turn around. You choose to sit either facing forward or backward. We showed him the seating arrangement chart, posted in the station. We located the dining car, and his car. He would be at the end of the track leaving, so he would arrive at the front of the train in Milano. There would be room to stash his luggage above his seat, we told him, but not enough room for his big bag, which he might have to leave in the aisle. We warned him to keep an eye on it.

When we saw the train arriving, we began to walk the distance to his car, which took several minutes. The train leaves "subito," almost immediately after arrival, so we pressed him to hurry. He wished to savor the last moments of his vacation. He dawdled. We urged him to walk faster. He looked spent instead of vacationed. When we reached his car, he turned to us and made a telling statement about travel in Italy. "Now that I know how things work here, I'd like to stay for another three weeks to enjoy myself."

Jensen and I felt lucky to be staying, though I suspected there would be new things to learn each day. The Italians have as many ways to flush a toilet as they do to cook a codfish. We shoved Robert onto the train and in seconds, the train pulled out. He gave us a surprised look from his seat, and mouthed "Thank you!" through the window as he blurred out of the station. We stood on the platform, watching the train until it was a dot. At this time tomorrow, Roberto would be on an airplane heading for home. I wondered what his thoughts were, what he would remember most, if he had enjoyed himself or only coped.

We were the only people on the platform. We walked the distance back to the terminal, stanke STAHN-kay; feminine plural for "tired." We drove straight back to San Gim, stopping at the San Gim Coop to pick up a few staples.

RENT A CART, GLOVE UP, AND BAG YOURSELF:
How Things Work at an Italian Grocery Store:

Renting a grocery cart: Grocery carts are usually kept outside the store and not necessarily close to the entrance. To use one, insert a £500 coin into the slot indicated on the cart. The coin releases the chain that secures the cart. When you return the cart, re-hook the chain, and you will get back your £500 coin. We kept a few £500 coins at hand in the car, and thought this rental practice was sound. You didn't see grocery carts on street corners in Italian towns, and the carts were in mint condition.

Pricing veggies: In the produce department, plastic gloves are provided, as are small plastic bags. Wearing the gloves, you choose the produce you want and put it into a plastic bag. You weigh your selection on a scale fitted with an electric panel that displays individual color photos of the store's produce. Select the picture that corresponds with what you are weighing, e.g., tomatoes. Put your bag on the scale. Press the tomato picture pad, and the machine will spit out an adhesive price strip. Use it to close the bag. Toss the gloves in the bin provided when you have finished buying the produce.

Buying grocery bags: If you do not bring your own shopping bag to the grocery store, you must buy the plastic bags that will hold your purchases.

They cost about £300 each (17 cents) and made good garbage bags at the villa. Estimate how many bags you will need (over-estimating is better and less embarrassing) and before you pay at the check-out, put the bags on the counter. Their cost will be added to your bill. Lastly, using your bags, bag your own goods.

The evening was cool. I showered and dressed for dinner, in the warmest clothing I had -- a new long, black hemp skirt and an older Calvin Klein two-ply black cotton knit wrap shirt with sleeves. I opened my armoire, selected the two pieces, noted that the blacks matched, and lay them on the bed. Something small, the size of a dime and the color of rust, clung to the skirt. I shook the skirt. The thing stayed. I looked closely. It was a scorpion. I asked Cristina, the bravest person in our party, for help. She took several tissues, pulled the scorpion off, put it in the toilet, and flushed twice. After that, I examined every piece of clothing before putting it on and, remembering "The Itsy-Bitsy Spider," who came up the drain again, I looked into the toilet before using it, but I never saw another scorpion.

Annie had cooked a wonderful dinner for us, a chicken stew, and risotto dripping with burro; butter, and fresh peas, and a salad. Rolf had set the table on their terrazza for our dinner. We gathered and toasted a safe return for Roberto. But the sky began to turn black alarmingly fast and Annie's terrazza had no overhang. As we ate, we kept a weather eye.

The storm hit as we were taking our last bites. We grabbed the platters and dishes, put them in Annie's kitchen, and Annie and Jensen and Crist and I took our wine glasses and wine to our covered terrazza. Rolf followed in a few minutes, using their outdoor umbrella to keep dry. We laughed, drank our wine, and watched the rain obliterate the landscape. The downpour stopped long enough to reveal the last stunning rays from the sunset, then continued through the night. Annie and Jensen and I stayed up quite late chatting and drinking the good Chianti, secure and cozy on our sheltered terrace, with lots of candles burning. I climbed into bed alone, and realized that I wouldn't talk to Roberto for a long time. He wouldn't call me when he got home. I had no phone.

Lunch at Lorenza de' Medici's

The grandmother still sat on the bench.

If it's Saturday, it must be cleaning day. We love the consistency of our living. The five of us headed out early for the Saturday market in Castellina. As Roberto had summarized, now that we knew how things worked, we'd just enjoy ourselves.

'Twas a fresh, sweet-smelling, clean, clear morning. We drove through the warm air with the windows open, stopping only to drop off an enormous amount of garbage and bottles. There were several areas along the roads for villa owners and renters to take their garbage. The nearest to us was about a kilometer away. There were bins for regular garbage; small dumpsters, plus bins for recycling glass and bins for recycling plastic. The Fiat's trunk was conveniently equipped with an elastic band on each side, perfect for securing wine bottles, both full and empty. We filled the bands with our empties and emptied the trunk into the bins, making the car much lighter and better smelling, then headed for Castellina. The Tuscans were rabid recyclers, even more so than in California. There were recycle bins for bottles and plastic on every town's street corners along with the trash receptacles. The towns were tidy.

The blue bow was still on the door in Castellina, and the old woman sat on the same bench, wearing the same clothes. What's the Italian for "déjà vu?" We visited the famous caves of La Castellina di Tommaso Boiola. I snapped a shot of Annie and Rolf in the cave, dwarfed by gigantic wine barrels. We said hello to our porchetta man, and bought some porchetta "a portare;" ah-por-TAH-ray, to go, plus fruits and cheeses and more of the golden green olive oil. I filled the shopping bag I had bought there.

Crist found saline solution for her contact lenses in a Farmacia; far-mah-CHEE-ah, pharmacy, and we stocked up on items that were in The Box -- film, one-use cameras, deodorant. I paid £15.000 (about $8.70) for two rolls of Kodak Gold film, which came packaged with a Kodak-yellow collapsible cup that would come in handy later in the trip.

There had been no need to send anything ahead to Italy. More and more, the world's products are becoming uniform, a plus/minus cultural convenience. The same brands we have at home were on the shelves of the smallest Farmacias in Italian towns where little or no English was spoken.

We dawdled in and out of shops until we started to get hungry. Our luncheon destination was Badia a Coltibuono; Abbey of the Good Harvest, the 12th century monastery, the location of Lorenza de' Medici's cooking school. I had heard there was an good, rustic ristorante there as well, and a store that offered the monastery's products: olive oil, wine, honey, and spices. Whether they were open, whether we could get in, whether we could even find Badia was to be determined.

We drove past Radda, headquarters of the Chianti League since 1415 (Lega del Chianti, the ancient organization that gave Chianti its name.) Soon after Radda, we saw a peeling, wooden sign appealingly pointing left to Badia. There was a stone building at the bottom of a steep road -- the monastery shop. An "Aperto," sign leaned into the window -- the shop was open. Another sign advertised chestnut honey. We'd stop in after lunch. Jensen put the car in first gear and powered us up and around and up some more. When we thought we might be on a wild goose chase, the road leveled out, and we were looking at the monastery. We parked in a lot under chestnut trees, the only car there. We walked past the abbey where the monks had cultivated the very first vineyards here in the heart of Chianti, to a grouping of white umbrellas; the ristorante.

About 20 tables were set up under the spreading chestnut trees. We were the only takers. We weren't sure the ristorante was open until a young man greeted us, "Giorno!" We replied, "Giorno!" I asked, "Cinque personi?"

(CHINK-way) Si. He gestured to sit anywhere. We chose the table with the best view to the countryside. The sight was spectacular, overlooking the gentle, never-ending hills speckled with vineyards. The entire Chianti valley stretched to the horizon. It felt cool under the umbrellas, a coolness we attributed to the altitude. We had all worn long sleeved cotton shirts as protection against the sun, and now our shirts took off the chill. Immediately after we sat down, a butterfly, exactly the color of the tangerine linen tablecloths, alighted on my arm; a lovely welcome. When he landed on Cristina's hand, I took his picture. To her delight, he walked around on her hand investigating her fingers for many minutes.

We drooled our way through the first reading of the menu. The day's prix fixe luncheon £45,000 ($26.00) included the house antipasto, ricotta gnocchi with sage and butter sauce, boned rabbit with olives, and dolce; dessert. We eschewed the prix fixe meal in favor of ordering à la carte. The wine list was extensive. Bottles of Chianti Riserva dated back to the early 1980's. The best 1990's were about £90,000 ($52.00). We ordered the vino rosso di casa (house red) for around $8. It was a good choice; the light tannin seemed right with the light chill in the air. I ordered braised duckling with homemade tagliatelli;

a huge plate of the thick, rich egg pasta in a dark, concentrated game sauce with a half a duckling; a perfect cold weather dish, I thought. Annie ordered the gnocchi with sage. Crist, a vegetarian, chose ziti with ricotta. Jensen ordered her favorite food, eggplant parmigiana, which she voted "best ever." Rolf chose some bruschetta and an order of bean soup. The food was simple, fresh, and tasty. Had it been our first meal in Tuscany, we would have been more impressed.

The Tuscan menus reflected the frutte di stagione, the fruits and vegetables of the season, and the game indigenous to Tuscany. What was in season was what was on the menus throughout Tuscany. The menus varied little from place to place. They offered us the season's end of the asparagus and squash blossoms, and the high summer harvests of peppers, artichokes, zucchini, eggplant, and tomatoes. Beans were featured on most menus and the dense bread accompanied every meal. The preparations were unpretentious, similar to the first "California Cuisine" that Alice Waters propagated in the 1980's. The fresh ingredients soloed and starred. We were accustomed to eating pasta with whatever was in season at home. Our daily diet was mostly pasta with something fresh. We made a lateral dietary move in Tuscany. We wondered how meat and potatoes tourists fared.

For dessert, Annie and I split a pear tarta with plums and strawberry sauce, as good as any dessert I'd had in Paris. We all had cappuccinos. By the time we were spooning up the last of the milky froth, the ristorante had filled with those who had reserved for lunch. We congratulated ourselves on finding our way here and getting here early enough to be seated without a rez

We drove back down to the monastery shop, but it was chiuso for the lunch time. Visions of chunky jars filled with thick chestnut honey flew on wings across the hills. Jensen, who was majoring in business at college, said it wasn't very good marketing to close the store when the customers arrived, and then drove us home on what Annie dubbed the "fusilli" roads. We napped, swam later, and ate the leftovers from the past few days, which turned out to be a feast, drunk with a two liter fiasco of Chianti from Pietrafitta. The Pietrafitta '95 DOCG was our current house wine.

We planned to burn a candle in our first fiasco each night, as we had in college, until the bottle was covered with wax. "Fiasco" is Italian for "flask." The straw covers of the first Chianti fiasco bottles were woven by hand. Maria told me that she and Max didn't bottle their wine in fiascoes. For them, the fiasco was a sign of cheap wine -- the *old* Chianti wine -- wine that couldn't be aged, and not just because the wineries couldn't lay a fiasco on its side. A fiasco was a "tourist thing" she said. I told her what the English word "fiasco" means. She said there is an Italian expression using the word fiasco and meaning the same as the English and shrugged "see what I mean?" She would probably prefer that we didn't burn candles in our fiasco while she was around.

After dinner, we heard music drifting from San Gim. It was an Italian band with a big band sound. They played song after song. A male vocalist sang in Italian. Occasionally, we could hear people clapping and cheering. The band was spirited, festive, and the sound so clear we felt they were playing in our vineyard. We agreed it was a probably wedding reception, and why not join in the celebration? We all danced, over to the side of the terrazza. We danced on until we were too stanke to stand. The music played late into the night. We remarked that until this evening, we hadn't heard a radio or watched TV. We didn't know what the "summer movies" were. We had not heard any recorded sound since we arrived. We hadn't missed it. Yet, we welcomed this musical intrusion.

High summer holds the earth.

Rolf went to the early mass and when we awoke, we found a tray of pastries on the kitchen table for us, a delightful present. I made some nasty cappuccino and ate a pastry on the terrace in the morning's beauty.

The church bells rang all at once from all sides. There was a special mass this morning at 11:00 a.m. in San Gim, a medieval celebration where costumes would be worn. I was too lazy to go. Sitting on the terrazza on this morning looking across the ripening vineyards, smelling the sweet air and feeling the pale sunshine was Kingdom Come.

Annie was all dressed up and ready to go to mass. My spirit was willing, I told her, but my body said to sit on the terrace in my jammies and do niente; nee-EN-tay, nothing. I apologized. Jensen slept late, a well-deserved rest. Her friend, Laura, would arrive Wednesday. Jensen had talked of nothing

113

else for days. She was exhausted from being excited about Laura's arrival.

We had no plans in particular for the day. I got out my maps, the Michelins, and the local ones, and the maps of the tiny towns that Gaynor had given me, and all the maps of every kind in the villa, and spread them out on the terrazza table. I leisurely traveled the roads and lanes from my chair and learned more geography. The day turned warm, so I went indoors to shower and put on a swimsuit. When I returned, the maps were gone, blown across the terrazza, caught in the geraniums. In moments, the wind had picked up, the innocuous fluffy clouds had become monsters. I carried the maps inside, folded them up, and turned on our small lamps to wait for the storm to pass.

Annie had brought along the journal her father wrote during his first trip to Italy. He was Roberto's age now at the time. I curled up on a leather sofa to listen to Cristina practice and to read the pages of curly, old-fashioned handwriting. Robert's grandfather's name was Alfredo and he lived in New York, as did all of Robert's family. When Robert was a child, his grandfather took him to the Italian operas at the Met. As I remembered that, Cristina's voice scaled a complicated run and I thought how proud he would be to hear his great granddaughter sing Donizetti. Crist and he had met only once. She was a two year-old. I have a photo of her squirming in his lap. He laughed and laughed as he tried to hold on to her. She fought and fought and finally won, scrambling away and into the yard.

His family called him "Poppy Fred." The family was originally from Bientina, the small town outside Pisa that Robert and Jensen had driven through. His wife's family was from a small town in the extreme south of Italy. Her name was Vincenzina. They called her "Jensie." I named Jensen after her and for a time we called Jensen "Jensie." I had met both Poppy Fred and Jensie, so the writing was evocative and lively for me. They are both dead now, Poppy Fred having died several years after Jensie, and many years after he wrote his journal.

In the early spring of 1955, Poppy and Jensie crossed the Atlantic from New York to Italy on the Andrea Doria. Poppy wrote that the ship pitched constantly and heavily coming and going, and that everyone on the ship, including the crew, became very ill. Jensie never left their stateroom. On arrival in Italy, Poppy and Jensie first visited Poppy's relatives in Bientina.

He wrote, "May 23, 1955: Left Bientina at 3:00 p.m., stopped at Certaldo and at San Gimignano, then continued on to Siena, returning to Pisa that night." The next day, they "stayed home, tired." I could well imagine. To visit one town in a day is filling fare.

I sank deeper into the sofa as the rain continued, and kept reading and listening. They took the train down south next and stayed on Jensie's family "chicken farm." The house had dirt floors. They shared the household with chickens and goats. Poppy described the chickens that scrambled over his feet as he wrote. He reported that he and Jens were served five eggs each for breakfast, and a whole chicken each for dinner. There was no running water. There were no indoor toilets. The relatives served them their best -- and only -- food. He wrote that Jensie's family "treated them like kings."

While I read, the sun came out and Cristina finished singing. The pools of water evaporated quickly. We went to the pool where Annie already sat sunbathing. I told her some about her father's journal. She chuckled at the thought of her father, a Manhattan manufacturer known for his sartorial elegance, staying on a chicken farm, and put on more tanning lotion.

Sundays, our property resembled a nudist colony. Max and Maria's two daughters and their friends came to visit and the daughters, their friends, and Maria all sunbathed nude for the afternoon. Rolf missed his nap.

We went back to the Osteria for dinner. I had pheasant with porcini mushrooms. This was a ragout of the fresh mushrooms, rather large chunks -- probably braised -- in a game sauce, probably rabbit. The pheasant was in the form of a cold terrine. Paper thin slices of the pheasant terrine were placed on top of the mushroom ragout, in layers, in a circle. The combination was perfetto; perfect. The others were not so adventuresome, choosing pasta and steak. I also had a vegetable soufflé that I shared. It was so good that I had only one taste to myself. We had been craving broccoli, and the soufflé came close to the taste. We thought we'd see broccoli dishes and broccoli-pasta variations on the menus, but we did not. We didn't know whether the Tuscans didn't eat broccoli or if it simply wasn't in season.

I had a recipe for ziti with broccoli from Roberto's other grandmother, whom we all called Nana, who was Sicilian. It was a favorite dish of ours and very easy to prepare: steam the broccoli, chop it, and toss it with olive oil and several sliced cloves of lightly-sautéed garlic. Cook the ziti in the broccoli steaming water and add it to the broccoli mixture with a bit of the steaming water, for consistency. Robert's grandmother sometimes boiled the broccoli and ziti together.

I ordered a pear poached in Chianti (wine) for dessert. When we returned to the villa, we again heard music drifting from San Gim. We were delighted, and decided there was a Festa, having to do with the costumed mass. We danced off our dinner. Jensen taught Annie and Cristina the Macarena, making the two of them the last persons in the western world to learn it. Jensen was both embarrassed that she knew the dance and pleased to teach it.

Shopping in Firenze

On this beautiful, clear morning, Rolf walked with Crist to Kate's. Annie, Jensen, and I drove to Firenze. Jensen easily found the train station. We parked there and walked to the Duomo, Baptistery, Campanile. It was Jensen's first visit to Firenze. She was doing reconnaissance for when she and Laura would come to Firenze together. We walked on to the Piazza della Signoria, past the Uffizi, closed today, so there were no crowds. Even the piazza was deserted. We took Kate's advice for lunch and stopped at one of the food shops on the Uffizi side of the Ponte Vecchio for foccaccia stuffed with tuna, and an artichoke pizza. We sat in a small garden in back. Kate was right. The food was fresh, inexpensive, and delicious, far better than the tourist ristorante. We liked the ambiance of the garden though the area was only serviceable to sit and eat something simple. It was crowded, and we sat in the midst of Italian shoppers who jabbered and ate. We felt "Italian."

We got gelati and walked across the Ponte Vecchio, up to the Pitti Palace, also closed, to the closed Boboli Gardens; more reconnaissance. The walking was easy with no tourists jostling us. We went to the shop Il Papiro and bought the richly decorative Florentine paper that is made by hand, one sheet at a time. I bought place cards, writing paper, and bookmarks with the Bridge of Sighs engraved on them and inscribed: "Here I fell to sleep." I also bought fancy Florentine paper "corners" to place on the page where one fell to sleep, and to greet the reader the next evening. Jensen chose a Murano glass dipping pen and a bottle of violet-scented, deep purple India ink. I sprang for some writing paper to go with her pen and ink.

We shopped for leather. I bought Jensen some well-earned leather driving gloves. Cristina's voice coach at home had requested that I try to find her a pair of red kid gloves to match some she bought in Firenze 10 years ago. She had lost one. I had the other one with me. The first shop we entered had an identical pair. The salesgirl took my one red glove and competently fitted it to a new pair. "Va bene?" Si.

I looked for a wedding present for my niece, Kelley, who would be married in Texas in September. Kelley would marry a young man who was the F-14 pilot running the Top Gun school in Texas. Jensen and I had met him, and we, too, fell in love with him. I thought that a present from the Ponte Vecchio would be a good choice for them. Kelley, who is six-feet something tall, had been in Italy a few years ago when she was signed with the Elite Modeling Agency. She came to Milano for some "go-sees," and ended up a runway model for Armani. She spent several months here. I couldn't make up my mind what to buy since I had nothing in mind.

Florence was much warmer than the countryside; too warm for us country girls. When we decided to go home, we were surprised that it was almost 6:00 p.m. In the car, I asked Annie what she wanted to do for dinner. She said she had shopped the day before and left Rolf in charge of cutting up a chicken, making barbecue sauce and a macaroni salad. Marvelous. We swam when we got home, then had a late dinner, courtesy of Rolfo.

The music festival continued into the night. Monday night's feature was American folk songs: Peter, Paul, and Mary, and Simon and Garfunkel. Whoever was playing was very good. I planned to ask the tourist office what was going on, to see if we could get tickets, maybe when Laura arrived, though we agreed that listening from our own terrazza would be hard to beat. Our dance floor wasn't at all crowded and we didn't need a dance partner.

Savoring

Church bells rang insistently this morning, and the rooster crowed what sounded like "up and AT 'em" or else "cock-a-DOO-dle," without the final "-doo." I watched a butterfly flutter around the vase of daisies on the terrazza table. I took in the way he flew. I watched him unwind his filament-like proboscis into the flowers to sip their nectars. All my senses concentrated on this small creature. He filled my movie screen. When he bobbled away, I lazily pondered what a long time it takes to gain knowledge and wisdom and to learn how things worked ... what the underpinnings and histories of things were ... and what a short time we had to savor the knowledge and to appreciate what we have learned and to clearly understand and to see. Today I planned to see and savor, to stare and wonder.

I have been in Italy 25 days; mostly in one place, unpacked. It has taken me 25 days to realize that I don't have to rush from one task to the next or from one place to another. That there is no schedule. No phone. No world news. There is no responsibility, except for Crist's music, which only she can do. I had reached "la dolce far niente;" the sweetness of doing nothing. It was easier to say than to do. I constantly thought of tasks and then checked myself. Dry the wine glasses? Let the air do it. Wash out some clothes? Wear something else. Drive to Siena? Take a swim.

I drove Crist to Kate's and Kate invited me to return early for a "performance." I shopped in town for a while. Few people were around before the shops flipped the signs to "aperto." The tour buses wouldn't arrive for another hour. The shopkeepers were moving their display wares to the street. The residents bought coffees and walked through the streets sipping, chatting, walking their babies and dogs. I said "Giorno's" to some, relishing sharing the local private time and being amid the natives, if not actually one of them.

I returned early to Kate's. Cristina sang her new Bellini piece, *Almen se no poss'io.* Her voice went through my ears and filled the part of my anatomy that aches for beauty. I was tongue-tied. My throat filled with tears. I didn't let them spill out. Crist hated any show of emotion from me. She found it juvenile. That is, if I became emotional toward her, she took it as an affront to her status as an adult. I constantly found myself wanting to do something for her, to reciprocate for how she moved me, but so far the best I managed without showing emotion was a dumb smile. I articulated my deep feeling, "That was nice." She smiled her Mona Lisa in response.

I bought her a fragola gelato and asked if she would like to get a new case for her music -- her old case had started to rip, I ad-libbed as an excuse for the purchase. I'd like to buy her a piece of the moon, or catch a ray of the sun and put it in a diamond box to slip into her pocket for safekeeping.

"Sure," she said. We went to the art store and she chose a heavy, plastic, purple art box with a suitcase-type handle, a work of art in itself, and perfect for carrying her music back and forth. We shopped for dinner, choosing homemade gnocchi and pesto for the main course, her favorite foods. We bought two bottles of Sangiovese, another bottle of Sambuca, arugula, tomatoes, peaches, and grapes, and some schiacciati, instead of bread. Schiacciati is similar to pizza or foccaccia, but much thinner and flatter and crisper. The flat bread was brushed with olive oil and sprinkled with rosemary and came in three, oblong sizes: large, much larger, and huge. For ease of carrying, I bought the smallest size, ample for all of us. I generally served it right from the tablecloth. We broke off crisp pieces.

We had a lazy afternoon at home and dined on the terrazza rather late. The music started while we were eating. It was Eric Clapton, or a terrific wanna-be. He played and played, we sang, we danced, we laughed, we sipped the Sambuca, convinced that Signore Clapton was performing in San Gim. I promised to find out first thing tomorrow.

Laura Arrives

Jensen left early this morning to drive to Firenze to pick up Laura. They would return for dinner, she told us, or else maybe they wouldn't return for dinner. Since they couldn't phone us, I hoped they would join us. I would make myself crazy by tracking their progress in my head all day.

Annie and Crist and I walked to Kate's and then Annie and I strolled around San Gim during Crist's lesson this morning, gathering food. We successfully bought olive bread, and it was as crusty as we had hoped. We shared a heel as we shopped. We picked up peppers and eggplant and foccaccia. This would be Laura's "Welcome to Italy" party. We went to Lucia e Maria to search for the perfect dessert. Annie bought a torta di nonna, a grandmother's cake, a confection of pastry stuffed with about 10 cups of their gorgeous custard and dusted on top with powdered sugar and toasted almonds.

When we picked up Crist, Kate gave me the information she had written for the program that the group would perform down south later in the summer and asked if I would translate it into English and edit it. Sure. I took it home. Roberto had brought along Cristina's hefty Italian dictionary. I got it out. I learned much as I went along, and not just Italian. The first part of the program would be music from Shakespearean plays, lyrics by Shakespeare, with the music written later by Schubert, Haydn, Schumann, Mendelssohn, and others: "Shakespeare added music to reveal the true character of his players through the lyrics -- that Ophelia is mad, that Desdemona is fearful, that King Lear is a fool," I translated.

The music of Shakespeare's time was simple, one or two instruments, a few notes. The actors were not singers. The "newer" music, written to Shakespeare's words, was far more complex and written for sophisticated opera singers.

The company would sing selections from *As You Like it, The Tempest, Henry VIII, Much ado about Nothing, Twelfth Night,* and *A Midsummer Night's Dream*, among others. Cristina would sing "Who is Silvia," a solo, from *Two Gentlemen of Verona,* music by Franz Schubert. She sang it crisply and sweetly and with authority, leaving a haunting impression of just who this Silvia was.

Crist is quiet and shy. That such beauty and talent reside in this simple, self-effacing person tangles me. In the ristorante, the waiters stare at her. Men on the street stop to look. She is oblivious to herself.

She and I sat at the table after our lunch and watched a black sky progress in a westerly direction over the vineyards directly toward the villa. The villa was still in bright sun. The thunder was profound. As the feathery white clouds accumulated and filled the blue spaces above us, the sky began to resemble something that Steven Spielberg's special effects folks might have created for a film version of *Noah's Ark.* Crist and I gathered our reading and writing materials, cleared the table of all our candlesticks, vases, the fiasco, which is starting to look like the product of a 60's Greenwich Village coffee house, and moved inside. We closed the shutters, and came back outside to sit together on the protected stoop and watch the show. The wind picked up quickly and intensely. The laundry rack blew over, the table skittered across the terrace like a toothpick, past us and into the geraniums, followed by six dancing chairs and two sudden chaise lounges.

My thoughts were of Jensen and Laura's progess through the storm when Crist nudged me and pointed left. Almost completely straight streaks of lightning shot violently violet from as high as we could see to the ground. Again and again, stripe after stripe, moving closer and closer. The thunder continued to clap and growl. The rain started. The wind blew us wet. We retreated inside and turned on our small lamps. Then we lighted all the candles. We sat together on the sofa, quietly listening to the thundersome storm.

Laura and Jensen arrived around 4:00 p.m. By then, the rain had stopped, the sodden sky was partly blue. They had seen no rain, heard no thunder. Tall, willowy, blonde, 22 year-old Laura looked fabulous. She had slept on the plane, and was ready to party. She unpacked, showered, had an aperitivo of chilled Rosata and told us about every second of her trip. The terrace dried quickly. I wiped off the table, re-set it, and it was as if the storm had never happened. I sautéed some stuffed olives for hors d'oeuvres, sliced the olive bread, and filled a small majolica bowl with olive oil for dipping. I cooked a simple tomato and porcini sauce, tossed it with pasta and Reggiano and served minced olives on the side. Laura loves olives. Annie prepared a salad, we sliced the foccaccia, and opened a two-liter fiasco of DOCG Chianti. Laura was impressed. Hours later, we sat back on the terrazza, sipping Sambuca, and listening to the evening's concert: all Italian tonight, similar to the first night. Again I promised to get info about the festa.

The next morning was warm, a bit misty, rather humid. Crist came out to the terrace while I was sipping my muddy coffee and gave me three sets of the alabaster cherries I was so enamored with, plus a hug. The hug smelled like sweetpeas. She said, "Happy birthday." I thanked her. The cherries were gold, shading to pale crimson, highly polished, and exactly the size, color, and shape of real cherries; Rainiers. The clever wires that twisted the cherries together looked like real stems. Crist brought out some toast that wasn't badly done, some butter and honey, and joined me for breakfast. Later, Jensen gave me a set of watercolors and a palette. Laura gave me some watercolor paper. They had wrapped their gifts in beautiful Florentine paper with flowers and the French words for love and garden sprinkled into the design. I wondered where they had found such sumptuous paper.

Laura treated Crist and Jensen and me to dinner at a famous ristorante in San Gim. The waitress chewed gum. The prices were high, the food was so-so. We didn't finish our dinners, but we had a grand time. Back home, an Italian band began to play loud folk songs. We opened some wine and danced until late. Partying with Gen- X's, I felt younger.

I painted my birthday cherries

We decided that our terrace was more a veranda than a terrazza:

it was broad, about 12' wide, and extended the length of the villa, about 50 feet, and it was covered. The veranda was paved with 12" squares of terra cotta. The "ceiling," about 12' high or so, was constructed of the same terra cotta tiles, and supported to the front by four sturdy, stucco columns. The villa's exterior was a combination of plain stone and stucco-covered stone. Two sets of double Chianti-red shutters framed the two sets of French doors that led from our villa to the veranda. Three glass globes suspended from metal supports shaped like flowers. They were meant to light the veranda at night. We didn't turn them on, preferring our corny fiasco with candle and our other candles. Besides, Maria wouldn't like it.

Large, white stone boxes of double red geraniums rested on the veranda's front steps. I covered our veranda table, which seated six, with a red and white tablecloth to match the geraniums and a white linen tablecloth topper. A locally-made green and white majolica pitcher filled with Maria's flowers sat at the center, holding the day's pick of flowers, with a bowl of new alabaster cherries to the side.

I looked closely at all of these objects, trying to decide what to paint first. I hadn't painted for a while. After moving to San Francisco from New York, I studied oil painting at U.C. Berkeley as a post grad and I studied acrylics briefly after that, followed by watercolors. That was years ago, and even then I knew my talent would never catch up with my taste. My taste kept improving, while my painting ability stayed flat. I didn't think painting would be like riding a bicycle, no. But like riding a bicycle, which for me means an old Schwinn, I was doing this only for fun.

I started by painting my version of the front of the villa and the Chianti-colored shutters. I marveled at using paint colors called "umber" and "Siena" in their native land. The beginnings were bad, the final strokes were not terrible. I painted the cherries. I painted the geraniums. The painting went fast. The shimmering sun dried the paper almost instantly. Painting is a good vacation exercise, requiring as much attention as you care to give it.

Crist, Jensen, Laura, and I went to Il Refugio for dinner. We had a wonderful time, a time that only four non-competitive women could share. There was another Italian band playing when we got home, so we opened wine, drank and danced and laughed in the balmy air until late. "Tomorrow," I promised, "I'll see if we can get tickets."

"Allora ..."
Partying with the Communists

The weather turned quite warm this morning and stayed warm all day. I wouldn't say it was overwhelmingly hot, just summer-toasty. The constant breeze refreshed, kept us comfortable. Crist and I drove into San Gim to collect some picnic foods and to continue the search for drinkable coffee. I bought Annie a small majolica bowl with a charming bird painted in its center and "San Gimignano" hand written and glazed into its bottom. I didn't have the inclination to take to her. I thought it might be a peace offering, but she wasn't upset with us, only Rolf had decided that he no longer liked us. He hasn't spoken to us since around noon on my birthday.

Crist and I went to the San Gimignano Tourist Information Booth to find out about the music festival and to see about getting tickets. The woman told us it was The Festa of Unity, celebrating, she thought, the unification of Italy. The festa would go on for two or three weeks, and was sponsored by the "far right." She said it was free, anyone could go, and explained how to get there.

"Far out," I asided to Crist.

"Righteous music," she said.

The woman informed us that the food and wine booths opened around 7:30 p.m. The music began around 9:30 p.m.

"Is there dancing?" I asked.

"Yes, I think so," she said.

We took our picnic home and told the others the good news. Annie came down to our veranda to chat. I gave her the bowl and told her about the Far Right Festa. She said if we were going, she wanted to come, but Rolf probably wouldn't. We picked our way through the picnic foods.

Laura had brought four new American summer novels with her on the plane, and offered them to me. In the afternoon, I read one -- more like binged on it. We swam and then dressed up somewhat for "The Far-Out Righteous Festa." We were all moderately politically conservative, in any event, more right than left. Laura's father was a well-known historian and history teacher and a somewhat conservative Republican. Laura enthused that her father would be pleased to learn that she was mingling with political conservatives.

I tried to imagine George Bush doing an Italian folk dance. We decided this would be a "cash" party, and we each brought £100.000, just in case. We hadn't spent more than about $20.00 a day for days and we thought we could afford to splurge a bit. We left around 7:15 p.m. Rolf decided to join the party at the last minute. While we stood in the parking area trying to figure out how to get six adults to the Festa in the Fix It Again Tony for four, Maria and Maximillian joined us. They were dressed up and going out, too. I asked if they were going to the Festa. Maria laughed, shook her head, and replied with a sentence that included the word "ridiculo," ridiculous. As they climbed into their Fiat, one of our party explained to the others that instead of going to the Festa, M & M were going to pick radicchio. This was how international misunderstandings began.

Jensen drove, making two trips. Crist, Annie, Rolf, and I were the first passengers. In San Gim, we followed the directions until we saw a sign that read "Festa parcheggio;" festival parking, with an arrow to the left. We drove down the lane, and came to a field of grass, trampled by previous Festa-goers. We got out of the car, the only people there except a few workers who were setting up. We told Jensen we'd keep an eye out for her and Laura when they returned. We walked into the fenced-off Festa area, maybe half the size of a football field. To the left were some tents. We could smell, but not see, the food preparations ... barbecued meats and fried something, maybe shrimp and zucchini blossoms? On our right were some booths. We walked over to take a look. The workers were setting up what looked like Bingo, maybe, and some card games. There was a large booth stacked high with displays of what we thought might be prizes for the winners of the games: large, beautiful house plants, vases of fresh flowers, lovely pieces of majolica.

Farther on, to our left, was a tented pavilion filled with about 50 long tables for 10 or 12 people each, similar to the set-up at the Festa in Venezia. Opposite the pavilion, a man was organizing a wine booth. A half dozen white plastic tables and a couple dozen white plastic chairs were arranged between the pavilion and the wine booth. A covered bandstand and a surprisingly large, smooth, wooden dance floor lay at the end of the trampled festa area. Chairs three-deep ringed the dance floor. We continued on, past the dance floor, and looked across the valley. Straight across was our villa; practically a stone's throw from the bandstand. No wonder we could hear the music so clearly. We went back and sat at one of the white plastic tables near the wine booth. Rolf gathered six chairs while I went to the booth. The man gave me an unlabeled bottle of Chianti and six plastic glasses. I gave him five Marias, he gave me change. Jensen and Laura joined us.

The festa-goers began to arrive. There were many local families. The people had dressed simply for the Saturday night festivities; the women in plain Polyester flowered dresses like those sold in the local markets, the men in neatly pressed, short-sleeved shirts and cotton trousers, the children in shorts, cotton shirts, and sandals. We stood a foot or so taller than any adult there. Crist, Jens, and Laura wore long skirts, cashmere sweaters, and high heeled combat-style boots. Annie and I wore country print, cotton wrap skirts with linen blouses. Rolf stood out because of his height and because he had chosen to wear a bright red Hawaiian shirt with gleaming white trousers. He generally wore something that screamed, "AMERICAN!"

Our group looked out of place, as if we had got off a tourist bus at the wrong stop. The tables at the pavilion were filling up, so we took our wine and walked over to stake one out. A waiter came by, and I asked for a menu. He explained that we had to go to the "Cassa;" cashier, near the entrance. Jensen and I were appointed to reconnoiter. Outside the food preparation tents, we saw a sign, 'CASSA.' Jensen said, "Mi cassa è tu cassa." We anticipated an evening of fun.

About 20 people lined up in front of the Cassa window. They chatted and laughed and they all seemed to know each other. This was like a huge, friendly block party. Jens and I figured that when we got to the front of the line, we would be given a menu. Then we noticed a crowd to the left of the line. They were looking at "Il Menu;" eel Men-OO, The Menu. The names of the dishes offered for dinner were handwritten on paper plates tacked to a board. The antipasti plates were grouped together, then the primi, the secondi, and so on. There were no prices.

It dawned on us that when we got to the head of the line, we might need to order. We would need to order six dinners and probably the wine, too. Jensen pulled out her notepad and pen, and started writing. We chose six salads, three antipasti, five pasta and five meat and seafood entrées. We'd sort out the food at the table. Jens wrote it all down in English. We counted up the items and added some potatoes and vegetables and another pasta. As we got closer to the front of the line, Jensen wrote faster. She filled a notepad page. She told me, "Order fast, and speak quickly. Act Italian. I don't want to be embarrassed."

"Si!" I promised brightly, dark with doubt.

When we were about three people away from the front of the line, we could see into the Cassa booth. Behind two male cashiers hung a circular, 5' diameter hammer and sickle flag. Far out. But not to the right.

The next question, after What are we doing here? was, Would we have to show our Communist Party card to order? Was there a password? A secret handshake? What was this Festa? Should we tell the others? Only one more person stood between us and the communists. We stopped gaping and speculating, to listen intently.

"Allora," the man ahead of me said. The equivalent of ... Well-ll-ll. He drew out his "Allora" to about 10 seconds. Then he ordered rapidly. The cashier checked off what he ordered on a form that was not unlike a racetrack betting form, and added up the total. The man carefully removed the correct amount of lire from his well-worn wallet.

We had to pay when we ordered! I asked Jensen if she had any money. Yes, a hundred thousand. I had left my money in my bag at the table. Hope that's enough, I worried. "Maybe they'll take Visa," Jensen giggled, and went on to whisper a description of a potential Visa commercial where you could join the communist party only with the Visa card. "The communists don't take American Express," she laughed, wiggling her eyebrows. Then she launched into the potential American Express commercial, starring a previously prominent communist, now dead, who banged his shoe and demanded, "Do you know me?"

The man in front of us was now buying what looked like raffle tickets, about four for a dollar. Remembering the majolica in the booth, I interrupted Jensen to say I wanted to get some raffle tickets, too. She rolled her eyes.

"Let's just see if we can get through the dinner-ordering, mommmmm."

Our cashier was a clean-cut man, about 40, wearing a pin-striped cotton shirt, button down collar, very Brooks Bros. He smiled disarmingly, nodded his head, and greeted us. "Sera," he said, pleasantly... Good evening.

"Sera," I blurted nervously.

He looked at me expectantly, and didn't appear to be waiting for me to say a secret password or to give the handshake of solidarity or to flip my Party card on the counter, so I took a deep breath and began:

"Allora," I said, as the man before me had. Gaining confidence, I stretched out my Allora a full five seconds, until Jensen jabbed me in the ribs. Translating haltingly from Jensen's list, I ordered as quickly as I could. The man cooperatively checked off each item and wrote a price next to it and Jensen checked off each item on her list, too.

"Wine!" Jensen coached me.

"Red?" I asked her. She jabbed me again. I asked for two bottles of vino rosso locale; local red wine, please. The man handed over the bottles and asked how many were in our party. "Seis," I told him, six. He added a cover charge, a music charge and a bread charge per person. The paper was covered with enormous, fancy numbers. Worried, I dug into my pocket and found a few Marias. He told me what the grand total was. It sounded astronomical. I stared blankly. Jensen covered by handing him her hundred grand. He gave her a few thousand in change and gave me the menu/receipt. We took one last look at the hammer and sickle, said "Sera" to the Cassa man, and moved quickly out of the line. Jensen, a good mathematician and a so-so history student, came up with a definition: "Communist party: An evening of wine, dinner, music, and dancing for about $8.50 a person." We agreed we wouldn't tell the others about the hammer and sickle, at least not until after dinner.

By the time we got back, all the tables were full and most people were eating. Jensen and I both thought that conversation stopped and a hundred eyes followed us to our table. We shrugged it off, told the group what we ordered, and we poured the wine. I handed our receipt to a waiter, and several people began to put things on our table. One gave us plates, flatware, and napkins. Another brought bread, another, salads. The food started to arrive -- large plates of pasta, grilled shrimp and lobster tails, roasted veal and pasta. It was all delicious. As we polished off each course, a man with a rolling cart of dirty dishes stopped at our table. He said, "Please," to me, in Russian, as he reached for the salad plates. Without thinking, I said "Thank you," in Russian, depleting my entire Russian vocabulary as I handed him the plates. Stunned, I told Jensen that the man was speaking Russian. We decided we should tell the others the whole story, "just in case." She also whispered, "Doesn't this party remind you of the festa on the canal in Venice?" We blinked at each other.

Rolfo laughed heartily to learn that we were probably being indoctrinated as we ate. Laura laughed that if her father knew she was there, he would probably be outraged. We finished eating and moved with our comrades over to the dance floor. We sat at the same table as before dinner. Rolfo bought more wine. I wished I had bought raffle tickets. The band warmed up and began to play a set of Italian songs we hadn't heard before.

The dance floor immediately filled with beautifully dressed couples who danced a formal, sweeping waltz. The couples moved together in a circle, clockwise, smooth as skaters. The next number was a fox-trot. They glided through it and on to another waltz. The crowd was clearly divided into dancers and watchers. The chairs edging the dance floor were all full and watchers stood three deep behind each chair. The dancers were tall and perfectly matched, like Ken and Barbie dolls. The women had swept up their hair in old fashioned Gibson Girl styles and wore tailored suits reminiscent of the Joan Crawford 40's look. The men also wore suits, of the Hans Conreid style. We thought perhaps they were the local Italian Arthur Murray Communist Party Dancing School demonstrating for the plebeians, except there were probably 50 couples on the floor. We watched, charmed and fascinated, for over two hours. The crowd swelled. As evening moved to night, younger couples and middle aged single men and women began to arrive, replacing the families. The well-dressed bourgeois dancers departed, and men and women who looked like "the workers" took over the dance floor.

Around 11:00 p.m., Annie and Rolf wanted to go home. Jensen took them, then returned for us. A half hour later, we decided go home, too, for a Sambuca and a listen from our veranda. Jensen stood up to leave first. A man bowed to her. He introduced himself. His name was Emilio. He asked her to dance. Emilio was about 50 years old. He was clean shaven and doused liberally with powerful after-shave. He was dressed simply but neatly in a short-sleeved cotton shirt and cotton trousers, no tie. Jensen smiled, firmly but graciously declining the privilege. Emilio took her hand, then her arm, and gently pulled her to the dance floor. We all stared as he led her to the floor and then we followed like dogs for a closer look. She waltzed with Emilio, looking like a princess, her long golden hair flowing, as they swept across the floor.

Jensen had been a Debutante four seasons ago in San Francisco, and had learned to waltz for the Ball. She remembered. We thought she was as good as any of the dancers, even with her heavy shoes. She was laughing and dancing effortlessly. A man tapped me on the arm, bowed, introduced himself, and asked me to dance. Another asked Laura, another invited Cristina.

"Why not?" asked Cristina. When the piece was over, other men asked us to dance, then other men after that. Between dances, Laura confided with a giggle that her first partner had reached his right arm all the way around her back to fondle her breast. I looked up and saw that the same man was dancing with Crist.

The men were all about Emilio's age, clean-shaven, their short hair slicked back neatly. They were more Spartanly dressed than the waltzing couples had been, but, we thought, equally good dancers. Each of my partners was a full head shorter than me. We danced until 12:30 a.m. and called it a night only when our dancing partners became amorous. One invited Laura to meet him afterwards, another invited Crist to his apartment in Poggibonsi, another asked Jensen to meet him at the Torture Museum in San Gim. Would we be in town long? No, we were leaving early the next morning; very early; at dawn; before dawn; subito. Now. "Sera!" We called over our shoulders as we quickly lost ourselves in the crowd and jogged to the car. The Fiat smelled like after-shave for days.

Vipere!

We dancers slept late and gathered on the veranda for espresso around 10:30 a.m. Annie went to early mass, and dropped off a tray of pastries for us on her way back. We sat in our jammies in the clear, warm morning, sipping, tasting, and listening to the bells for the 11:00 a.m. mass, wondering why the bells always ring about a quarter of each hour. We decided to stay home for the day. Annie and Jensen painted together, Laura and I read, Crist practiced and read some new music. She reads music the way I read a book, her eyes dancing from measure to measure. I wished I could hear what she was hearing.

Later, I started an overly-ambitious watercolor of the hillside to the left of the villa, a rise of vineyards topped by a single, poignantly crooked little tree. I saw the shapes clearly and understood the shadow patterns, but the translation to paper would take many more years of practice, years I wouldn't have.

The crooked little tree atop the hill

In the late afternoon, Laura and Jensen went into San Gim to do some shopping. Annie began to prepare eggplant parmigiano and veal for our dinner. Crist swam laps. I went for a swim with the 5:45 or 5:46 p.m. bells. Rolf stared at the nude bathers from behind his book. The aromas from Annie's kitchen floated out to me. It was a perfect lazy Sunday.

After the swim, I walked up the 10 steps that led to the olive grove and the hammock. I turned around at the top of the steps, to gaze out, to figure out how to compose the best photo of the pool with the vineyards in the background. As I stood there lost in my thoughts, a very long snake lunged from his coil on the second step to the top, past my feet, and into the grass. It took me no longer than an instant to jump from the top step to the middle step. Another long snake uncoiled from the middle step and streaked past me. I leapt to the bottom, unglued, screaming.

Maria, who was sunbathing nude nearby with her friends, came over to see what the problem was. My Italian had slithered away.

"Vipera!" I cried, pointing to the steps. "Due vipere!" Two vipers, I clarified, though it was not a good time to come up with a plural feminine noun ending in front of a naked woman.

She calmly interviewed me, asking if they were long and thin or short and thick. Long and thin, I gestured, reaching my arms out to their full extent. She smiled clinically and explained that "vipere," poisonous vipers, are short and fat. What I had seen was "serpe," serpents, the long, thin, *non-* poisonous snakes. It didn't help.

Her natural sciences lecture concluded, she turned her naked back to me and returned to her sunbathing. I stood there feeling awkward and stupid, wondering why I should be the one to feel awkward and stupid. I took a long, hot shower, deciding that the pool photo would be better taken from the opposite side, looking toward the snake-infested olive groves.

We dined on the veranda, Annie's cooking was meraviglioso; mare-ah-vee-YOH-soh, marvelous. I practiced saying that word many times before I could roll it off my tongue. Jensen and Laura went back into San Gim to hang out for a while. They hoped they wouldn't bump into their dance partners. The rest of us stayed outside listening to the music that drifted over from the communist party. We reminisced about our evening, and planned our assault on the Prada outlet the next day.

Prada or Bust

Prada Outlet Day, 7:00 a.m.: Beautiful, warm morning. Sipped insipid coffee with an apricot stuffed croissant, then woke up Jensen and Laura and cooked them breakfast. Lighting the propane stove in the early morning was a challenge. The Italian matches which, by the way, are not free, and must be paid for at the tabaccaio; tobacconist, are short, flimsy, round plastic sticks that are difficult to light and which extinguish themselves almost instantly after you have struck them. To light the stove while half-awake in the dim kitchen took many tries and many matches.

Crist wanted to walk to Kate's and back alone this morning, and to spend some time shopping in San Gim by herself, a fair request. I hadn't meant to be crowding her. Annie, Jens, Laura, and I were going to try to find the Prada Outlet. Crist had no patience for such a project. I had picked the directions to the outlet off the Net, and carried the print-out with me.

The print-out read, "The Prada Outlet is between Rome and Florence: I Pellettieri d'Italia, Localita Levanella, Montevarchi."

I assumed that "I Pellettieri d'Italia, Montevarchi" was Prada's address, and that Localita Levanella would be the street. We easily found the small town of Montevarchi on the map, just a Post-It south of Firenze, and drove there. Once in Montevarchi, the road signs informed us that Levanella was a suburb of Montevarchi. We were confused. We asked several people if they knew where the Prada Outlet might be: "Posso comprare Prada qui vicino?" Poh-soh cohm-prah-ray Prada kwee vee-CHEE-noh (Pigeon Italian for "Can I buy Prada near here?") Various Italians gave us a variety of answers. Following one person's advice, to drive back toward Montevarchi, Jensen saw a small sign "Pellettieri d'Italia." She turned down the street the sign pointed to.

Two hours after we left the villa, we found a complex of warehouses and loading docks, all locked and closed. The parking lot was empty. We spied one open door. Jens parked, and I went inside to repeat for the -enth time, "Posso comprare Prada qui vicino?" I walked through the open door and into a garment factory. There were no workers. Half-sewn garments lay at work stations. Dozens of sewing machines sat idle. Bolts of fabric were stacked around the room. A stout, dark-haired woman came out from an office, and clicked her heels across the floor toward me, glaring.

"'Giorno, Signora," I said brightly.

"'Giorno," she said, clicking ominously toward me.

I asked my question.

She shook her head, the Italian leitmotif for "Americans are so stupid," and gestured for me to follow her. She walked me to the door. She pointed to a door across the parking lot. She gave me a sharp look. She turned around and went inside, closing and locking the door behind her.

"Molto grazie," I called to her.

We walked to the door she had indicated. There was no Prada sign. There were no signs at all. The door was locked. We spotted a neatly typed paper taped to a window, written in Italian, stating that the store would re-open August 18 after Feria; holiday. We wondered, What store? Three folded, terry cloth bathrobes were stacked on the floor near the door. We squinted to read the labels: Prada, Prada, and Prada. We had found the outlet. We could find it again, and quicker, too. We scrutinized what we could see of the outlet. It was large, and set up like a real store rather than a factory. The right half of the store was devoted to women's clothing, bags, and shoes, and the left to mens' wear; suits, jackets, shirts, and shoes. There were several glass cases in the center of store whose contents we couldn't see, peer as we might.

We drove back to Montevarchi "Centro;" downtown, for lunch. We found a very old bar on a corner, the only place of any kind open in the sleepy town, the Caffè Fontana. There was no fontana; fountain, but the tall, good-looking barman suggested, in English, that he might make up something special for us, some fresh panini with mozzarella and prosciutto, perhaps? We thanked him, ordered cold Danish beer, and sat alone in a booth upholstered with well-worn leather in the 1930's dining room, enjoying our well-deserved lunch, and planned our return to Prada. Shopping can be more demanding that culturing.

What we had was not an address, as we had thought, but merely an indication of direction. "I Pellettieri d'Italia, Localita Levanella, Montevarchi" translates: Italian leather goods, near Levanella, a suburb of Montevarchi. That we found it was pure luck or, to be more precise, determination.

We enjoyed the drive back, speeding past medieval villages, vineyards, and silvery olive groves with Jensen at the helm. At home, we read, napped, and swam. Crist had shopped for dinner and whisked a perfect gorgonzola sauce for us, entirely different from the sauce she makes at home; lighter, yet richer tasting. She tossed it with some fresh fettuccine she had found in a small San Gim shop, made a tomato and basil salad, sliced some bread, and opened some Vernaccia. We danced on the veranda to the communist party's American rock and roll. The words "communist party" have taken on a fresh meaning for us. The party would continue through August 17, the Cassa poster had said.

Tony Blair comes to Town

I awoke to a clear clear blue blue sky and a light chill at 7:00 a.m. The tractor began creaking at 6:00 a.m. and the roosters doodled. I made a large cup of coffee to take off the cold edge and finished it at the moment the sun popped over the hills. The landscape brightened, the veranda warmed as if Maria had turned on the heat. I'm not actually sure that we have heat.

I have now tried all the variables for making coffee. I have used both the on-stove espresso pot and the funnel with the coffee filter in all combinations: different types and amounts of coffee, different kinds and amounts of milk, heated and cold. I have tried tap water and several bottled waters. I tasted no difference between any of them. I concluded that Italian coffee is different from American coffee and I say the hell with it.

I painted all day and read another book. Was I bored or relaxed? Kate was having dinner with Tony Blair and his family tonight. All of San Gim was ga-ga over the British Prime Minister's visit here. Crist hummed and cooked pasta with a rich red sauce for our dinner. She seemed very happy. Annie said she loves to see Crist and me together. She said we remind her of two bees buzzing happily around a beautiful rose. I made a note to think about that.

The breeze piped up around 6:30 p.m. every day and didn't slack until about 8:00 p.m. If we could persuade our group to eat after 8:00, we would dine more comfortably. Maybe I was cranky.

Next day, Crist and I drove to Kate's and I walked to the chiesa St. Agostino while she worked with Kate. I was to return early. As in many of the simple, smaller churches, the walls of St. Agostino were frescoed. They were as beautiful as the more elaborate inlays or oil paintings that the large cathedrals boasted. One fresco had a "frame" painted of vertical, hanging swags of fruit that resembled contemporary Williamsburg decorative art. What looked like raffia bows connected the bunches of fruits and vegetables. One bunch was composed of a bouquet of lemons with bay leaves (laurel) trim. Another was pine cones with pine bough trim, another an artichoke bouquet with rosemary trim. I sketched them to remember. I'd like to try making such swags at home.

A recording of the *Ave Maria*, sung by an a cappella choir, floated through the church and into the flowering courtyard where I sat daydreaming. I woke up and had to walk fast to get back to Kate's in time for a performance. As I left the San Gim archway, I ran straight into a pale green Mercedes station wagon, or maybe a pale green Mercedes hearse -- I couldn't tell which because the vehicle's back and sides were obscured by funeral wreaths wider than my open arms. The wreaths were composed of a nightmarish mix of candy colored pink-orange Gerber daisies, red orchids, and pink rubrum lilies. The mourners gathered behind the hearse; handsome people of all ages, dressed in somber Armani and vivacious Versace. Only a few wore black. I watched as the hearse started up and slowly proceeded through the arch and into town, the group following. I snapped out of it and hurried to Kate's, wishing I could have joined the group, maybe walking on to St. Agostino.

Kate had a surprise. "Sit down! Listen!" She beamed with pleasure.

It was a new Rossini piece, from *The Barber of Seville*, as hauntingly beautiful as the *Ave Maria* in the church. Crist was able to learn a new piece every two days. She picked up each nuance and pronunciation fillip after Kate told her once. Kate was pleased. Cristina was soaring. I said, "That was wonderful." I was sure that Kate thought of me as an inarticulate boor.

Kate showed me the menu from last night's dinner with Tony Blair. It was "tipico;" typical, local San Gim cibo, CHEE-boh; food. The starter was fried zucchini blossoms, the first course was pasta with porcini mushrooms, then Florentine steak, and for dessert, torta di nonna; our humble, everyday fare.

Crist and I shopped a bit on our way home, got gelati, and came home to swim and nap. We all went to Il Refugio for dinner, and sat staring at stars, listening to the music, and tasting Sambuca far into the night. We were surprised how late it was when we finally went to bed though more and more, time meant less.

Culture, Shopping, Stealing

Crist had the day off. She planned to swim and sun. Kate was having lunch with some politicos from London. Annie and I drove Jensen and Laura to the Firenze Stazione; train station, for their weekend trip to Venice. I suggested that they take the Orient Express, an old dream of mine, but they are of a generation that prefers the new and sleek. They opted for the Eurostar.

When they had their tickets in hand, they quickly dismissed us oldsters. Annie and I shopped our way through the city. A little culture, a little shopping, a bite to eat: repeat to coda. Most stores were having sales, 30%-50% off. Several shops were closed for Feria, including Giannini, the famous Florentine paper store across from the Pitti Palace. Wandering toward Centro from the train station, we came across a sidewalk shoe sale. Annie helped me balance while I took off my old shoes and tried on new ones. I bought a pair of handmade penny loafers, square toe, that fit like Florentine gloves, for about $35.00. Annie said they were identical to some Ralph Lauren's for which she paid over $200.00 stateside. I was happy with my old shoes. They were good, leather flats I had bought and worn constantly at home before leaving on this trip. I wore out the soles and had the shoes resoled just before we left. They were as comfortable as the proverbial bedroom slippers. I had high hopes for the new loafers, too.

I bought a very small, square, alligator Ferré bag for half price. Each Ferré bag is numbered. The numbers are large. Annie joked that the number is the price. We walked to the Boboli gardens for lunch high above the city. We sat at the Boboli caffè with many other Americans in the midday heat, under muslin-colored (or un-colored) umbrellas and sipped peach iced tea and drank in the red tiled rooftops. The food was dreadful. Our frittatas were a scrambled egg devoid of flavor on a stale roll we couldn't chew. No matter -- the setting was idyllic. We left the food to the many yellow jackets and explored the gardens. Annie was disappointed that only dead grass filled the Boboli's trim parterres. As we were leaving, we saw a small parterre filled to the brim with blooms. The Boboli are all structure; architectural gardens. There is only enough water for the fountains, which splashed and helped us feel cooler.

We used the rest of the afternoon to find a wedding present for my niece, Kelley. We scoured the silver stores on the Ponte Vecchio. I found a graceful, utterly useless .997 silver basket, hand-hammered inside, smooth outside, with a delicate handle formed of dainty bunches of silver grapes. A few more grapes decorated the rim of the bowl. The shop's silversmith told me he had made only one such basket -- he makes only one of each piece -- except for his sets of silver goblets. The shop girl gift wrapped it. I'd have to hand-carry it home and mail it to Texas from there. Without a use, it should last for generations.

We shopped our way back to the parcheggio, admiring for many moments the perfect marzipan fruits and vegetables in the fancy shop windows and wondering if it would be at all feasible to bring some home. We pushed our decision to another day and moved on to the train station parking lot. The sidewalks became more and more congested as we got closer to the station.

Two blocks away, we were shoulder to shoulder with crowds walking to the station and coming from the station. We could not walk next to each other, so we continued single file, bumping our way between people. A young girl walking toward us caught my eye. She looked about 10. She fixed her eyes on me, making me uneasy. She had a newspaper spread over her outstretched arms. She approached. Wary, I clutched my bag and spun around to see if Annie was OK. She was pushing away a child of about six who was trying to open her fanny pack. When Annie shouted at her, both girls retreated. Annie said that the snap on her pack is difficult even for her to open. "It takes practice," she said breathlessly. We locked arms until we got to our destination.

I was carrying the shopping bag I had bought in Castellina. I carried no purse or wallet. I had a soft, nondescript sunglass case that I had filled with all I would need for shopping that day: my ATM and VISA cards, cash, a solar pocket calculator, a pen, and my checkbook record, which I used to keep a running tally of amounts spent and lire taken from ATM's. The case was at the bottom of the bag. My purchases, which included a bakery bag, were on top. I wasn't so naïve to think my "system" was theft-proof. But most women carried a handbag or wore a fanny pack. A local shopping bag would not be as attractive a target. My bag could be stolen, true, but not without a fight, and I thought it unlikely that anyone could reach inside the bag and fish out my sunglass case while I held the bag. I was wearing sunglasses. The thief might think the case was empty.

We talked of nothing but our attack on our drive home. It made us hungry. We stopped at the ristorante called da Nisio, about 5 k from the villa, to see if we could get a dinner rez. Da Nisio was the ristorante where Kate had dined today with San Gim's mayor and the head of Britain's Labor Party. The manager said they could take us at 8:00 p.m. The ristorante didn't have a terrazza, and we hated to break our perfect record for eating outdoors every night, but Kate had promised it was the best ristorante in the area, so we made the rez.

When we arrived at 8:00, the ristorante had been transformed into a terrazza. The windows and doors had vanished; sliding back to the corners. The clientele was all

Italian. Tables were set with exquisite crystal wine glasses. A superior wine list matched them. This was the first ristorante we had been to that had good, crystal stemware. I ordered saddle of pork with a piquant red currant sauce, roasted potatoes, and a lemon cream with blackberries and strawberries for dessert. It was the best food we had tasted so far, yet the price was about the same as the simpler fare at Il Refugio. We dined for hours. Back home, we sat on the veranda and had some wine and a drop of Sambuca. The communist party served up Italian folk songs along with unfamiliar, lighthearted Italian music played on unusual instruments, heavy on percussion.

I awoke at 4:00 a.m. sweating from the memory of a dream in which I grappled with hollow-eyed, long-haired little girls who turned into vapors. I turned on the hall light and left it on for the night, then worried that it might attract enormous crawling and flying bugs. I didn't get back to sleep.

Volterra: Ghosts from the Past

In the very early, very warm morning, I washed a surprisingly large number of wine glasses, considering we were out for dinner last night, so that I could use the sink to do some laundry. I thanked myself once more for bringing a sink stopper. Actually, I brought two, and gave one to Annie. There are no stoppers in any of the bathrooms or in our kitchens and I haven't seen any at the stores or at the market. I used a powdered Italian detergent, the brand that was most popular with the Italian women at the Coop, who were emptying the shelf when I walked by. I thought it would be the best one, but it was probably only the cheapest, or on sale. The clothes seemed dirtier after I washed them than before. I hung them outside and they often blew off the drying apparatus, picking up more dirt.

I think I have worn everything I brought. I wished I had a sweater or two and some warm jammies. I packed two silk nighties plus cotton pajamas, a poor choice. Next time I'd bring flannel pajamas. I organized this morning, counted my money, and recorded recent purchases in the checkbook record that I brought for that specific purpose. It was a good device and it didn't take up much space.

Whenever I made a purchase or took money from a Bankomat; ATM, I saved the receipt, tucking it into my checkbook record to record and deduct from my balance later on. I had spent about a fifth of my budgeted money in Venice. San Gim is not an expensive place, and the goods are not as tempting as those in Venice. According to my records, four weeks into the trip, I was comfortably ahead of budget.

We dropped Crist at Kate's, and I snapped some shots of Annie and Rolf in the cloisters of the Duomo, where a young man played the harp. Many people had gathered for the holiday mass today; Assumption Day. When the bells pealed to announce the mass, the harpist continued playing, soundless to all, drowned out by the anvil chorus. Annie and Rolf went to mass while I picked up Crist. Kate asked her to "do" her new Mozart récitatif for me, to demonstrate the pronunciation of her new Italian "T's." The double Italian "T" was quite different from the single Italian "T," Kate explained to me. Both are difficult for non Italians to pronounce; much less, to sing. Crist complied, and from the rosy look on Kate's face, I guessed she did so to a "T." I turned to mush and said, "very nice!" Kate must think I am an idiot. It is important to pronounce the récitatif perfectly, as it is the "spoken" introduction to the aria and must be crisp and easy to understand.

After Kate's, we met Annie and Rolf at the mass. The church was full, many people had to stand. It was extremely warm, close, humid. The smell of incense was stupefying. Back home, I could still smell it on my breath and on my moist arms as I sat on the veranda in the still of the midday heat.

Baby shadows sprouted from under the olive groves. All along the roads, families were picnicking on this feast day. Everything was closed, including most of the ristoranti. Occasionally, we heard a voice, a mother calling, a child laughing or crying, men shouting. There were two picnic parties on our private road just outside the gate. The families had set up card tables and folding chairs on the entrance to our driveway. They borrowed our view and breeze all afternoon.

We had a picnic, too. Annie made some tuna sandwiches using the dark tuna that is packed in oil, the tuna called for stateside in Italian recipes such as Vitello Tonnato; the tuna that is found at home only in Italian delis and costs several dollars for a small can. Here it was under a dollar a can. We drank cold Moretti beer with our sandwiches. We felt fortunate to be here. I wondered what Jensen and Laura were doing, if they liked their hotel in Venice, if they had problems in transit, if the Orient Express would have been more glamorous than the Eurostar, if they would have encounters with tall, dark strangers or short, wily girl thieves.

After lunch, I napped and swam. My naps are not more than 10 minutes, enough to refresh. Crist doesn't nap, but she "disconnects." Before we wanted to, Crist and I began to cook dinner for Annie and Rolf: Veal with succulent, enormous local capers with their stems on, and a light lemon sauce, plus fettuccine with fresh tomato and basil sauce, and a green bean salad; al dente beans tossed with olive oil and lemon, a splash of Balsamic, a dash of salt and pepper. We ate early, unfortunately, and it was rather windy. Later, we sipped Sambuca, a lubricant we have become devoted to -- and listened in on the communist party's Italian bands, similar to the music last Saturday. Annie and I laughed, danced, gazed at the gibbous moon, and looked forward to watching the full moon's rise over our veranda.

Saturday morning, we stripped our beds and put all the sheets and towels in a stack on the living room floor, and headed out before the maids arrived. Rolf walked to San Gim for the day and so did Crist, but separately. Annie and I drove through the beautiful valleys of the Era and Cecina Rivers to Volterra, a half hour down the road and 1780 feet above sea level. We saw no other cars. The driving was smooth and easy, with nobody tailgating or coming toward us on the wrong side of the road as we sped around the curves. We passed the county Penitentiary, composed of several low, modern buildings with a central (high-fenced) soccer field that we could look down into. The parking lot was full. Saturday must be visiting day or maybe the inmates were having an invitational soccer match?

Alabaster is King in the medieval walled town of Volterra. The Etruscans began digging the stuff from the surrounding hills in the 8th century B.C. and they honed their carving skills to fine and highly decorative art. We stopped at Ali, the largest artisan shop in the town and the nearest to the town entrance; in other words, the main tourist shop. Annie bought a carved elephant to add to her collection of elephants and we admired the other carved animals -- sculpted fruits, lamps, accessories, boxes, hundreds and hundreds of objets d'art carved from this heavy, beautiful natural stone. One sculpture captured a ferocious fight between two life-sized horses. It was carved from a single slab of alabaster, with variegated colors ranging from white to black.

We learned that the more transparent the alabaster, the purer it is, and the more expensive. I tried on one of the transparent necklaces with perfectly matched, clear, round beads. It was uniquely beautiful, quite expensive, and after I wore it about a half-minute, it felt like a millstone around my neck. As I put it back in the display, a craftsman was arranging several delicate, three-strand bracelets in the display. He had made them of jade and fresh water pear!s. They were reasonably priced. I bought three; one for each of "my girls."

Narrow cobblestone and brick streets led us to Centro, the center of town. We stopped to sit in the Piazza dei Priori to look at the 13th century Palazzo and to soak up the local flavors. Volterra is well kept by its residents. Their pride is reflected in the freshly-swept streets, the flowers that sprout from their window boxes, the neatness of the shops and squares. You could hear it in their laughter as they gathered in groups to chat, show off their babies, and to catch up on local gossip.

Wherever we went, we saw young families playing with their babies and small children. We walked on, through the Palazzo Viti, a palatial home built by the Viti family, an important alabaster importer. The home is open to the public. From the living room floor rose two enormous columns of elaborately carved alabaster -- a meter in diameter, 12 feet tall -- a commission for the King of Mexico, who was assassinated before the pieces could be delivered. Vittorio Emmanuel slept here. He was a guest of the Viti family. The guide told us that his bedroom was exactly as he left it. The room looked rather like Marie Antoinette's frou-frou bedroom at Versailles. A bust of the Italian King, not alabaster, sat on a dresser.

An oil painting of a voluptuous woman, reminiscent of Ingre's Odalisque, hung on a dining room wall. The artist, "A. Puccinelli," had signed it with a flourish. Puccinelli is Annie's maiden name. Intrigued, she asked the guide if he knew anything about the artist. He didn't. She speculated that the artist's name was the same as her father's; Alfred.

We were far from Centro, and ready for lunch. Rather than return to the fancy town square restaurants, we stopped for a quick bite at a pizza place, then proceeded to the famous Museum of Volterra, the Guarnacci, named for its principal benefactor, who donated his then already-famous collection of Etruscan artifacts to the town of Volterra in 1761. We were standing directly in front of the museum when I asked a passerby where it was. He pointedly pointed behind us. Grazie. The museum's artifacts were arranged from oldest finds (2300 B.C.) to newest (2 B.C.) The oldest objects -- arrowheads -- were Neolithic, from the Bronze Age. The museum had one of the world's largest collections of cinerary urns; the archeologists concentrated their searches for the Etruscan past in Etrurian necropolises.

The Etrurian civilization burned their dead. The earliest burial urns were simple, small, local clay vases with a bowl on top; a lid. They resembled the Amaryllis kits you buy at Christmas. As the years moved ahead, the vases became larger and more elaborate. Carving was added to the cineraries. The materials became richer, moving from terra cotta to stone to alabaster and marble, culminating in cineraries resembling Roman sarcophagi; lidded, rectangular boxes. The lids bore elaborate sculptures of the deceased, lying down, lounging; enjoying a well-deserved rest in the after-life. The cinder box was carved to depict the deceased's work and hobbies. Often, the artisan carved several horses into the scene; mounts to speed the dead to his next life.

The departed's possessions were buried with his or her ashes. Weapons were buried with the men along with tack for their horses. Toilet articles were entombed with the women's ashes. The earliest possessions were primitive, humble; an arrowhead or two, a rudimentary comb. The progression of possessions through the years was fascinating. Chic perfume pans, belt buckles, and silver earrings slowly replaced the rough combs. Finely wrought knives and well-turned bits superseded the arrowheads.

Common through the earliest to the latest possessions were "fibulae," the Etrurian version of safety pins; fasteners for their draped clothing. I had always wondered how togas were held together. The first fibulae were utilitarian, made of bronze and iron. The last were exquisitely fashioned of solid gold; as decorative as they were useful. The moment Etruscan jewelry was born is recorded. Modern Tuscan shops sell souvenir fibulae, in gold and brass; brooches.

After stepping through three stories of cremation urns, we needed some fresh air. We strode forward 350 years, in search of the Roman amphitheater. Confused by the map, I stopped to ask a shopkeeper where we might find the amphitheater. She gave me the sad, "Oh no, another stupid American" head shake,

and without a word, cut her eyes right. We rounded the corner she indicated, 10 paces away, and in the field below, just outside the town walls, we saw a dozen or so sentinel columns. The amphitheater's original outline was apparent. There were no postcard kiosks, no shops, no tourists smudging its boundaries. We drank in our first real Roman amphitheater, pictured on page 147.

Back at the Piazza dei Priori, the complexion had changed. The town now bustled with gelati-slurping tourists, but no Americans. We continued to be a novelty. Many of the locals took us for Germans. The shopkeepers greeted us in German. Other Italians in the shops also spoke German to us. I understood enough Italian to know that they didn't like us Germans. I corrected them, telling them that we were Americans, not Germans. As Americans, the Italians thought of us as allies and as their liberators. We were noblesse oblige. By asserting our nationality, I felt an edgy alliance with the Italians, that we were all still fighting the war.

We walked along the ancient walls, the Tuscan hills spread below, dark clouds curling over them. With no schedule and no time frame, we poked through shops away from the touristy parts of town. In the back streets, we passed a frutta shop. Wooden crates of perfect, ripe fruit were stacked high outside the door. I couldn't resist an apricot. The shop's owner wasn't in sight, so I helped myself. Annie chose a fig. The fruits were made of alabaster. It was the best work I had seen. I chose a fig, too, and a small bunch of grapes whose stem was a real grape stem, knowing it wasn't practical to carry such heavy items home but being unable to resist them. I took the pieces inside to the shopkeeper, and asked, "Who made them?" He said they were all his work, he was the artist. I told him they were the loveliest I had seen. He was pleased, and flushed red. He wrapped up the fruit for us and autographed the wrappings with a flourish.

The sun felt strong around 4:00 p.m., and we felt like a swim. We made our way back to the parking garage through the enchanting side streets. We walked down a precipitous, narrow street where hollyhocks forced their way between the cobblestones to tower several feet taller than us. The stalwart stems were like small tree trunks, over three inches in diameter. Peeking down the side streets, flowers tumbled from every window box, pots of geraniums were banked in front of every door.

We left Volterra through the Porta all'Arco, reputed to be "the best preserved Etruscan gateway in Italy," dating from the 4th century, B.C. Several photographers stood near the arch, their cameras on tripods; serious shooters. We marveled at the ancient stonework, the artistry of antiquity. Three heads jutted from the arch in the town wall, their identities long since eroded. I thought they might be lions, but no doubt they were the eroded heads of men. These heads might have cast a warning to any who entered unamicably. Their stance alone evoked the Etruscan pride whose mysterious roots are still strong as the hollyhock trunk. I satisfied myself with a postcard photo of the arch. It was an old postcard. The heads were clearly those of men, not lions. How soon, I wondered, until the heads would be completely eroded?

We were lost. We asked two women who were coming from their house along the wall if they could tell us where the parking garage was, hoping they would give us the "Oh no, another stupid American" look and point across the street. Instead, they told us we were many kilometers from the garage, and offered us a ride. We accepted, gratefully, agreeing that we much preferred the industrious grace of the tiny Italian towns to the indolent idleness of the big cities.

Once home, Annie sunned while Crist and I swam. We showered, dressed, and had a Campari and soda, erring dinner on the late side, in case Jensen and Laura arrived in time to eat with us. They had planned to take the train from Venezia to Firenze to Poggibonsi, and then a taxi to the villa, a full day of travel.

At 7:30 p.m., their taxi driver honked at our gate. I pressed the button to open the gates. They tumbled from the taxi with packages and shopping bags and stories. We kissed and hugged as if we hadn't seen each other in weeks. I poured them Campari and sodas and they breathlessly spilled out the details of their trip to Venezia. The train was crowded but clean. Nothing romantic happened on the Eurostar. It took forever to get to Venezia. They shopped Dolce et Gabbana, "did the Rialto," hated their hotel, describing their room as "literally, a broom closet!" They had a gondola ride, fell in love with gondoliers. They modeled the clothing they bought. We ate on the veranda, drank wine, and danced to Italian folk dances courtesy of the communist party. Jens and Laura were glad to be home. I slept better.

La famiglia in Marlia

On this cool, overcast morning, we awoke to find a pastry package from Lucia e Maria on our kitchen table. This had become a routine, and was becoming a serious addiction. Just the sight of the softly mounded, tissue-covered tray made me ravenous.

Though I was swimming nearly every day as well as walking what seemed like miles on many days, my waistbands were shrinking. Annie generously offered that the cause of the problem was the Italian detergent. I had a tummy bulge. It was growing. Nonetheless, I couldn't resist Annie and Rolf's offerings. They bought an extra piece or two of pastry each Sunday. No matter how many pieces were on the tray, they were all gone by noon. Waste not, no waist.

Annie had attended the 8:00 a.m. mass, bought and dropped off the pastries, changed from her pretty pastel suit into her swimsuit, and joined us on the terrazza with a big sigh of satisfaction. Life was good. We were still in our pajamas, working on the mound of pastries when she sat down with us. Between bites, Annie said that only old women, "like me," she giggled, attended the early mass. They all dressed identically; street clothes' nuns, wearing straight black skirts hitting just below the knee. Flowery polyester blouses sprouted above; the same clothing sold at the San Gim open air market. These loose blouses were gaining practical appeal for both of us.

My trim haircut was sprouting out unevenly. My sunburn was peeling. Makeup was out of the question over a flaky face. I had gone native.

We now called Laura "Laah-OOH'-rah," similar to Allora; Ah-LOH-rah, because of the popular song by the same name, a tune that played over and over on every station on the car radio. Kate had informed us that the song's name was "Laura" and not "Allora."

The Italian car radio, by the way, displayed the radio station's name, rather than its number. E.g., ROCK rather than say, 88.5.

After breakfast, Laah-OOH'-ra and Jensen drove to Marlia; Mahr-LEE-ah, a suburb of Lucca, to meet Laura's relatives. Laura's last name is Granucci; Grah-NOO-chee. The San Francisco Granucci clan had arranged the get together with the Marlia Granucci famiglia months before. Dozens of phone calls and letters to Italy followed by many San Francisco family dinners where translations were attempted, then more phone calls and letters and dinners had preceded the summit. We gleaned from the stack of paperwork she brought with her that Laura was descended from Dante Alighieri and that her kinsmen's Marlia manse was once Dante's. "Cool!" We concurred.

If nothing else, the preparations had brought the family members closer together. The Marlia family were in the shutter business these days, likely a lucrative commerce since every house in Italy had shutters on every window and on many doors. The two travelers left with reams of instructions from San Francisco and Marlia, a few letters written in Italian from older San Francisco relatives, a camera, and an album of old and new family photos carefully culled from San Francisco collections. "Ciao!" we waved wistfully, wishing we could see Dante's manse, too.

Since the genealogists took the car, we kicked back. Annie did laundry, Rolfo read another World War II novel, Crist read music and practiced her récitatif. In the afternoon, I accompanied my camera cen' metri up our lane to the hamlet of Racciano. There was a stone church (locked) and two small stone houses (all shutters closed), and the ristorante Il Refugio, meaning "refuge," which it had been for us. That was all there was to Racciano. It was not on any map.

In medieval times, these rough refuges, way stations, were set up for travelers and minstrels who had the daring to make their way from one hilltop fortress to another. The pilgrims would stay safely there for a night or two, dine, pray, then continue their journey.

Our potential villa

On the way to Racciano, I took pictures of the chicken coop that Robert had idly suggested we should buy and "fix up." The coop was a crumbling two-story, two-room stone structure, previously (that is, about a hundred years previously) a Contadino's house. Behind it was a smaller stone house, also two stories, that once lodged a working frontoia; olive press. Only three walls of the smaller building still stood. The dilapidated olive press had become a roost. The siting took good advantage of its "lot." Our potential villa nestled on a gentle, down-rolling hill that looked to San Gimignano. Ducks and geese swam in a pond to the side of the house. Vineyards zigzagged down the hill, then disappeared into a small forest of oaks in the valley below. I guessed there could be four acres or a couple hectares.

Max had explained to us that Tuscany has strict rules for building and remodeling, most strict if you are not a Tuscan. Rather than build from scratch, you have to remodel the existing structures. You must stay within the villa's original footprint.

You must keep the original structure's use -- or darned close. He told us that it was a good idea to become a member of the local Town Council if you wished to do any extensive remodeling. He said that best of all, you should become Mayor. That is how things are accomplished in Tuscany and in the rest of Italy, too.

I realized that the project was futile, but in a romantic mode, I had daydreamed a renovation. I had joined the San Gim Town Council and turned the chicken coop into a house. When I became Mayor, I added a third story and converted the olive press into a greenhouse with a sprawling terrazza. The duck pond, of course, became the swimming pool during my second term as Mayor. While I was considering the possibilities of the transformation and the difficulties of getting elected, I began to see the cracks that crazed the coop more as structural problems than photographic opportunities. That was when the rain began. Putting away the camera, I escaped to an oak for refuge.

The potential villa's greenhouse

The turkeys and chickens and geese and ducks stayed outside the coop to peck in the mud. A fat, colorful rooster strutted from inside the house to its doorway. He reviewed the damp situation, puffed himself up, and crowed an announcement, like a bugler: "Get in out of the rain you birdbrains!" He fluffed his feathers, turned on his heel militarily, and retreated inside. The hens obediently followed him, one by one. The turkeys, a motley rearguard, filed inside behind the hens. The geese left the pond and called to the ducks. The ducks waddled from the pond to follow the geese in their pecking order. The waterfowl remained outside with me, eyeing each other, perhaps taking the first watch. "We don't mind the rain," they seemed to be chuckling. Each of these birds had its own personality. I could see why Beatrix Potter was so fascinated by her barnyard animals. You can see the world in a drop of water if you look closely, and on the face of a wildflower, too.

When the downpour stopped, the birds returned to their previous stations. I took a few more pictures. As I did, the adage, "room service, not debt service" hit home. I was happy as could be in our simple stone house. I had enough work to do at our own home in California. We didn't need to buy a fixer-upper villa. And I'd make a lousy politician. I'm much better at taking pot shots than at dodging bullets.

Jensen and Laura returned from Marlia around dinner time, somewhat disappointed. The ancestral house was closed up for Feria; vacation. The carefully crafted communications were for naught. The relatives were all away except for a 90 year-old aunt who was in the care of a distant cousin. When they got to Lucca, Jens and Laura phoned the numbers they had been given by Laura's San Francisco relatives. The distant cousin answered. He was unaware that they were expected. He spoke and understood some English, but they had trouble understanding what he said. He asked them where they were. They told him. He said to wait there. He drove to meet them. He was a handsome young man exactly their age. They followed him in their car to his apartment. Both Jensen and Laura fell in love with the young man at once.

It rained in Marlia, too. They couldn't tour the manse. Deeply infatuated, Laura and Jensen sat on the sofa with the cousin and slowly turned the pages of Laura's photo album.

Laura knew all the faces' names and family positions. The cousin recognized everyone, too, either by name or face. It was as if they were watching an old, favorite movie together for the first time. The old woman was deaf, but she understood that Laura was from San Francisco and that she was famiglia. She alternated between weeping and clapping her hands, crying, "San Francisco!" The Italians we met all seemed to be familiar with San Francisco, whether or not they had relatives there. Jens snapped a few photos of the cousin and Laura together. They each kissed the aunt's wet cheeks, and drove home unrequited.

The two went out to dinner while we ate indoors for the first time. The thunder growled nonstop, often roaring through the villa as loudly as the ugly black Bosnian Airforce planes that almost daily did maneuvers overhead. I set the table with flowers and with a flowery damask tablecloth that Laura thought might make an excellent long skirt. Laura, who kept ahead of the fashion curve, wore only long skirts. Annie and Crist and I chattered by candlelight until late, not meaning to wait up for Laura and Jens but doing just that. They were happier when they got home and they joined us to talk until the candles burned out.

Clouds

Last night's storm scattered golden hazelnuts all over the patio, a hazard to navigation, and also brought out the yellow jackets. I made tea for me and coffee for Jens and Laura in the odd little one-cup stovetop pot and whipped up some French toast for Laura. With these rich staples -- eggs, milk, butter, and bread, plus a dab of the Pietrafitta wildflower honey -- French toast became fairly haute and heavy cuisine. Laura, who is tall and skinny, is trying to figure out how to get some of the creamy Italian butter home to her butter-loving father. Others of us are wondering how to get it off our hips and tummies.

Jens and Laura drove into Firenze for a last shopping spree, leaving us to our own devices. I chose painting: the fuschia petunias, the red geraniums. My paintings do not show how shockingly bright their true colors are. Even if I had the ability to mix such vivid colors effectively on paper, the results would not suit my taste. I was stunned at the intensity of the colors in the masters' restored works throughout Tuscany. For me, the standard in Italian renaissance paintings was a dark, subdued, slightly mysterious surface.

The Italian vegetation, the sky -- all of Italy -- is luminously bright and best viewed in nature or somewhat smudged or aged, like the Reggiano.

Awesomely huge cumulus clouds cavorted close. Everywhere within the clouds and between them, figures constantly alliterated, formed, dissolved, formed anew. God and Adam on the Sistine Chapel ceiling scudded past, overtaken by Raffaello's angels and the Pearly Gates and Casper the Ghost. An updraft separated Venus from her half shell. Disembodied faces and attenuated extremities passed wondrously as in an art survey course featuring fast-shuffling slides of unfamiliar sculptures and paintings. Who needs museums? Michaelangelo simply released the shapes he saw inside his beloved Cararra marble, the story goes. My hunch is that he got some ideas from these billowy clouds, too.

The day began hot and sunny. Perfect watercolor weather. I'd hold the paper in the sun for a few seconds and it was dry, ready for the next treatment. After lunch, I felt a few sprinkles.

The air chilled. Rain followed, clearing in time for Cristina's solo walk to Kate's. Halfway home on the rustic path, a gullywasher caught her. She arrived at the villa at the storm's peak. She stripped off her clothes and muddy shoes and got into a hot shower. I quickly rinsed out her spattered clothes and sneakers and hung them inside, on the back of the closed shutters. They were wetter before I had washed them. We congratulated ourselves on buying wash and wear clothes, and complimented the originators of wash and wear silk. The sun finally overpowered the clouds, drying off the patio in minutes.

Jensen and Laura returned around dinner time, laden with leather goods. Jensen wore a sleek, new black leather jacket. Laura showed us presents of handbags for her sisters and mom and more shoes and sweaters for herself. While I was dabbling, Annie had slaved over some memorable pasta primavera -- the flavors of the mushrooms, zucchini, and peppers were so concentrated that a few slices flavored an entire pound of pasta. A quarter of a clove of garlic had the same potency as three or four whole cloves at home.

The communist party was over, alas. They had packed up their hammers, sickles, and axes, and moved -- maybe to another venue. We watched a sunset louder than the amplified music and sipped some darkly delicious Brunello di Montalcino. Tomorrow, Prada.

Silver San Gim

Jens & Laura's last day here. A dazzling morning, I made some espresso, trying a new kind of coffee that Jensen bought in San Gim, and moved to the terrazza at 7:00 a.m. All was fresh and clean, a masterful watercolor wash. The sun cast long shadows across the olive groves. It was early enough to catch a shot of San Gim backlit by the incipient sunrise. The town was a black silhouette on a glowing, silver background.

More birds out this morning; the first time I heard actual birdsong -- a singular sound and a singular noun. I snatched a few minutes to sip and soak up the surroundings like the nubby paper that absorbs my watery paint, before waking up Jens and Laura and starting breakfast. I wanted to make sure they were well fed and ready to shop. Crist would sleep in and have some privacy today. She finds clothes shopping a bore.

Jensen found the Prada outlet easily, having made the trial run. We arrived at 10:00 a.m., along with a few other cars. The outlet was a first class store, nothing low-rent about it, with both Prada and MiuMiu labels. The dresses and gowns were exquisite: soft, pastel organdy and chiffon creations with meticulous hand-beading at the hems and sleeve ends. Most of the clothing was diaphanous, made for 19 year-olds who were very tall, extremely thin, rich, and bold. Two of them, beautiful British models who had driven up from Rome, were having a marvelous time trying on evening gowns. One young woman had a thick, golden mane of hair and a deep tan. She modeled a low cut, long, skinny, cream-colored panne velvet gown. The only trim was a dark brown, transparent seam that ran the length of the gown from the bodice to the floor and matched her tan perfectly. The effect was striking. The garment seemed to have been created especially for her. She blanched at the price, about $600.00, but her friend convinced her to buy it anyway, promising her it would retail for thousands in London.

The outlet would close at noon for three hours, so we turned our attention to ourselves. We bought shoes with square toes and tall, triangular heels that we probably would never wear and that reminded me of the cartoon shoes the Beatles wore in *Yellow Submarine,* and conservative cashmere sweaters that we would wear. We had just started to look at the handbags and accessories when it was closing time. I glimpsed the men's clothing briefly, wishing Roberto were here to model a few of the handsome pieces. We barely had time to hand over our Visa cards to pay for our goods before the salesgirls pushed us out the door. Outside, many cars were arriving. The doors were locked. A salesgirl flipped over a sign that translated, "We open at 3:00 p.m." We didn't wait.

Back in San Gim, Laura wanted to buy some majolica for her relatives. I took her to the store where Roberto and I had admired a majolica patio table. She and Jensen talked me into ordering the table. While they shopped, I made the arrangements. The table was round, with a diameter of 54". The majolica top would be custom made (and signed by the artist!). The design would include a large nautilus at the center and other sea shells and kelp woven into a circular pattern around the nautilus. The colors were pale terra-cotta and aqua, plus sand and peach, on an off-white background. The tabletop's base would be heavy black wrought iron with simple Florentine curves. The shopkeeper assured me that my tabletop and base

160

would be ready in about six weeks. He would ship the heavy pieces by boat to San Francisco, to the Port of Oakland, which would take another six weeks or so.

If his time table was accurate, the shipment would arrive by Thanks-giving; no small reason to be thankful. While the shopkeeper did the paperwork, Laura chose a few large pieces of majolica for her mother, for her aunt, and for her grandmother: the classic "Four Seasons" plaques and two tall, ornate water pitchers. I asked if her pieces could be shipped along with the table. Yes, no problem, no extra charge. The shipping total would be $250, a few dollars more than the amount I paid to send my small box from San Francisco to San Gim. The merchant had a "tax free" sign in his window and accordingly lopped off the tax, amounting to about $250, a coincidence that made the shipping "free." Laura also liked a majolica pomegranate, a table centerpiece that the owner gave her as a gift. She would carry it home.

I tried not to think of all things that could go awry with our shipment. The shop owner would crate the table and send it to Livorno, the port nearest San Gim. From Livorno, the table would board a ship to New Jersey. From New Jersey, the table would transfer to a warehouse. From the warehouse, a truck would transport the table to the Port of Oakland, where I would pick it up. The shop owner told me if anything was broken on arrival, just take a photo of it, and he would replace it, pronto. It seemed easy to choose magnificent Italian goods, flip a credit card on the counter, and say, in an Eloïse tone of voice, "charge it and send it home, please."

To Ship say, a Table from Italy:

Later on in the summer, I bought a dozen majolica fruit plates and paid around $50.00 to ship them home. Six weeks later, FedEx delivered them to my California doorstep in perfect condition. However, for large purchases such as the table and wrought iron base, it is more complicated than charge and send. Merchants will send large purchases to your home by ship or by air. To ship by sea costs a fraction of air freight, but shipboard is slower and more steps and stops are involved, with more chance for loss and breakage. Here is what you can expect if you make a large purchase such as a table:

At the time of purchase, give the merchant your name, address, phone and fax numbers, clearly printed in upper case letters. Keep the receipt in a safe place, along with the merchant's name, address, phone, and fax numbers.

A shipping agent (in my case, the agent was in New Jersey) will take delivery of your package from the ship and transfer it to the port warehouse. The agent will fax or send you a bill for this service, which must be paid before the shipment can continue on to your home. (The transfer bill for the table was $125.00.) When the shipping agent has received your payment, he will have your goods transferred from the warehouse and trucked to the destination you have chosen. The agent will mail or fax you the payment confirmation number, the approximate time of arrival, and the address and phone number of the warehouse where your goods will be delivered. Without the nine-digit payment confirmation number, you cannot begin to make arrangements to pick up your purchase.

You have five days after your shipment arrives at its final destination to arrange for customs' clearance and to pick up your goods -- or to have them picked up for you -- before warehouse storage charges begin. The shipping agent gives you an approximate date of arrival, but the warehouse will not necessarily advise you when the shipment arrives. You must phone them, citing your nine-digit number.

You can do the customs' clearance yourself or hire a customs' broker. The warehouse can help you find a customs' broker. The broker's fee is about $100 and does not include delivery of the merchandise to you. If you don't live near the port or can't pick up the merchandise yourself, the broker can make arrangements to have it delivered wherever you wish.

When you pick up your merchandise, you will need to present the original bill of lading. The merchant from whom you made your purchase will send or fax it to you when they ship your goods. If you do not receive the bill of lading before your merchandise arrives, you must advise the shipping agent and present your original receipt for verification.

In any case, when you pick up your goods, take along your original receipt plus the documentation from the shipping agent, as well as the bill of lading sent from the merchant. Bring a credit card, some cash, your check book, and your passport. Leave your watch at home. You will go back and forth between the warehouse and customs, getting verifications. There will be handling charges, form filling-out charges, and a forklift charge, if you have say, a table. These charges amount to $100 or more, and you must pay in cash. Only U.S. customs will accept a check. Customs charges vary, depending on type and value of merchandise.

On November 24, almost exactly 12 weeks from the day I bought the table and base, the two pieces arrived at the warehouse in San Francisco. We decided to pick them up ourselves and to do the customs clearance ourselves. Jensen and Laura drove a borrowed truck to the dock. Roberto and I followed in a Jeep. The table top fit into the truck, the base fit (barely) into the back of the Jeep. It took the daylight portion of a November day to fill out forms, clear customs, transport, and uncrate the table. The table and the base arrived in perfect condition.

<u>Shipping and receiving cost summary for a table and base*</u>:
Shipping (boat & truck) $250.00   (shipping by air is more)

Shipping Agent:	125.00	
Customs:	45.00	
Forklift:	25.00	
Warehouse charges	85.00	(not including storage)
Total	$530.00	

* To the west coast. Delivery to the east coast is less.

When buying large pieces in Italy, remember to factor in all the potential extra charges. The above charges amounted to 1/3 of the store price for the table and base.

Italian brand names, such as Gucci and Armani, sell for about the same prices in Italy as in the States and the merchandise is largely the same as that offered by stores stateside. I confined my purchases to items I had not seen in American stores and items not available in American stores and craft items and original art that is exponentially marked up in American stores. And maybe one or two irresistible items.

An Antinori Tour

Home from shopping at Prada, we put on our new sweaters and opened some Rosso di Montalcino (£5,000) and lighted the barbecue for some steak slabs. In her book, *A Table in Tuscany,* a cookbook sealed away in my box somewhere in Livorno, or possibly being puzzled over at this moment by an Italian stranger, Leslie Forbes has a recipe for sautéed courgette blossoms; zucchini flowers. I remembered reading that you beat flour and water together with a sprinkle of fresh spices, coated the blossoms, and sautéed them in olive oil. I had picked up a package of 30 blossoms for about $1.50 at the San Gim grocery store. At home, I paid about $.50 per blossom during our brief season.

The San Gim grocery store was called the Coop, as in Co-operative, a chain with a link in most Tuscan towns; more expensive than the Super-All over in Poggibonsi, but more conveniently located; just outside the San Gim wall. We called it the coop, as in chicken.

The zucchini blossoms were about six inches long. While the barbecue coals were heating, I prepared the hors d'oeuvres; our antipasto. I whisked some flour and water and added a small amount of egg white for body, whipped the batter to a froth, and sprinkled in snippets of thyme. I dipped and turned the blossoms until they were thoroughly coated, then placed them into about a half inch of sizzling extra virgin olive oil. In a few seconds they were golden. I turned them once, drained them, and sprinkled the deep fried blossoms with salt and pepper. The first batch was good.

For the second batch, I experimented by adding more flour to the batter and some whole, beaten egg. This batch produced a crisper crust and was just what we had in mind. I learned that if the oil was hot enough, the blossoms opencd up, a felicitous side-effect. We popped the crunchy blossoms hot and whole into our mouths. They tasted like essence of fresh garden. Annie contributed her famous home made French fries, also prepared in the wonderful olive oil, and tossed a big salad to balance our steak feast. We ate until deep dark.

While Jensen and Laura helped Annie do dishes, Rolf spotted the full moon rising the color of a red-orange Tuscan egg yolk. We joined him on the veranda, lining up our chairs to face the moon as if it was a TV, and watched the moon's progress. I tried to take a photo, a time exposure. Having no tripod at hand, I sort of propped the camera on a chair and guesstimated a 26 second finger-on-the-button. Rolf suggested that it might look like a scrambled egg, but it didn't turn out badly.

Next day, I was up with the bird, who sang again. It was more poignant today. Jensen and Laura would leave for home. I loaded my camera with 200 ASA, and took the first light shot of Annie and Rolf that we had been planning since the morning I first saw them standing in the open window of their bedroom. They had looked out, laughing and waving, framed by the Chianti colored shutters set on the ageless stone wall. Long, crimson geranium tendrils laced their way down from their window box.

"Don't let this happen to you."

The early sun this morning gave a fresh light, highlighting the stonework's texture and purifying the flowers' intensity. For extra Tuscan color, I asked Rolfo to wear his purple shirt and Annie her grass green shirt. My vision was a Christmas photo for them to send to all of their family. Rolf said he would write the photo caption, "Don't let this happen to you."

Annie planned to take cuttings from the bright geranium blossoms. She envisioned growing the geraniums at home, and passing along another generation of cuttings to her five children and six grandchildren. Two years later, she would bring me my own cuttings.

I finished the roll of film, shooting Jensen and Laura and their many bags before Rolf and I filled the trunk with the bags. We stopped in San Gim to get traveling money at the Bankomat, and while the girls were punching buttons, I stopped at Lucia e Maria to get them a last custard donut for the road. We drove to Florence, parked at the Stazione; train station, the only practical place to park in all of Florence, leaving the bags in the locked trunk. The security in the station's garage seemed good. The signs said that nobody could get into the garage on foot without a parking ticket. (One could, if one knew the ropes.) We hoped the girls' precious goods would be in the trunk when we returned.

Our goal was Michaelangelo's David at the Accademia museum in Centro; the center of town, a walk of about Cen'Metri from the train station. We took a shortcut through the underground walkway, circumventing the station traffic. It was a long and rather narrow tunnel, lined with shops, Bankomats, and cambios. Toward the end of the tunnel, just before the stairs that returned you to the street, the lighting was dim. A gypsy woman sat on the ground, leaning against the wall on our right, her legs stretched out into the tunnel. She had placed a pot holding a few £1.000 notes in front of her feet. She held a baby. As we stepped to the left to avoid her, a pack of four little girls quickly stepped toward us from the shadows on our left. This time, scarves disguised their nimble fingers. I warned Rolf and the girls, and fled up the stairs. Jens and Laura and Rolf shouted at the girls as if they were vicious dogs. The waifs slunk into the shadows. It was like a sad dream.

We followed the street named Ricasoli, one of several eponymous streets in towns throughout Italy that paid homage to the mid-19th century Italian Prime Minister; the man "whose fine hand finalized the components of Chianti wine." The famous Brolio wine of the Barone Bettino Ricasoli's estate has been produced since the 12th century.

As we crossed street a couple blocks later, a man on a motorscooter, talking on a cell phone, obliviously caromed through us pedestrians, missing us by inches. As my heart was slowing down, another group of girls came toward us, two blocks from the Accademia. Instinctively, I ran. Jens and Laura and Rolf strode through the pack of beggars again. Rolf was their target. He is six feet three inches tall, a big man. He growled and shook them off like naughty puppies.

The museum line at 10:30 a.m. was short. We were inside gaping at Michaelangelo's prisoners and the David within 10 minutes. Though signs everywhere said "No Flash," and guides repeated the words in every language every few seconds, dozens of flashes constantly bombarded the sculpture and us. We saw spots where Michaelangelo had put no spots. It was as if all of Europe's paparazzi had gathered to take pot shots at the giant.

Jens was eager to move on, so we were back on the street within an hour. By then, the museum line was around the block. I had vowed -- and promised -- that I would not impose Culture on the group. I kept quiet and kept up as we goose-stepped past the glamorous Pucci headquarters, the Piazza San Marco; Savonarola's turf, and the Medici tombs, housing what is arguably Firenze's most important sculpture -- past a century of fascinating politics, religion, and art, to the train station. We retrieved the girls' luggage from the trunk and they disappeared quickly to do some (more) last minute shopping at the Stazione shops. For them, Italy was a series of shopping malls connected by bumper cars and motorscooters.

Driving from the station, Rolf and I decided to stop somewhere for lunch. As I drove, I ruminated. The contrast of Jensen and Laura's first Italian experience with my first trip to Italy was black and white. I had hoped for gray, at least. Had I done the right thing? Should I have been more insistent about Culture? Or was this a generational thing? Does art matter? I was sunk. Art animates life. Art makes the spirit exuberant. To pare it from life leaves a lean skeleton. Is art necessary? I brooded. Crist's song, "Who is Silvia" popped into my head. It was ludicrous to think that art didn't matter. Mothers do not stop working as mothers for a minute.

We found a handsome ristorante a few minutes out of Centro, in San Casciano. Only one other couple was there, young Italians. The owner seated Rolf and me with a flourish, handing us heavy menus. Rolf asked me to choose the wine.

"When in Florence," thought I, morphing from mom to wine maven. I chose an Antinori, Fattoria Cigliano. We raised our eyebrows when we tasted it -- blackberries, currants, "frutte di bosco," fruits of the woods -- jammy, impressive. I ordered ravioli stuffed with "ricotta casa," lavishly bathed in a sauce of tiny zucchini slices, fresh tomato, and a touch of pancetta that enlivened the tomato. For antipasto, Rolf ordered "salucci di casa," which translated as eight thin slices of different kinds of prosciutto plus four of salami; an ample picnic for several people. For a primi piatti, he ordered ziti "formaggio casa;" house cheese, a rich handling of the simple dish. It was all delicious, but too much to finish. Next to us, the Italian couple ordered antipasto, primi piatti, secondi piatti, contorni, and dolce. We lingered, attempting to finish our huge servings and taking small sips of the wine in a futile effort to make it last longer. I wondered again how the Italians stayed so slim while eating so much.

When the waiter came back to see if we had enjoyed our Pranzo; lunch, I asked him if this Antinori fattoria was nearby and if we could visit. "Si!" He drew a map, and said, "due kilo," two kilometers, a couple minutes. We left. A few curves of the road, a few drops of rain, and we were driving through the gates of Antinori's Fattoria Cigliano toward a massive stone mansion set on many hectares of rolling vineyards.

We circled the wine estate, but all doors to the mansion were closed. The only person around was a young man repairing a tractor. I parked and asked him if we could taste some wine. He shrugged his shoulders indifferently. I changed my tack -- "Possiamo comprare di vino?" Can we buy some wine? "Si!" He gestured to follow him. We walked to the main house.

He shouted to a shuttered, upper window. A woman threw open the shutters, listened to his request, and shouted back that she would phone the Padrone -- give him 10 minutes. We thanked them both. The mechanic returned to the tractor while we wandered for the 10 minutes or so, admiring a nectarine orchard, the trees drooping low with ripe fruit. We ducked into a work area to avoid a sprinkle of rain, and even this space was beautiful. The workers' wash basin was hewn from a five foot long slab of rock. Above, a stone angel dispensed water through her angelic mouth. Pressed linen towels hung nearby.

The padrone arrived in his Range Rover, all smiles. We introduced ourselves and shook hands. He knew San Francisco. He had visited the Napa Valley. He had relatives in Los Angeles. Choosing a heavy key from a ring of many keys, he opened a room. He invited us inside. It was cool and dark and cases of wine were stacked taller than Rolfo. The padrone wanted to know where we had drunk this wine that we wanted. We told him, "Ristorante Antica." He was delighted. The restaurant owner was his friend. He handed me a case of our luncheon wine. I didn't have much cash. I asked, "Quanta costa?" How much? He said £97.000; about $55, or $4.60 a bottle. I gave him £100.000, he gave me change. We chatted a bit. We thanked him, put the case in the trunk, and drove home with our new house wine, to replace the Pietrafitta and Santa Cristina, the latter a personal favorite of mine.

The Santa Cristina estate boasts Antinori's finest vineyard, the Tignanello. Marchese Piero Antinori originated the wine nearly 30 years ago, outside of the DOC rules and regs for Chianti. At the time, Chianti was an inferior wine, requiring a considerable portion of white grapes. The wine did not age well. Sig. Antinori created his new wine from Sangiovese, blended with Cabernet Sauvignon and Cabernet Franc, aged it in French oak for 20 months and then some more in the bottle. The Tignanello is the seminal wine of the new, rich DOCG's, and Sig. Antinori is the father. God bless him.

Back home, I helped Crist choose which clothes to take with her to Umbria. She would be leaving on Thursday, driving South with Kate. Kate said the car was full and that Cristina could bring only a small suitcase with her. She asked if I could bring the rest of her things down to her later. Certo. That would give us an excuse to see her before the performance. She and I chose enough clothes to get her through three days of unknown activities.

We had a farewell dinner for Crist at Il Refugio. Rolf ordered the spaghetti carbonara as a primi -- the egg, almost raw, had been incorporated into a light béchamel sauce; a preparation that, because of the new cooking standards for eggs in the States, would not be possible at a restaurant at home, but I was sure I could duplicate the technique in the privacy of my kitchen. The bacon was bits of pancetta. The dish tasted far lighter than the carbonara we had eaten stateside. Rolf's wild boar cacciatore (which we now knew meant "hunter," because we had seen all the No Hunting signs, vietate cacciare) really*was* wild boar. After all these days of asking Rolf if I could taste what he ordered, I had worn him down. He consented to let me taste almost everything. The boar was quite good, and not too gamy.

The waiters knew us by now. They brought a tiramisu to Crist after dinner, a farewell present. We toasted her with Santa Cristina and I thought of my three Colombian gardeners at home. If they should be working while Cristina was practicing, they stopped and politely asked my permission to stand outside the room where she worked to listen. I stood there listening, too. We all stared at the same spot on the wall to her practice room. "She is an angel," José confided. "It is the voice of God," his workers whispered: "Santa Cristina!" The three men crossed themselves when she finished her practice and continued on with their work. They didn't charge me for their listening time.

Cristina was suffused in happiness at her farewell dinner. We came home in time to watch the full moon rise red and to taste a thimble of grappa before bed. I fell asleep hoping all was well with Jens and that tomorrow would be the beginning of a successful, maybe even stellar experience for Santa Crist.

On Empty

As I sat on the veranda with my good, English tea, the chameleons scampered around me in circles like leaves being blown in a hurricane. Warm and clear, with a light breeze, every morning felt like Sunday morning, and not just because of the crazily ringing church bells. I drove Crist and her small suitcase to Kate's at 8:30 a.m. Kate's husband would drive the four women to their destination -- Kate, Cristina, Simona (a mezzo soprano), and a Scottish woman to whom I wasn't introduced; elderly, snow white hair, very attractive, beautifully dressed, sparkling eyes; someone I would love to know. Kate's husband was taller than me, handsome, spoke good English, and was kind and chivalrous toward the women. I could see why Kate had been attracted to him. He put the bags in the trunk along with all of their linens for the week and had trouble closing it. They left subito. Immediately. Precipitously. I didn't have time to say good-bye to Crist. I waved as they drove around the corner, feeling a mix of scared happy empty hopeful?

Back in the car, the gasoline reserve light was on, another empty. I drove a block to the San Gimignano benzina (gasoline) station. The young attendant pointed to where he wanted me to park. I was relieved I didn't have to pump, though one pumps in Italy only if the benzina is closed. "Pieno?" He asked. "Si!" Fill it up. I asked him to check the "petrolio," the oil, and for lack of a better word, "tutti," everything else. I sprang the hood, a new skill, to reveal the car's insides. Two older gentlemen began to confer on its contents. They took turns measuring the oil, discussing the matter seriously. They spoke with the young attendant, whom they elected to inform me that there was no oil. "Niente!" Nothing. Leaning into the engine, one of the older men lit a cigarette and gestured "BOOM!" He wasn't talking about an explosion caused by his cigarette. The attendant poured in two quarts of petrolio, I paid (more than £100.000 for the benzina alone), thanked them 1.000 times, and drove over to the parcheggio. Gas was sold by the liter. The average cost per gallon was about $5.00. The Fiat was small and a stick shift, so we got fairly good mileage.

The morning was clear, balmy, perfect. I wandered through the Thursday market. The fishmongers were slicing fish open, removing scales, skin, entrails, cutting precise fillets to order. The porchetta man caught my eye and held out a morsel to taste. As I was crunching, a man who looked like a circus performer; short, heavily muscled and tattooed, handed Signore Porchetta a Maria and asked for a taste of the skin. The vendor waved away the money. The man insisted. The vendor took the lire and lopped off a big piece of skin for his paying customer. The man grinned wide and took a huge bite that sent grease running down

172

his chin. He wiped it with his hand and shouted theatrically, "molto bene!" Very good.

I watched as the local women laughed together and jostled in the early morning, arguing and bargaining with the merchants, filling their shopping bags, and congratulating each other on a purchase "bene fatto;" well done. This was local time. The local men lined the streets, gesticulating, chatting, smoking, greeting their neighbors as if they had all just arrived at a very special party:

"Giorno!" ('Morning! They don't say *buon* giorno; good day.)

"Giorno!"

"Allora," (Any conversation begins with Allora, stretching the -o into several seconds. Ah-LOH-rah is the rough equivalent of "So ..." As in, "Soooo. How's the family?")

"Come va?" (How's it going?)

"Va bene." (Good -- fine, OK.)

"è caldo." (Hot enough for you?)

"è vero." (That's the truth. This is accompanied by a small, understanding nod.)

"Absolutamente." (You can say that again. This is supplemented with an emphatic nod.)

"Si, si, si." (Yeah, yeah, yeah.)

"Ciao!" (See 'ya.)

The locals jostled each other like children on a playground as I stood at the fruit stand contemplating the tiny, lemon-yellow pears. The fruit vendor pushed a bag toward me. "Dica!" Speak! As if to inform me that this was a place of business, not an art gallery. I pointed to eight separate works of art, careful not to touch them. The woman put the pears into the bag, weighed it, and said it would be £800; about 50 cents. I paid her and walked across the way and selected four plump tomatoes, warm and fragrant, the same as when you pick them from the garden. The aroma of spit-roasting drew me next to the roast vendor, separate from the Porchetta van. Inexplicably, I bought an inexpressibly beautiful roasted chicken.

I looked around for Annie and Rolf. They had planned to walk to town this morning. It was caldo; quite warm now, and I was hoping I could find them to see if they'd like a ride home. I thought they might be at one of the two bakeries, so I headed down the twisty, cobblestone street that led to them. On the way, I discovered a Florentine paper store I had not noticed before. Though San Gim comprises only a few blocks, each day I spotted a store that was new to me. The shop owners took their Feria; vacation, in July and August, closing their stores for a week or two, then reopening. I bought some Florentine wrapping paper in the shop, embellished with long, elegant pastel lilies gilded with gold and noticed the paper with the flowers and the French writing that Jensen had wrapped my birthday presents in. She and Laura had gone to some trouble over my birthday. I felt a sharp loneliness for them and for Crist.

At the bakery, I was able to buy the last loaf of the excellent olive bread, but unable to find Annie and Rolf. I picked up a few croissants and stopped next door for a pizzetta and some marinated mushrooms. Loaded down, I hiked up to La Rocca, the 13th century fortress. I was alone there at 10:00 a.m. I walked the inside perimeter of the old walls, peering through the small archers' slits to the Tuscan countryside. The alcoves from which the archers zinged their arrows were waist high, about 4' deep, 2-1/2 feet wide, 3' tall. Presumably, the archers, smaller than me, crawled inside the alcoves to take aim, then crawled out quickly to avoid detection and the enemies' arrows. I peered at their targets. One slit framed our villa. What a shot!

What a shot!

I sat on a stone bench looking out as an archer would and ate a pear, then a pair, then three. Swallows flew continuously to the sheer wall, clung there momentarily, then sheared off. They were sipping rainwater caught in crevasses eroded over centuries by more rain water.

A strong aroma wafted to my nose from the chicken, a delicious warning. I retraced my path through town and headed home with my goods. While I was daydreaming of archers, the market had filled up. The mountains of fish had eroded. The piles of produce had shrunk. The honey merchant beckoned. He wanted me to taste his golden acacia honey, his sun-yellow sunflower honey, and his own wildflower honey. He offered me tastes of bee pollen. "Molto bene!" I repeated after each taste. All the jars were too heavy and too large to add to my shopping bag. I tried to explain the situation to him. He laughed and waved me away. "Domani!" Tomorrow, he said. "Domani," I promised. As I exited the main town entrance, I wondered if I would have a domani in San Gim; another empty feeling.

At home, I watched one of our "pets," a fat, green chameleon, as he caught minuscule bugs for his lunch. He was at my feet, in the same space that Romeo occupied at home. I smiled, thinking about my huge black lab's devotion and all of me ached the way my teeth did when I ate the sweet pears.

I was dog-sick, but excited about our adventure to Spoleto.

Rolf was sitting on the veranda smoking a cigar. We had all acquired the "noble rot." Instead of reserving his cigars for after dinner enjoyment, Rolf was smoking them during the day, too, like the San Jimmy locals. We swam, sunned, napped, had our last veranda dinner -- the market chicken was crisply succulent and made a good pairing with Annie's arugula salad. We shared a bottle of our new Antinori house wine.

The Shadow People

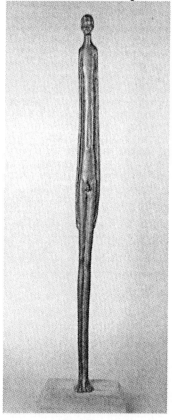

On our last day at the villa, the hazelnuts crunched under my feet when I went outside to have my breakfast. I tasted a nut. It was bitter. The air was noticeably cooler this morning, or maybe I was warming to the idea of moving on. I was now alone in our part of the villa. I missed Cristina's humming and Jensen's laughter and Laura's glamor. It was too quiet and the rooms seemed immense without all their stuff on every chair. The kitchen table was bare of bowls brimming with fruit. No heels of bread, no hunks of cheese sat at the ready.

Crist's watch had broken so she took both my watch and alarm clock with her. All day and night I had no idea what time it was. I rose with the sun and fell with the sun. It seemed the natural thing to do. About today, I knew only that Jens and Laura would arrive in San Francisco and that Crist was awakening in a town none of us had never seen. The feeling was familiar. I recognized it from the time my daughters became teenagers, softly and subtly moving away from me, becoming grown-up strangers with secrets I would never share.

After washing my dishes, I sat at the barren kitchen table, getting organized -- tossing receipts and counting lire. Italian law dictated that you must leave the restaurant where you have dined with the receipt in your possession. I had wads of restaurant receipts. I had thought of saving them as souvenirs, but far too many had accumulated. I jotted down their totals to see where I stood with my budget and then tossed most of them. When I finished my calculations, I was still ahead of budget. I spent the morning organizing, packing, keeping busy.

I wrapped up the Deruta candle holders to use in Spoleto, along with several candles. I padded and packed the alabaster fruit that had served as our table's centerpiece. I made a mental list of objects I was pleased to have brought along on our trip: the large, round, flat rubber plug for the drain remained at the top of the list. Next came a flashlight, then the Ziplock bag of Tide that ran out so quickly. My print-out of friends' and families' addresses and phone numbers was useful as well as reassuring. If I had to, I could get in touch with them. I had sent postcards to most of the people. Printing out six copies of our itinerary with all phone and fax numbers was a sound idea. Each of us needed the info individually at some point. Robert took a copy with him when he left as did Jensen and Laura.

Bringing so many clothes was not a good idea. Next time, I promised myself, I'd bring only one of everything, except for underthings, and buy whatever I needed here, maybe even underthings. I'd pack only a simple carry-on bag and buy an inexpensive bag or two here for carrying purchases home. As I packed my clothes, I knew I'd break my promise.

I went up to La Rocca mid-morning to photograph the villa from a medieval archer's point of view. While in town, I assembled our last San Gim picnic: grapes and melon and sciacciatta sandwiches of tomato and buffalo mozzarella. For dessert, I chose the local special, mandorlatto -- similar to the famous panforte, but richer and less dense, more like cake. I bought an etto of the chocolate mandorlatto and an etto of the orange at Lucia e Maria, their own recipe.

I dawdled over my purchases as the locals did, chatting with the shopkeepers, reluctant to leave San Gim behind. I found the honey vendor and bought a pint of his wildflower honey, pleased that I had a "domani" in San Gim. Back at home, I finished packing my bags, spread out our Pranzo on the veranda table along with my Michelin map, and began to plan the drive to Spoleto. Soon Annie and Rolf wandered down. I opened a chilly San Gim Vernaccia. "Will Umbria be much like Tuscany?" was the topic of discussion over lunch. "How long is the drive?" "Where should we have lunch?"

I poured the remains of a lovely, chilled Lambrusco to accompany the dolce. (If you buy Lambrusco, make sure you buy a corked bottle. The large bottles of Lambrusco with screw tops tasted like strawberry soda that had "turned.") The mandorlatto cakes resembled fancy candy. We sliced tiny tidbits and held the morsels in our mouths until they melted.

"I can't believe we've been in San Gim for five weeks," we repeated over and over between tastes. There was much that we didn't cover in Tuscany, saying, "We have plenty of time," as we turned over in our pool "beds" to tan our other sides.

We didn't visit the source of Michaelangelo's materiel, Carrara, but we viewed the Carrara slaves and the Carrara David. We didn't explore the medieval walled town of Monteriggioni, almost walking distance from the villa, but we ventured the difficult fusilli drive to Badia a Coltibuono.

Had we gone nowhere, being at the villa amid the olive orchards and vineyards would have amply served up the Tuscan experience. The Europeans we met came to Tuscany for the express purpose of sitting in the sun for a week -- they swam, stared at their surroundings, drank wine, and went home tan. They didn't dine out as often as we did, they didn't do culture or even much shopping. Many drove their own cars to Tuscany, bringing their own linens and often their own food, to briefly borrow the sunshine.

Our landlord Max had begun to build another rental villa to the front and side of us. He had closed it in and "dabbled" at finishing it. It would be complete by next June, he told us. His schedule was the same every day. In the early morning, he went to San Gim to stand or sit in the square in front of the Duomo, to smoke and jabber with his friends. He drove home around 1:00 p.m. to eat the lunch that Maria had spent the morning preparing. They napped afterwards. He began work on the new villa around 5:00 p.m., while Maria began dinner preparations. Occasionally, a worker came to help Max. To paint the crooked tree that crowns the far hillside, I had moved one of our veranda chairs near Max's work site so I could sit under an oak, out of the sun. As I painted, the two men worked, unselfconsciously whistling and singing bits of the songs they carried in their heads and chatting in their dialect, adding color to my painting. Occasionally, I'd burst into their song. They didn't mind.

Max was building the new villa to match the old -- with the same stonework as the medieval walls of San Gim: a line of mortared bricks, some stone, another line of bricks, more stones, and so on, with a red tiled roof. Max seemed expert at trowelling in the cement between the building blocks. His sharp-edged trowel marks were identical to those on San Gim's walls, where the marks still existed.

"The Tuscan Three" sat by the pool on our last afternoon, gazing at the clouds. The clouds are the predominant, common feature of the Tuscan landscape. "Maybe the clouds are very low to the ground," Annie conjectured, "and that's why they appear so enormous." They seemed to be within an arm's reach. Maybe the clouds were the same as those at home, and we never noticed. Maybe we looked too hard for red giants and black holes and missed the simple surfaces.

I thought of shooting a series of cloud photos. Who would take the time to look at the images? Who took the time to look at the originals? Photographs couldn't capture the clouds' changing shapes and colors, but you could look at them any time of day or night, rain, shine, or snow. I took a few "cloud shots," thinking that maybe we hadn't seen many Americans here because Americans couldn't slow down long enough to be here. Americans had to be doing something constructive at all times. We Americans didn't want to miss anything, and so we missed what was between the things we raced to see.

"Festiva tarde," said the Tuscans; make haste slowly. A warning sign at a ristorante in San Gim read, "Slow Food." After five weeks, we understood. We understood and we could say out loud without hesitating, "la dolce far niente" -- the sweetness of doing nothing -- and many other words and phrases that were not on the tapes. For example: "Poggibonsi." But we couldn't say that without laughing.

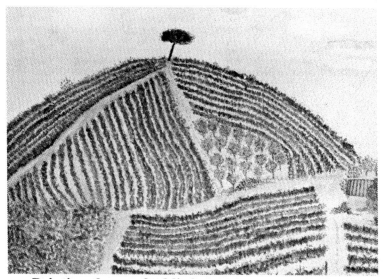

Painting the crooked little tree was too ambitious

I finished transferring the image of the crooked little tree onto my watercolor paper in the last light of the afternoon. Some things are best experienced in nature instead of on paper. I then drove to Il Refugio to get a rez for our last dinner in San Gim.

The evening church bells were ringing and the shadows slanting very tall, reminding me of the Etruscan "shadow people." In the Etruscan museums, at least one glass display case contained examples of the Etruscan "shadow people" -- mysteriously tall, skinny metal sculptures of men and women. The unusually attenuated figures are similar in style to Giacometti's work. Maybe Giacometti was descended from the Etruscans. The modern souvenir versions of the shadow people sold in the shops were virtually identical to those in the museums. The Etruscans were fascinated by the effects of the Tuscan sun, too.

Time on my hands, I veered off-piste onto a narrow lane with overgrowth so thick I could do nothing but press on until the road widened. A line of wild turkeys blocked my way. I wasn't in a hurry, so I waited patiently to see what they were up to. In a few minutes, they gangled to the brush at the side of the lane, leaving behind their tall shadows. The lane led to the gates of a villa, locked, of course. Italian villa gates opened electronically. It was ironic to press a gizmo and watch enormously heavy antique gates respond by grandly swinging open. Do you suppose castles now had similar electronics for opening portcullises?

I had planned to paint our beautiful gates, on paper that is, but I didn't have the patience. I drove back down the lane through the turkey shadows and on to Il Refugio. Nobody was outside. I walked inside.

"Sera," I called out to the dark room.

A very old man stood in the back behind the bar, drying wine glasses. He worked by the faint light near a window.

"Sera!" He waved a dish towel at me.

"Vorrei una prenotazione per questa sera, tre personi ala oto, o mezz' oto per favore," I rattled off. "Si, Signora." The man picked up the reservation book to record my reservation for three people at around eight o'clock and asked me to write my name in it. I stopped congratulating myself on what I thought was my newly-excellent Italian. "Puccinelli," I declared. "Allora," said he. "Molto bene." He wrote the name in the reservation book. He knew at once I wasn't Italian. I'd never truly fit in here, hard as I tried, no matter what I called myself.

Annie decided it was imperative to take a cutting from the long-stemmed geraniums that crowded the boxes at Il Refugio. The flowers were pale pink. Allora -- we went to the ristorante prepared. I had my shopping bag from Castellina, the one that could hold four bottles of wine or oil upright, without spilling. Tonight, it held one water bottle half-full, and Annie's folding scissors. When the waiter had taken our order, we ambled over to the flower box. Annie quickly snipped off three stems. I put them into the bottle, an accessory after the fact.

Over dolce, we thanked the waiters for our wonderful summer dinners. They surprised us with big hugs. They sent their best wishes to Crist and told us it was a piacere (Pee-ah-

CHAIR-ay); a pleasure. I told them we had not forgotten our first dinner there, how kind they were to give us a bag of bread and butter, coffee, milk, and fruit. I said we would remember every meal there, because each one was the best. Hurry back, they said. "Festiva tarde," I replied, shrugging my shoulders.

Perugia to Spoleto

We packed up the car for Spoleto. Annie brought every bite of leftover food in the villa, every ounce of olive oil and vinegar, every candle end, all the terrible matches, our unopened bottled water, the fruits and vegetables, salt and pepper, sugar, and flour. We snipped most of my basil, wrapped it in damp paper towels and put it in Saran Wrap. We sandwiched the Antinori bottles between her bags. I put my precious presents on top of it all. The trunk was full, the inside of the car was overfull. I wondered how we would manage once Cristina was back with us and we had another person plus at least another suitcase. Most of all, I wondered where we would fit all of the majolica that I planned to buy.

We chose Perugia as our lunch destination. The Red Guide led us to the peak of the town. From there, we looked out on our new Umbrian countryside. We parked, the only car on the street. We walked to the main square. Everything was closed except the ristoranti. A few vendors had set up majolica from Deruta on the steps of the Duomo, near the famous fountain. The fountain was covered with the famous Italian scaffolding. There were at least 500 pieces of majolica on the steps -- Deruta is only a few miles south of Perugia -- bowls, plates, and pitchers, in many patterns. Annie and I lost ourselves looking at the bounty. Rolf was impatient and hungry. He said he'd meet us over at the corner, and pointed to a pasticceria. We looked at the pieces and the prices and pondered if we should buy here or wait until Deruta. We decided to wait until we had time to make the hard decisions. Besides, the car was already full.

We walked over to the corner to meet Rolf. About 15 paces from him, an attractive young woman around Jensen's age was checking the seams on her stockings. She tenderly ran her hand from the heels of her four-inch spikes to her buttocks, working first up one leg and then the other, bending and twisting so that her bountiful breasts spilled from her low-cut silk blouse, directly in Rolf's sight of vision. Annie and I stopped before we reached Rolf, to watch this show. When the young woman was satisfied with her seams, she took off her sunglasses and polished them on her very chic, very short skirt, lifting it to her waist, toward Rolf, to accomplish the task efficiently. It was then we noticed that she wore no stockings.

We joined Rolf. He was oblivious to us. He continued to stare at the young woman, slack-jawed. When she saw Annie and me, the young woman walked away from us, across the piazza, mincing exactly like the runway models, crossing her right foot in front of her left, left over her right, and so on. I had read, and it was now confirmed, that Versace fashioned his clothes after those worn by the Perugian streetwalkers.

Rolf said that the young woman had asked him something but he had no idea what she said. "Well, not precisely," he confessed. We found a table at an outdoor caffè for lunch. Annie and I ordered hamburgers. They were made of minced ham and served with ketchup. We got some lire at the Bankomat, and drove on to Spoleto hungry, arriving in the late afternoon.

Our Spoleto rental was described as a 17th century "palace" with modern bathrooms and a view and a terrace. We knew nothing else about the place but we referred to it between us, facetiously, as "our palace in Spoleto." The person I communicated with by fax, the owner, didn't speak English. He had phoned me a few times in California, but back in February, I couldn't understand what he said. In rudimentary Italian, I had confirmed the dates and the price, and I had sent a down payment check in lire.

When we turned in our villa keys to Gaynor in the morning, she was kind enough to phone the manager of the Spoleto palace for instructions. We learned that the road to our palace was unmarked. We would follow the perimeter of the stone wall that enclosed the town. We would enter the town by crossing the bridge, a right turn, and enter the walled city. Next, we would take a left at the house covered with ivy and continue until we saw a driveway. The driveway led to the palace. We followed the instructions without a hitch. But we didn't know that the driveway was straight up and that it was modeled on one of those circular metal staircases that connects two or three floors in a loft. There were four corkscrew turns. The walls of the drive were sheer, steep stone. Though cars could go both up and down the drive, there was room for only one small car going in one direction.

I wasn't prepared for the ascent. I didn't know there were four turns. I couldn't tell if a car was coming down the drive. I couldn't see beyond the hairpin turns. I had to stop and back up on the 45 degree slope at each turn and, using a combination of slowly releasing the hand brake and quickly releasing the clutch and slamming on the brakes, I screeched haltingly up the twists. Rolf alternately said, "This isn't good" and "Jeez," his head in his hands. Annie didn't say a word. When we got to the top, I stopped the car. We three sat silently. I was dripping wet. My hands and knees shook. I couldn't get out of the car. I looked at Annie. She was woozy; seasick.

"We are not staying here," I stated flatly. Annie and Rolf agreed.

A handsome young man bounded from the palace to greet us. He called to two other young men. The three of them opened our doors and began carrying our suitcases and grocery bags inside. I was too weak to protest. When I stopped sweating and shaking, only the thought of having to drive back down the slippery slide got me out of the car. Annie and Rolf slowly followed.

The main young man returned.

"Giorno!" He enthused.

"Please phone and get us a hotel reservation right now," I commanded him shakily.

He shrugged his shoulders. "Completo!" he grinned charmingly; full. The hotels were all full. He didn't speak any

English. He couldn't understand why we were upset. I was unable to explain about the driveway. He was confused. He said we had a reservation here. Come, he said, let me show you. He was the owner's son, he told us. His father had put him in charge. We had to stay, he explained. In a daze, Annie and I followed him inside to survey our accommodations. Rolf got back in the car.

The palace was a large, square edifice with a smooth, simple stone façade. It sat on the slope just below the famous Spoleto Duomo. The outside of the palace was original 17th century. The interior held a faint smell of new paint and of pine and was state-of-the-art 20th century Italian design. We meekly entered the living room. Our enthusiastic young guide opened his arms, indicating spaciousness. He smiled at us expectantly.

The living room was larger by far than our entire villa in San Gim. The table surfaces were marble. The dining table could seat 12. An enormous, whimsically carved, pine sofa looked as if it could seat six normal people or sleep one giant.

The young man ushered us through the rooms. There were three levels and three bedrooms. Each bedroom was furnished with handmade pine armoires seven feet long, capacious dressers, and capriciously carved king size pine beds. The same talented carpenter who made the beds had also hewn and carved the end tables, lamps, and side chairs from the same handsome pine. One bath had a Roman tub -- six feet long or so, narrow, and several feet deep; a soaking tub. An outdoor shower carved from stone led off the bath.

There were phones, color TVs, a marble kitchen with an oven and a dishwasher and a full-size refrigerator with a freezer and real ice. Our shuttered windows opened to a bird's eye view of Spoleto's red tiled rooftops.

We cautiously explored outside. A stone slab terrace table could seat eight. A porchetta could fit neatly on the outdoor barbecue. On the breakfast terrace, a white faïence China drum balanced an octagonal, beveled glass table top. Four curvaceous, white wrought iron arm chairs with white-on-white crewel cushions were arranged around the table. Our terrace looked out on Spoleto's rooftops and up the valley to the hills beyond. Out the back door, broad, cobblestone steps led up to the Duomo.

"Molto bene," very nice, we hesitantly admitted to the young man. Annie and I conferred. Our bags and groceries were already inside. We decided to stay. I thanked the young man. "Va bene," I said. "Va bene?" he beamed at us, clapping his hands. "Va bene."

We enticed Rolf inside to take a look. He was baleful. I opened a bottle of the Antinori. I looked for wine glasses. I found a China cupboard with a shelf of fine China and one of crystal wine glasses. I poured a glass of wine and handed it to Rolf. I suggested he sit on the giant, curvaceous sofa. He sat. He sipped. He said, "OK."

We chose bedrooms, one each, on separate levels, what luxury, and unpacked. We had brought along all our household goods from San Gim, so there was no need to drive out for provisions. There was also no way I'd do it. Annie and I unpacked the Antinori, some Campari, Moretti beer, pasta, salad greens, tomatoes, anchovies, olive oil, vinegar, peaches, melon, and bread. I blessed Annie's frugality and put our food in the fridge and the handsome kitchen cupboards while she tossed together some pasta. I got out our candles and candleholders, carried plates, flatware, wine glasses and water glasses, napkins, and wine and water to the long terrazza that overlooked Spoleto. We ate and drank, watched the sunset, then the town's lights blink on, and later, the stars. We settled into our palace.

Annie's favorite geraniums

The Finest Place, the Best Moment

While Annie slept late in her palace bedroom, Rolf and I were out the back door early in the dewy morning to explore our new home town. We walked up to the Duomo, and on to the piazza where the market was held every weekday morning. We watched pigeons dive from the rooftops to the fountain to drink. We investigated the narrow, medieval streets. We walked under the Arch of Drusus (23 A.D.) commemorating Spoleto's victory over the Germanic tribes, and explaining why the name of the shop across from it has the word "Germanic" in it. At the end of the main street was a Roman arch (300 B.C.) and the Church of Sant-Ansano. The church was pristine, a recent restoration. Mass was in session, so we wandered elsewhere.

An interesting alley drew us past the open doors of the Sant-Ansano refectory. One of the priests -- or a higher-up -- appeared to live there. A pot bubbled on the stove, his breakfast porridge, perhaps. His black clothing hung on pegs. We felt like intruders, so we moved on past the door. At the end of the alley, we unintentionally ambushed the occupant of the refectory who, barefoot and attired in his long underwear, was watering his plants. We apologized in English, and beat a hasty retreat, pausing only briefly to examine some window boxes overflowing with long, salmon geraniums. I was pretty sure that Annie would want a few cuttings.

At the only store open at the early hour, I bought juice squeezed from blood oranges, truffled fresh mozzarella, salami, and bread. The eggs in the case were laid that morning and displayed on excelsior, like jewels. I chose five and praised my hard burlap shopping bag. Back home, we tasted the dark red juice, scrambled the eggs with salami, ate bites of cheese with bread, while reporting all to Annie.

Rolf summarized simply, "Spoleto is the finest place I have been."

After lunch, we were to drive to Montefranco to see Crist and to bring her the rest of her clothes. I assured Annie and Rolf that I would be up to the challenge of the "driveway." I went a bit overboard. I told them that I drove roads such as the corkscrew driveway all the time in California. I was scared yesterday only because I didn't know what to expect. Now that I knew, I assured them, it would be easy. They actually believed me.

I hoped that I hadn't blown out the clutch or ruined the brakes during our ascent. I tested both before we left. I believed that going down the roller coaster would probably be even more difficult -- and scarier -- than coming up. I imagined free-fall. I also worried that another car might be coming up while I was going down.

I put Cristina's suitcase in the trunk and cheerfully called to Annie and Rolf that I was ready whenever they were. All I saw as we drove down were the steep walls. I brushed within scant fractions of inches of them on each side of the car. The descent was far more difficult and seemed much steeper than the ascent. I rode the brakes and turned the steering wheel 360 left, 360 right, 360 left, 360 right all the way down, riding both clutch and brake all the way. Annie and Rolf cheered when we got to the bottom. I shrugged offhandedly and said, "See? No problem." Sweating, I dreaded the trip back up the roller coaster.

The 15 minute drive from Spoleto to Montefranco was like a dramatically shortened trip from San Francisco to Yosemite. We meandered through forests and smooth, green hills that were almost mountains, dotted with tiny hilltop towns. A waterfall that looked like Angel Falls presented itself in the distance, a cataract plunging thousands of feet. We rounded a hairpin and it was gone. We met no other cars.

The opera company had no phone. But in San Gimignano, Kate had assured that it would be easy to find Cristina. She said the performance would be in the Montefranco church. The church was on the piazza. The place where Crist and the others in the company were staying was across the piazza. I had a clear picture in my mind. As we entered town, I saw a sign that said "Chiesa;" (Key-AY-zah); church. We followed the sign to the church and parked. There was no piazza. We asked a man who was walking his dog if there was another church in town. "Si," he replied, and pointed toward Centro. We drove to Centro and followed the next "Chiesa" sign down a narrow cobblestone lane that deadended at the church.

The town buildings were on our left, the town wall and a steep, defensive precipice was on our right. There was no piazza. We walked up some stone steps next to the Chiesa. Through the open door of a house along the steps, we saw a family having their Sunday lunch. They waved and said, "Giorno!" A man came out and, as unlikely as it seemed, he said in English, "Hi! Americans?" Yes, we told him. I asked if there was another church in town. He described the only other church as the one we had already been to. "This church," he said, pointing to the church, "is Montefranco's main church."

He asked where we were from. We told him, New York and San Francisco. He told us that he was originally from Rome, but had married a woman from San Francisco, and now lived in San Francisco, a rather strong coincidence. He was visiting his mother. He wanted to chat. I asked him if he had seen any music students. No. Heard anyone singing? Nope.

I left Annie and Rolf there to chat with him and began to search through medieval streets de Chirico might have painted. Down an alleyway, up a side street, not a soul around. As if in a dream, I thought I heard Cristina's voice. She was singing something familiar. But the streets were narrow and twisty, the medieval stone houses made solid walls, and the sound fooled me. I turned one way and the singing stopped. I turned the other, and I heard her voice again. I followed the sound as a dog would follow a scent. Up an alleyway, down another side street, I came to a medieval building with an open door. Cristina's voice floated from within. I walked inside. I followed her singing up three flights of stairs and found her sitting in a circle formed by three young women and a young man who played the guitar. Crist sat in their midst, singing American folk songs, teaching the songs to the Italians -- early Joan Baez -- songs I didn't know she knew. She looked up, pleased to see me, and came out to the hall to chat. "This is the best time I've ever had," she said. I smiled at her speechlessly, and then told her I was glad, and that we would be there for the performance on Friday night. We hugged. She smelled like garlic.

I asked her about the food. "It's fabulous!" she said, giving me the details. They had their own cook. Breakfast was rolls and coffee. Pranzo was pasta and salad. Dinner was served at 8:00 or 9:00 p.m. -- a hearty soup, then salad, then pasta. Most of the meals were vegetarian. Wine was served with dinner. The music was easy, she said. She had already learned most of it. They worked about six hours a day, taking turns singing and playing. She had her own room -- clean but tiny. She shared a bath. All the singers and musicians went out together at night. There was a farmacia where they drank Cokes. Last night there was a street dance. The others didn't speak much English, but she was getting along "just great."

She was wearing a T-shirt and jeans. They were not clean. I handed off the suitcase containing the rest of her clothing, doubting that she would wear anything but her "very cool" American jeans and T-shirt for the remainder of the week. "Nine-thirty on Friday," she reminded me, as she returned to the room with her new Italian friends. One of the young women began to hum a tune. Cristina picked it up and sang the words. The young guitarist picked out the harmony. I ranked the moment as one of the best in my life.

Making a few wrong turns with no music to guide me, I walked back to where Annie and Rolf were still engrossed with the man who lived in San Francisco. I asked him which he preferred -- living in Italy or living in the U.S.? He laughed and said it was too difficult to live in Italy after living in the U.S. He came to Italy only one summer week a year, he said, to visit his mother. He brought his children. He waved to the children, who sat at the dining table with their grandmother. They shyly waved back and said, "Hi!" We invited the man to come to Friday's concert. He declined. He was leaving for San Francisco the next day.

I remembered Roberto's parting words: now that he knew how things worked, he'd like to stay and enjoy himself. Except all of it *was* difficult; things worked differently in each place.

There was no pattern to rely on. Each toilet was a challenge to flush. At our palace in Spoleto, there was a button on the wall above my toilet. A chain also dangled overhead. The button or the chain? The tiger or the lady? Nothing happened when I pulled the chain. Nothing happened when I pressed the button. Frustrated, I banged the button twice, hard. The toilet flushed agreeably. Each Italian faucet held its own secrets, each door its own mysteries, especially in ristorante rest rooms. Windows were the worst. As in France, all French doors opened inward.

We drove back to Spoleto. I was joyous at Crist's happiness. The air was sweeter, the scenery even more beautiful on our return trip. I confidently Andretti'd my way up the roller coaster driveway.

We walked to the Duomo in the early evening, when it was most dramatic. The sun glinted on the magnificent gold fresco at the peak, turning it umm, golder. Mass was getting out when we arrived. We waited for the attendees to leave, then walked to the door. "Hi!" said a familiar voice. It was Cristina. She said she was just hanging out with her friends, adding, "Ciao for now!"

We did the 101 survey tour of the 12th century Duomo. Here was Filippo Lippi's Assunzione, to my eye, one of the world's greatest wonders. Super-imposed on it I saw another wonder in my mind's eye, Vermeer's *The Letter*. Lippi's tomb was also here, designed by his son, Filippino. So his dad could keep an eye on things in the Duomo. On our way out, we glimpsed Bernini's bust of Pope Urban VIII. Annie and Rolf were hungry, so we pressed on, but we hoped we'd be back and that Cristina would, too.

We found an outdoor ristorante that was open earlier than the others, and had what Annie referred to as "a good dinner." That would be great, homemade pasta. The wine came in a Deruta carafe, starting a conversation about "When do we go?" In a day or two, we decided. Let's enjoy Spoleto.

After dinner, I went to a "Bar" and ordered some Benedictine, Sambuca, and some Strega "a portare," to go. We had no leftover Sambuca and I had neglected to buy it this morning. The woman behind the bar was amused. She put the liqueurs into individual espresso-to-go cups, put lids on them, stacked them, and wrapped them up in a paper cone. On our way back to the palace, we stopped to sit on a Roman wall to listen to a symphony rehearsal, then walked back to our palace to share tastes of our syrupy drinks on the terrazza by candlelight, looking at the lights of the city. We were as happy as we had ever been.

Porcini mushrooms at the Spoleto market

Annie and I got up early to go to the market. We did some sightseeing along the way, our usual culture, shopping, eating tour de force. The market rivaled the sights. We admired heaping bowls of fat, fresh truffles, wooden fruit boxes filled with bursting ripe black figs, green figs, and green figs tinged with black. Mounds of squash blossoms neighbored plums of all sizes and colors with a veneer of what looked like frost, same as the alabaster plums. Adorable baby purple eggplants and smooth green and purple junior eggplants and chubby mature melanzane shared a box. The British called eggplants "aubergines" as the French do. If a menu had a translation, eggplant was listed in Italian, "melanzane," and translated "aubergine."

The signs shouted, "No tocare!" (No Toe-CAH-ray) Don't touch! The vendors selected well, and tucked a generous bunch of freshly picked basil (basilico) into each bag as a garnish. I bought pomodori piccoli; literally, "little tomatoes;" cherry tomatoes, and chose some figs and grapes. The vendors used an antique weighing device that looked like a combination doctor's office scale and copper plate. It didn't look very scientific or accurate but we gladly paid for the vendors' interesting show of weighing.

A display of cheeses lured us into the Alimentari; grocery store, where the grocer displayed a tray a meter wide groaning with rounds of "ricotta salti." The cheese rounds were about eight inches across, six inches high. They were covered with what looked like saw dust; the "salti." The white aproned grocer bustled over to explain that there are two kinds of ricotta salti: ricotta made from cow's milk and ricotta made from goat's milk. He cut off a chunk of the former, doused it liberally with the sawdust stuff, and plunked a piece in the palm of Annie's hand and a piece into my palm. We began to pinch off a bit off to taste, but he said, "No, no, no." He indicated that the correct way to eat ricotta salti is to pop the whole thing in your mouth, sawdust and all. We obeyed, palms up. The cow's milk ricotta was soft and sweet and the "salti" was delicious -- only slightly salty with a nutty after-taste. It dribbled down our blouses. Then he gave us each a chunk of the goat's milk ricotta, dusted with the salt dust. It was harder, and sharp. While we savored our samples, he cut about a half pound of each kind for us and wrapped them up.

He explained that one eats the sweeter cheese with cookies, and the goat's milk salti with bread and wine. He went behind the glass case that displayed a dozen kinds of cookies. I said we would take due etti of biscotti. He shook his head. "No, no, no." He chose about a kilo; 2.2 pounds of the cookies, two of each kind, put them into a paper bag, and asked what else we wanted, as if he was offering us a choice.

I asked if I could take a photo of the ricotta salti. "No, no no!" He shook his head. "Esperta!" Wait. He went to the back of the store and after a few minutes returned with two skinny, seven foot long salamis. He handed one to Annie, he kept the other. He put his arm around her waist, and positioned himself with Annie behind the salti, smiling broadly. "Va bene?" He asked me. "Molto bene," I laughed. Very good. I took a few shots of the pose he had set up for me, then asked for a bottle of Strega. Last night, we decided we preferred it even to Sambuca. "Si!" He said, for the first time. I told him that we'd be back Domani; tomorrow (Doh-MAH-nee) "Ciao!"

We shopped back through town. I chose some plump, homemade ravioli pillows, an etto of fresh pesto, some oven-warm rosemary foccaccia. At home, we cooked the pasta, doused it with pesto, spread out the other foodstuffs on the table, opened some cold Pinot Grigio, and as we ate our interesting lunch, we decided we all loved Spoleto best. That our Italian was improving and that we were pre-conditioned to medieval hill towns after our weeks in San Gim had everything to do with our high comfort level in Spoleto. As much as we had enjoyed our countryside swimming pool and vineyards, we loved being in town.

Annie and Rolf had not eaten fresh figs before. They marveled at the taste and consistency. We have excellent figs in Northern California and I bought them all year 'round, but these figs were figgier, squishier. We spent the afternoon napping, sunning, sitting on the terrazza, savoring the lunch aftertastes in the still of the afternoon. The light breeze had followed us to Spoleto. The sky was clear, church bells clanged, tolled, rang, reminding us that time passed here, though it didn't matter to us.

On the terrazza this afternoon, looking out at crumbling medieval walls, I glanced through a guide book, gleaning info about Spoleto. Among other facts, the book reported that Hannibal tried to take Spoleto, but was unsuccessful. The text didn't say if he brought his elephants. If so, I understood why he didn't succeed -- too steep for elephants.

Before dinner, we strolled up to La Rocca -- the peak of Spoleto -- a 14th century castle that was once home to Lucrezia Borgia. It was closed. We went on to the magnificent Roman bridge. We rested on a bench next to the bridge -- in a small park that looked out on the countryside -- a spot where the locals gathered. In town, the crowd was cosmopolitan, artistic, well-dressed, highly-cultured; town was a true artist's enclave. Up here, the group was less sophisticated, but equally colorful. Men zoomed by on motor scooters, shouting to each other. A man walked his dog over to a group of his compadres, who sat on a bench near us. He made a joke about his dog peeing on one of the men. He said the dog would pee on command. He looked down to see the dog wetting his own shoe. He laughed as loudly as his friends and so did we.

We dined at the same ristorante as last night. Looking through my Michelin Red Guide, I noted that it was among Spoleto's best. We walked home slowly, stopping again to listen to the symphony practice. The concerto would be Saturday night. We'd be in Arezzo on Saturday night.

Back on the terrazza sipping Strega, we listened to the amplified sound from a vintage drama being performed in a piazza below. The voices were all male. It sounded more like the men at the Roman bridge squabbling good-naturedly in rhyme than a drama from another time. The night was chilly. In my huge bedroom, in my enormous bed, I read for a while, trying to sort out the feud between the Guelfs and the Ghibellines back in Tuscany. Reading about Italy in Italy is compelling stuff. In the abstract, on the patio in California, where the clock next to me scrupulously measured my minutes, my Italian reading didn't stick.

I pulled all the covers around me to make the bed seem smaller and warmer. I read about the battle of Montaperti, in 1260. But my reading experience was incomplete. For 20 years, I have not read without a cat. Twenty years is the age of my oldest cat. I am a reader who reads lying down; on a sofa or a loveseat, in bed, or seasonally, on the patio chaise. My cat senses when I am about to lie down to read. She watches while I gather my reading material -- a magazine or two, a book -- and she follows me to where I'll read it. When I am settled, she jumps on me. She lies across my chest and tummy, her nose touching my chin. I associate reading with having a warm tummy and chest and a tickle on the chin. When she bathes' herself, I hold my book overhead to accommodate her movement. When she lies flat and limp, sleeping, I bend my knees behind her and lean my book on my thighs. From habit, I do the same now without her. A cat completes the pleasure of reading.

Montaperti was the only battle of any century that the Sienese won against the Florentines. Dante recorded the details. The Sienese won because many Florentines changed sides mid-way in the fight, thus increasing the Sienese odds against the Florentines. The turning point of the battle was when a Florentine named Bocca degli Abati rode his horse up to the Florentine standard bearer and lopped off the bearer's wrists with a stroke of his sword. The standard fell to the ground, and I imagine that the standard bearer did too, and that blood splurted everywhere; on the horse, on the standard, on the ground, on his fellow soldiers. There is probably an idiom of a Latin word derivative that means "a cutting off of hands," similar to the word decapitation or defenestration or related to Procrustean, but I don't know the word. Maybe its root is "Abati."

Anyhow, the dramatic hand severing (abatation) signaled to the Florentines that Bocca had changed sides. The standard's ignominious descent, and probably the blood, was a dark warning to the others to follow Abati's lead. Many Florentines turn-coated. Confusion ensued. The Sienese and Sienese-Florentines moved in for a decisive kill of the nonplused Florentine chauvinists. The Sienese still celebrate this Quisling victory. The Florentines rub their wrists and look the other way.

In the still of the night I padded across the cold marble floor and took a long, hot bath in the deep tub to wash off the blood. I toweled off and pulled my cozy Prada cashmere sweater over my nightie. I placed an extra pillow on my tummy to hold the blankets close as a cat. Buona notte.

Deruta

Annie and I left Spoleto for the legendary Deruta at 9:00 a.m. sharp, wondering how Deruta could possibly live up to the expectations we had built over the past several weeks. We drove north, past three storybook hilltop towns, only one of which, Spello, was on the map. The other two were called Eggi and Trevi, like the Roman fountain. The towns looked like drip sand castles. A tower rose from the top of the town. Identical, sand-colored driblets; houses, spilled down the hillside, helter-skelter. We drove past Assisi, glimpsed Perugia's perfect, sky blue Duomo, then turned south to Deruta, home of the ceramics known as majolica; in Italian, maioliche. Artisans made majolica from the local clay. They hand-painted their pieces, then fired them, resulting in one-of-a-kind ceramic tableware. The pieces were heavy, and very strong.

Large, modern showrooms lined the road for a kilometer or so at the outskirts of Deruta. We drove past them and parked a few feet from the stone archway that was the entrance to the medieval town.

We arrived at opening time, 10:00 a.m. Artisans' shops lined the narrow, cobblestone streets. I don't recall that there was any other kind of store in town except a bakery. We went from shop to shop, admiring the work. There were only a few other tourists, an American couple on their honeymoon who were selecting "their pattern," and a few German couples who looked to be buying souvenirs. The American couple chose a pattern sprinkled with lemons. Annie and I admired their choice, which pleased them.

Most shops were fairly small. Shelves ran floor to ceiling, crammed with majolica bowls and plates and cups and pitchers and tiles and serving pieces of all sizes and shapes. Most of the work was new, straight from the kiln. Some of the pieces were reproductions of antique pieces. There were a few real antiques. They were the most delicate. The work on the antique pieces was more like lace than ceramics and the antiques were astronomically expensive; museum pieces.

According to the literature I picked up,*"Even before the 15c, it (majolica) was a well-established and widespread industry, enjoying its heyday during the 16c and 18c."*

But majolica's roots began to grow in Etruscan times. The Etruscans must have been good miners, or maybe in the course of burying all those cineraries, they ended up with piles of alabaster and the terra cotta that is the base of majolica, and in an idle moment or century, an imaginative artist or 100 decided to make the piles useful. Thus, majolica.

Most artisans in Deruta created pieces of the classic majolica patterns: "Bordato," a crisp yellow, white and gold geometric pattern; the eponymous "Green Rooster" pattern; "Ricco," a flowery orange, blue, and yellow renaissance pattern; and most famous of all, "Raffaellesco," painted with golden dragons, and taking its name from the artist Raffaello; Raphael. The dragon represented "a benevolent power that protects its owner from adversities" -- but not, unfortunately, from breakage, should a dragon drop. "Siena" was another well-known pattern. The pattern was mostly black and white, with touches of brown and gold. The design was a serene, sitting deer; the same deer that was inlaid in the floor of the Siena Cathedral. This deer was "the symbol of humanity in its search for peace and wisdom."

I had shopped through the San Gim thrift store and found an old "Siena" candleholder (yes, there are thrift shops in Italy. San Gim's is located behind the Etruscan museum, near the old well.) I paid £500 for my Siena thrift candleholder; about $1.50.

In addition, or in some cases instead of their versions of the classic patterns, each artisan created his and her own unique shapes and patterns. Each shop brought surprises. Each shop had to be shopped. A bowl painted only one color and with a simple pattern was inexpensive, say £10.000 ($5.00 and change). As an artisan added colors and embellishments, the prices rose. An artisan or two was hard at work in each shop. We watched while men and women, old and young, painted pale colors in intricate designs on pitchers and plates. When the pieces were fired, the deep, true colors would emerge from the ceramics. The artisans sat working at large tables, with pint-jar-sized paint pots and many brushes in front of them.

Each piece of majolica was handmade and signed. The artisan wrote on the bottom of each piece he created:

FATTO A MANO   MADE BY HAND
IN ITALIA   IN ITALY
DERUTA G   DERUTA
G was the artisan's name. In this case,
 Giovanni's initial

My good friend Robin took care of my best friend, Romeo, at her house while I was in Italy. She has two children, ages one and three, who adore him. He licks them, and loves them, too. Her dinnerware is Raffaellesco. I scoured all the shops for a unique piece to take her, as partial thanks for having my 110 pound dog come live with her for two months.

Before we left, we had a "practice sleep-over," to see if Romeo would be happy staying at Robin's house overnight. The next morning, Robin found her husband, her three year-old daughter, and Romeo sleeping curled up together on the living room floor as they probably were right then while I was shopping in Deruta.

At Giovanni's, I found what I was looking for. Giovanni had come up with the idea of making a "breakfast set" in the Raffaellesco pattern. His set consisted of a cup and a large saucer with a round indentation for the cup plus a crescent-shaped indentation for a breakfast pastry. The cup was large; a double cappuccino size. I bought two sets for Robin, and Giovanni let me take his picture. His assistant then enfolded the sets in plastic bubble wrap. The result was two extra-large football-sized packages that I would carry home.

Annie and I browsed for a couple hours and then remembered that all the shops would close for lunch. We had to make some hard decisions. I chatted with an artisan who created the majolica for the local San Francisco store, Biordi. He showed me the patterns he was creating for Biordi's next catalogue, and told me that Deruta artisans imported their majolica directly only to Biordi and to Neiman-Marcus. Biordi was the shop in North Beach where I had previously bought a few pieces from Deruta, and where Robin bought all of hers. The man was also a salesman: he wanted to give me a special deal on an entire set of majolica for 12. A place setting consisted of three pieces: a large dinner plate, a large soup plate (so large that I might use such a bowl to serve pasta family-style) and a "fruit plate," which I would use as a salad, dessert, or luncheon plate. Instead of the soup plate, a cereal bowl could be substituted for the third piece of the place setting. The bowl was also quite generously sized; a small, flat, serving bowl, really.

The artisan said he would create any piece for me in any pattern I wished. He would be pleased to custom make pieces, too -- with my initials, perhaps? He showed me a sample of what he meant -- a plate with one of his signature designs. He had nuanced the buyer's initials into the center. The set of majolica would be an heirloom to pass on generation to generation, he insisted. I was tempted. I knew he was right and the prices were reasonable -- less than one-third what I'd pay at home, including shipping. But I wasn't in love with the patterns and I didn't need more dinnerware. Though it was a rare opportunity and I would probably regret turning him down, I did. To buy would be Mount Everest shopping.

Farther down the street, another artisan showed me plates and dishes she had painted with a rabbit pattern. I fell in love with the rabbits. The background was off-white, the rim was rosy-goldenrod. A rabbit was centered on each plate, surrounded by cabbages and other yummy bunny food. The border was the naïve, signature majolica dark blue trim. Each rabbit, and consequently each plate, was unique as the birds at Racciano. Each had its own artistic personality and individual choice of rabbit foods painted alongside each cock-eared animal; various flowers and cabbages.

There was also a duck pattern that coordinated nicely with the rabbits.

A small duck stared out at me disarmingly from tiles and from a chunky pitcher. I pictured wildflowers stuffing the pitcher and a new tile wall in my kitchen randomly sprinkled here and there with the sweet duck tiles. I bought a set of rabbit luncheon plates and a few duck accessories, all to ship home. I didn't need these pieces, but I did love them, which made up for the need. Besides, with shipping, the price was under $200.00 for about 18 pieces.

Later, at home in California, when we had finished the tomato and avocado sandwiches I served on these plates, Crist and I made up silly stories about the bunnies on our plates based on their differences in appearance and choice of foods.

Annie chose a piece or two of majolica from almost every store, and by the Deruta bewitching hour of 1:00 p.m., we had finished our shopping. The shopkeepers told us they might reopen at two, or maybe three, or thereabouts, at any rate, some time after lunch. Annie and I decided that we could come back another day.

We popped into the bakery just as it was closing and bought the last pizzetta and panino, both pomodoro and mozzarella. We walked back through the town's medieval arch, locked our purchases in the car, and continued to the park across the street where we found a shady bench. We ate and recapped our shopping coups, wondering who among our friends and relatives would be the lucky recipients of our precious majolica gifts or if we should keep all of it for ourselves. I filled my plastic, collapsible Kodak cup with water from the public fountain, and we drank and then washed up, as the locals did.

ASIDE: A collapsible cup is a nicety and can be a necessity for trekking around Italy. There are public fountains everywhere. The water is clean and good. We saw businessmen in suits, children, and people of all manners washing up, filling cups, and cooling off with water from the public fountains.

Back at the palace with our treasures, I opened our last bottle of the crisp, light, delicious, ice cold Vernaccia of San Gimignano and we sat on the terrace above the rooftops, sipping, tasting sweet grapes, figs, truffled cheeses, and biscotti. It was sunny, with a light breeze, the middle of a perfectly satisfying summer day in Italy.

I took a long bath in the deep Roman tub, and was just getting out when the phone rang -- my first direct phone call in seven weeks.

"Hello? Pronto? Yes? Si?" I poured out breathlessly, hoping everyone at home was OK. I had given our phone numbers to only a few "emergency" people.

"Hi, it's me, Phoebe. How are you?" Alexander Graham Bell was a genius. My friend Phoebe had phoned the number I had given her for the palace -- the owner's home -- and he had given her our direct number. I could have done the same, but I had no need for a phone. I asked my friend what our number was and wrote it down, just in case. She told me about her day in San Francisco and I described my day. She reacted as if I had taken the shuttle to Saturn instead of the Fiat to Deruta. For me, it was just another day in Italy. I promised to give her one of the bunny pieces, or possibly a duck.

We took a walk before dinner, down a narrow street where we had not ventured before. To our left, a small Roman piazza opened up, a carved stone fountain at its center. A royal lion dispensed the public waters. Above, a forest of hazelnut trees was filling with hundreds and hundreds of swallows. The swallows swept over the rooftops to their night's refuge, darkening the sky. We stood amid the spectacle, watching wave after wave of swallows arrive. Their chatter was high decibel Dolby. A thin old man, impeccably tailored in a dark, three piece suit, walked past us and laughed.

"Ecco!" He shouted to us; Watch this! He clapped his hands three times. The bird chatter immediately stilled. When it started again, he indicated that we should clap. We did, and the chatter stopped again. He laughed, we laughed appreciatively, and he walked on. "Sera!" He called to us.

To the right, our eyes followed beautiful, stone steps leading down a crooked path. They were irresistible. Hidden half way down the steps was a ristorante. We entered. The staff sat in front of the indoor wood-burning grill, eating their dinners. We walked through the entrance, onto the ristorante terrazza, where tables were set with smooth white linens, gleaming flatware, and Baccarat-style Bordeaux glasses. A tent framed eight tables at the terrazza's edge. The tables overlooked the rooftops. A young man asked if he could do anything for us.

Si. A rez for three at eight?

Si.

Under the tent?

Certo.

Grazie mille.

We returned to the top of the stairs where the swallows continued to fill the trees. We walked on. Another piazza opened to the right. A few families sat on benches in the twilight, talking and admiring the view. The families represented three generations: grandma, parents, parental siblings, children, grandchildren. We joined them on our own bench, in the corner of the park, and watched the swallows swoop to the trees beyond.

A rainbow filled the sky, stretching from the Duomo to the rooftops below. Rolf said, "This is the best cocktail we've had. What's next?" I had decided that in Italy, if you waited for 10 minutes, something always happened. I laughed, "Wait 10 minutes." The rainbow melted as the sun began to send out shards of deep pink and purple from behind the clouds, dappled with late-arriving swallows. Wow.

We felt a few sprinkles of rain. Finding cover under the hazelnut trees, we walked from the little park past the swallows, clapped, laughed, and continued down the steps to the ristorante.

When I asked him, the waiter recommended a local Umbrian wine, Sagrantino di Montefalco. He opened it slowly and showily, as one would a vintage bottle of Champagne. He then decanted it into a carved, crystal pitcher, and we tasted heaven. He told us that the Sagrantino grape is grown only in the

Montefalco area. Montefalco is fairly close to Spoleto, and I hoped we might drive over for a degustazione; tasting. The Montefalco wines have been produced for a very long time. I.e., Pliny wrote the praises of Montefalco wine in A.D. 50.

I thought of the contrasts between our Napa Valley wineries and those of Tuscany and Umbria. The new and the old. Napa's carefully engineered, brand new wood and steel vine supports, for example, as contrasted with the Tuscan vines that as often as not were held up by old, patched vines. I thought of the thoroughbred John Deere tractors powerfully plying the flat fields of the Napa Valley and the creaky mongrel Italian machines jigging up and down the lumpy Tuscan countryside. We drank to wine.

Rolf had a truffled frittata as a primi, enough for a meal. I had a bite. It was an omelet tossed with the jarred truffles I had seen in the Spoleto stores. The truffles were minced and covered with olive oil. I wasn't sure what to do with minced truffles, but now I knew. I had a panzanella, a twist on an old classic: fresh, tiny, fresh veggies, chopped up with only a few chunks of bread, and presented in a radicchio leaf. We all ordered something from the great-smelling indoor grill. I had a veal chop with sciacciatta di patate, translated as "smashed potatoes," similar to hash browns, but with a wood fire taste. They had been cooked on a stone like a pizza, inside the wood-burning stove. Annie ordered a filet of beef in green peppercorn sauce with a rice-stuffed tomato, Rolf had the mixed grill. It all went well with the Sagrantino di Montefalco.

Italian Alliteration

An early morning drizzle over the rooftops, an early knock at the door.

Three young women equipped with mops and brooms and carrying stacks of towels and sheets requested entry. This would be our organization day, filled with packing and making reservations for the last days of our Italian summer. But first, we had to get out of the way so that the young women could do their work.

Rolf headed out for a walk while Annie and I moved to the terrazza, me with maps and books, she with postcards and stamps. My new friend, Piera, and her husband joined us. Piera and her family were staying on the floor above us. The palace had three floors of tri-level apartments. There was a main entry door to the palace, and an entry foyer. Our door was to the immediate left of the entry. Across from our door was a small office for the manager, whom we never saw. A long hall led to the back of the palace, to the back door we used to walk up to town, and to the staircase that led to the apartments above.

How did I meet Piera? Our first evening out, as we were leaving, Annie closed our door, which locked automatically. Our only key was inside. A young couple passed by, and asked if they could help. The woman used her cell phone to call the owner, who told her where the extra key was. This was complicated. In a chest near the front door was a key that unlocked the office door. In the office was a key that would unlock our door. We found the key in the chest, but we couldn't unlock the office door. We all tried and failed. Piera phoned the owner again. The owner assured her that the key in the chest drawer unlocked the office door. We all tried again, and, using some force to pull on the door while Piera manipulated the key, Piera's husband was successful. We entered and searched the office, found the key to our door, and got it open. This took a couple hours, during which time we all chatted, laughed, and got to know each other. To thank Piera and her husband, I gave them a bottle of our Antinori. They acted as if I had given them a thousand dollars (not lire.) They refused, I insisted, they refused, I insisted, and by then we had become friends.

The woman who became my new friend, Piera Angelino, came from a town called San Antino, down near Naples. She was on vacation with her husband, their new baby, Giuseppe, whom they fondly called "Beppo," and Piera's mother, who took care of the baby a few hours each day so the couple could go out and spend time alone together. Piera's family had a vineyard down south, where they made a white wine from what she described as Champagne-type grapes. The label was "Asprini," and it was sold only in Naples. Piera had attended college in Rome, where she had been an English major. So we spoke English together. We also spoke Italian. I understood her quite well, but I couldn't understand even the simplest words her mother and husband used.

When we were together, I usually flirted with Beppo while Piera and her husband asked me questions about California. When her husband spoke, she translated for me. When I spoke, she translated for him. As we sat on the terrazza rapt in our simultaneous interpretive manner, Piera translated a question from her husband: Was there anything they could do for us? Did we needed help with anything "Italian?"

I told her that my current project, making reservations for our last few days in Italy, wasn't going too well. I explained that Rolf wanted to tour the Ferrari factory when we went to Modena (MOE-den-ah) in a few days. I had found the factory's phone number in one of my guidebooks and I had called to see if I could line up a tour. Here was the problem: After many rings, the phone was answered by either a machine or a real person, I couldn't tell which. Whichever it was, a woman spoke for about 30 seconds. I couldn't understand what was said. There was no beep. If it were a machine, what message would I leave anyway? I hung up when the talking stopped. Piera translated and explained the situation to her husband. They discussed the matter seriously for several minutes.

I watched enviously as they chatted, listening to the lilt, to the mellifluous sounds they made; as much music as language. All the words seemed to rhyme. The words didn't simply fall from their mouths. They went to some trouble to speak their language. They moved their tongues to various parts of their mouths. Their lips shaped and reshaped and configured to change the sounds. To speak the Italian language well requires some artistry, like playing the piano or painting. To know the translation of English words into Italian is nothing. More and more, I felt gawky speaking English; American English. It sounded flat, overly simple -- primitive, by comparison to Italian. My Italian accent was equally sophomoric by comparison.

Though the American vocabulary grows more colorful by the day in slang and metaphor, the sound we make becomes duller. Yeah. I dunno. Our tongues touch only a few parts at the front of our mouths. We barely move our lips ... unnhuh. We don't rhyme at all.

Piera said they had decided that she would phone the factory for me. She said that the Ferrari factory was in the small town of Maranello, a kilometer outside Modena. She asked me for the number I had already called. I invited her inside to use my phone. "No, no," she said. It was cheaper to use her cell phone. She explained that there are so many cell phones in Italy because the rates are so cheap. Resigned, I gave her the number and she dialed. She got a machine. She summarized the message: the factory was closed through the month of August. She looked thoughtful and then said, "Un momento." She phoned information, and asked for the Maranella Polizia. She got the police on the phone, told them the number she had dialed for the Ferrari factory and asked them if there was another number for the Ferrari factory. Si. She called the other number, and spoke for several minutes.

Piera told me that the fattoria; factory, was on feria; vacation. Fattoria, feria ... fah-TOE-ree-ah, fair-EE-ah ... It would re-open on September first, but it was necessary to reserve at least a week in advance for a visit. She said the Japanese, especially, reserved for tours months in advance. She was sincerely sorry she couldn't be more useful. I wished I could thank her more poetically than "Thannkssoomuch".

I asked her why she would call the police for information, rather than say, Information, and she told me that the police are the only reliable resource in such matters. I made a mental note. We chatted on, with her translating for her husband, then talking to me with their mutual opinion on each topic. They hadn't met any Americans before. We were a novelty. They were very interested in the U.S., and especially in California. They had tasted California wines, she told me, and they liked our Merlot. I guessed that they hadn't tried too many California wines and were being polite. I told them we loved all of their wines, especially the Barolos.

Piera said that Italy is insular as well as provincial. That Italians dislike the Germans intensely. She said that anyone who grew up in Italy had heard stories about cruel German behavior in both World Wars. Neither war ever really ended as far as the Italians were concerned, she said. Her husband nodded gravely.

I asked how they felt about the French. They both laughed. She said they also disliked the French, but the feeling was more one of rivalry -- you know, she smiled, over cars, fashion, food, and especially, wine. Piera's mother came outside to take Beppo. The young couple left for lunch and I went inside to phone for hotel reservations.

The women had finished cleaning. They had left a dozen towels for us. When we arrived, there were only three towels. I found the linen closet down the hall, and using the key that opened the office door, I was able to open the linen closet and took out more towels. I didn't know where to put the used towels. They accumulated each day. We folded them and stacked them outside our bathroom doors. The women had replaced all of them.

I organized my notes and books and maps on the large, marble table next to the living room phone. The Michelin Red Guide was invaluable for making reservations. Dialing the AT & T access code worked perfectly, and so did our phones. I was able to ask for reservations in Italian, to understand what the hotel manager said, to answer his questions, and to confirm the reservations.

My first call was to Arezzo. I dialed, and immediately an operator from Alabama got on the line to help me. When I told this to Piera later, she was astonished. She said, "Just use my cell phone." To call Arezzo via Alabama was preposterous to her and made me wonder, too. I chatted with the operator from Alabama. I told him I was calling Arezzo, in Italy, and I spelled it for him. I might have said Moscow, or Djakarta, or Reykjavik, but it was all the same to him. The next call, to Pistoia, brought another operator in the States. I spelled Pistoia and told her only that it was in Italy. She connected me instantly. I asked the manager of the three star Pistoian hotel for two rooms with baths for four people, single beds, for Sunday evening, with parking, and spelled my name in Italian when he asked. The manager said, "Si! Perfetto Signora." "Molto grazie," I beamed with relief.

My work done, I walked up to town. I went to the shop that had the most jars of truffles in the windows and, by the way, large "SALE" signs ("SOLDE.") The owner, a handsome woman of about 40, came from behind the counter to help me. I told her that I had tasted a frittata made with minced truffles and, "How do you prepare that, per favore?" She smiled broadly. She handed me a quart jar of minced truffles in olive oil, which she called "truffle sauce." She explained that for a appetizer for four people, I would whisk together four eggs. Any milk? No, unless you wish. Pour olive oil into a pan. Add the eggs, and four tablespoons of the minced truffles. Turn as you would an omelet, and serve. Molto facile; very easy. The truffle sauce was on sale for £40.000, about $22.00. How long would it last? Three months in the refrigerator, after you have opened the jar. Va bene. Another thing to carry home.

I also bought a small jar containing two whole, fresh black truffles, which I gave to Pinchas Zukerman at dinner the night after I returned from Italy. He was in the Bay Area to perform with the San Jose Symphony on their opening night. "Truffles? From Spoleto?" he swooned. At our supper after the performance, he recalled performing in Spoleto at the Festival dei Due Mondi; Festival of Two Worlds, the Gian-Carlo Menotti music festival that takes place in June and July each year.

The items I would have to carry with me on the plane were mounting. Down the street from the truffle sale, I looked into the window of a small jewelry shop, hoping to find a thank you gift for Kate. A pair of earrings sparkled at me. They were delicate music staffs dotted with notes. The gold staffs spiraled two inches. The musical notes were tiny, real jewels; diamonds, rubies, sapphires, and emeralds sprinkled through the spaces of the staffs. I bought them for Cristina, a splurge, but quite an appropriate souvenir of the summer. She hadn't bought much on the trip, only a present for her voice coach at home and one for her drama coach, and my birthday cherries, nothing at all for herself. I picked out an antique brooch, shaped as a gift bow, for Kate, and had both presents wrapped.

Later in the evening we went out to dinner. We wandered through the back streets, discovering new territory. Someone played a saxophone from a rooftop. The sound followed us through the neighborhoods. We found an outdoor caffè near the Savanna Hotel. The owner gave us menus, then took them away from us after we had deliberated but before we were ready to order. He said to forget the menu, he would bring us something. He brought us each a plate holding a dozen baby octopi, a matched set, each an inch and a half tall, sitting upright on their plate in a dark red sauce, like a circle of chess pawns in a pool of blood. Losing my appetite, I asked if I could have an insalata verde, hold the octopi. The house red wine, served in a maioliche pitcher, was like vinegar, and I sent it back. The owner whisked it away, and brought us an unlabeled bottle of red wine, opened it with a flourish, and I tasted it. Molto bene, grazie, Very good, thank you ... we'll keep the wine, ma no ho fame; but I'm not hungry. Rolf loved the baby octopi.

I decided to place here a typical check from a more delicious evening that Annie, Rolf, Cristina and I shared a bit later in the summer. Service was included in the price.

# of items ordered	item cost	
4 COPERTI	10.000	(cover charge)
1 VINI	14.000	(wine)
2 BEVANDE	6.000	(beverages)
4 PRIMI PIATTI	44.000	(first courses)
3 SECONDI PIATTI	40.000	(second courses)
2 CONTORNI	9.000	(vegetables)

TOTALE	123.000	(total: $69.00)

This check was dinner for four, at an Umbrian ristorante recommended by the Michelin Red Guide. The COPERTI, cover charge, was 2.500 each. We had one bottle of wine, costing nearly $8.00, meaning that it was not vino di casa, which runs around $4.50. Instead, we had a bottle recommended by the waiter.

The BEVANDE; drinks in this case, were two bottles of water. We ordered four PRIMI PIATTI, first courses, of pasta. Three of us also had SECONDI PIATTI, second courses, veal and beef. We ordered 2 CONTORNI, vegetables, this time, two salads that we shared. The total check at that day's exchange rate was $69, or $17 per person.

Not shown above were the other items on the menu that we did not order:

ANTIPASTI	(antipasto/appetizers)
FORMAGGI	(cheeses)
FRUTTA	(fruit)
DOLCI	(desserts)
CAFFÈ	(coffee)
LIQUORI	(liqueurs)
PASTI A PREZZO FISSO	(fixed price full meal)

A Prayer in Assisi

Francesca, the 20-ish daughter of our palace's owner, who helped out in the office when her father was traveling, arrived up the corkscrew drive on her motorscooter with her terrier on board and knocked on our door at 8:00 this morning. We had a phone message, she told me. It was on her machine. The message came in early this morning. I took my coffee, which was the Tuscan coffee's mediocre equal, and went to the office. Francesca pressed some buttons on her cell phone, alternately muttering about cell phones retrieving voice mail and shrieking to her terrier who tore around the terrazza, "Viena qui;" vee-en-ah-KWEE, come here! We still referred to these phones as "car phones" at home. Here they were as common as wallets.

I had finished my coffee by the time Francesca handed me her phone. I heard beeping, blipping, and then I heard Annie's daughter Tina ask, Please could her mother phone her as soon as possible? I thanked Francesca, who ran outside yelling "Viena qui! Viena qui!" and quickly went to find Annie. It didn't sound like a "Hi mom!" call.

We phoned Tina, who lives in California. It would be around midnight there. I dialed, and handed Annie the phone. Tina answered immediately. She told Annie that Renee, Annie's sister, was going to be OK, but she had a heart attack and was going to have bypass surgery that day in New York City. Annie was overwhelmed. She mutely handed me the phone and sat down, her head in her hands. Tina repeated the news to me. I rotely wrote everything she said. I gave her our direct number. We phoned Christopher, Annie's oldest son, a practicing physician in Massachusetts, and left a message for him to call us. We sat quietly for a while, helpless.

"I think we should go to Assisi," I said to Annie. "By the time we get home, there might be news."

"St. Francis is Renee's favorite Saint," she said hopefully.

We would make a purposeful pilgrimage.

We arrived at the walled city within half an hour, before 10:00 a.m., but the parking garages were already full. Directly across the street from the main garage was a caffè. We didn't see a "Vietato Parcheggio" (no parking) sign, so I parked in front of the caffè.

We walked the short distance up to the Cathedral of St. Francis, or San Francesco, entering into the lower Cathedral. Construction of the lower building was begun in 1228, two years after St. Francis's death. The interior was dark. The only light was from candles. The candles flickered, casting eerie shapes on the low, vaulted ceilings. A mass was in progress. Two priests sang the liturgy. It was pure and heartfelt, the only sound in the Cathedral. Visitors sat on the pews, praying, or walked slowly through the lower Cathedral, silently respectful. Many priests glided soundlessly past us; black ghosts. It was very warm, in the sense that the human body is warm, and the human spirit is warm. It was a Holy place, a living church, not a museum. The devout assembled here to worship, not to sightsee. There were no tour guides, no knot of foreigners in front of Cimambue's Madonna with St. Francis, the portrait that has become known as the "real" St. Francis. It seemed natural that the famous portrait hung there, an organic part of this sacred place.

We held hands as we followed the stone steps that led down to the crypt of St. Francis. His simple stone casket sat on a plain stone support. An unadorned altar was in front of the crypt, that day flanked by two large vases of tall lilies that sweetly and strongly scented the warm air. The dim light came entirely from candles and was sufficient. We felt we were seeing and experiencing this place as the Franciscans who originally lay St. Francis to rest had. The crypt was dug out; rediscovered, in 1818, and opened to the public. For over 300 years, the tomb had been hidden. Annie and I sat on a pew near the altar and prayed, then held hands again.

After a while, we rose and went to the relic room, where St. Francis's robe was displayed in a large, glass case. Made of burlap, the robe had many patches, evenly stitched onto the garment. The neck was a simple slash in the burlap, not finished with a seam. The white robe he died in was also displayed, of less mean cloth, along with his sandals, a few religious relics, and a nasty-looking cat o' nine-tails device which, an Italian man explained to me, was used in self-flagellation. Oh.

We made our way up the excessively steep back stairs to the upper Basilica, wondering why the steps in the medieval towns are so arduous. Was it easier to hew fewer steps or was this punishment akin to the cat-'o nine tails? We couldn't climb one foot after another, but as children do, we proceeded by placing one foot onto one tall step, then the other foot onto the step, and so on.

The Basilica was built directly on top of the lower Cathedral, and completed in 1253 -- 23 years after the lower

Cathedral. But entering it from the lower Cathedral was like going from an ancient past to a modern penthouse. Brilliant sunlight filled the enormous, airy space. Perhaps a thousand tourists, maybe more, assembled into groups with their guides. Many of the guides were priests. The guides spoke German, Japanese, and Danish, and, though it was not dark, shone their flashlights from fresco to fresco, to highlight the details as they explained them. The languages bounced back and forth in the bright room, as noisily as the swallows in the trees. I wanted to clap my hands and make it stop. We stared at the magnificent dome, blinking like nocturnal animals.

When we became used to the sensory bombardment, we followed the Life of St. Francis frescoes by Giotto, a monumental piece of work. We had not seen so much art nor so many people convened in one place before. As the Germans would say, the experience was "aufgeputz," too much much. We decided we were not very good tourists, preferring small chapels and unvisited back streets to the en masse crush. As we left, we stopped to consider our feelings. What was wrong with us? We realized that our visit to the St. Francis Cathedral was a private one that we couldn't share with strangers. Another time, under different circumstances, we might feel differently.

We walked quietly for a while after leaving the Basilica. We stopped at a take-out pizza place because the smells were tantalizing. We each bought a piccola pizza and got a Coke from a machine. Down a few steps was a beautiful library with a partner's desk and a view of the valley below. We took our pizza and Coke and sat at the desk to eat. Nobody seemed to mind. There wasn't anybody there to mind. We didn't talk. We had found a private room for reflection.

Returning to the car from the opposite direction we left it, we noticed we had parked in front of the police station next to the caffè, not in front of the caffè. A large sign informed that parking there is strictly illegal. How had we missed this sign? We hadn't been ticketed. We gingerly walked past the police station, where several officers stood, quickly got into the car, and drove off, only to find that all the streets were one way, the wrong way. We drove in circles, finally returning to the same police officers to sheepishly inquire how to get out of town. I told them that I don't know anything because I am a foreigner. They laughed and directed us out of Assisi. Ignorance is bliss.

We drove to the pretty walled town of Trevi, up to the tippy top of the hill, then changed our minds about exploring the town and drove right back down and home to Spoleto. We were anxious to learn if there was any news. We spent most of the evening on the phone. From what Christopher said, Renee would be fine, but it was a close call. We determined that the surgery was taking place at the same time we were praying in Assisi.

We went to the outdoor ristorante at the top of our steps for our last ristorante dinner in Spoleto. We had disregarded the ristorante previously in favor of dining further "downtown," where we presumed the food would be better than at our neighborhood hang-out. The food was the best we had eaten on the trip. The waiter chose an excellent bottle of Rosso di Montefalco, the second Montefalco wine, a blend of 75% Sangiovese, with Trebbiano Toscano, Malvasia, Merlot, Barbera, and Montepulciano -- plus about 10% of the sensational Sagrantino. A truffled pasta, a light veal dish, and the wine were sublimely Spoleto.

Piera and her family strolled by the ristorante while we were eating. They planned to leave early in the morning. We waved at our friends, who came up to the restaurant to say good-bye. I asked Piera to leave her address under my door, and thanked her for her many kindnesses. She handed over Beppo for a good-bye kiss. Beppo and I had become rather close. I hugged him, smelling the good baby smell. We said good-bye to our friends. Soon afterwards, we heard thunder. We finished our wine, an easy chore, and headed down the steps to home.

An impressive rain storm started as we arrived, and continued all night.

I went to bed to read and warm up. The thunder drowned out even the church bells. Lightning painted and repainted the walls of my room. A cricket had come inside to weather the storm. He sat near my bed, keeping me company, chirping between thunder volleys; a small, sweet comfort.

The Performance

I was up early, beside myself, practically on the other side of the palace, with the excitement of seeing Crist tonight -- not just to hear her sing, but also to hear all about her experience with the opera company. I missed her very much. I threw open my bedroom shutters to see if the storm had changed anything substantially. I watched the sun artistically edge the black clouds on the horizon with a golden pink border. I saw it as a good sign. I made coffee, and poured it into a large bowl with milk, as we have only espresso cups. Is this how trends get started?

Over breakfast, Annie, Rolf, and I made The Plan for the evening. We decided to eat at home early and to leave by 7:15 p.m., so I wouldn't have to drive both ways to Montefranco in the dark. The drive would take about 15 minutes, and the performance wasn't until 9:15 p.m., meaning, probably, 9:45 p.m. Italian time. Meantime, we had a whole day to fill. Piera had left her address and written a reminder that we must see Spello. "More beautiful than Spoleto," she wrote. I asked Annie and Rolf if they wanted to pop over. Rolf was a No, but Annie said Yes. We both wanted the day to pass quickly.

Annie and I drove from our Spoleto palace, careered down the corkscrew driveway and over the moat and through the medieval wall, where we bumped into the "New Town" market. We had heard about it, but had no idea it was in our front yard. I parked. This market was completely different from the daily market in the Old Town and much larger. Vendor booths and tables and displays ran along the entire side of the town wall -- outside the wall -- for blocks -- as far as we could see.

The first objects we came upon were wire cases of baby turkeys, exotic, multi-colored adult chickens, paper boxes filled with fluffy ducklings and baby chickens, cages of doves, of finches, and of parakeets. Children crowded around as if it were a petting zoo, playing with the ducklings, clucking to the turquoise parakeets. This market was for people who lived in the countryside, the modern Contadini, the farmers. There was no produce, no Porchetta van, no food sold at all. The Contadini raised their own. The animals were not for tonight's dinner. They were livestock and pets. The vendor offered the appropriate feed for each, along with advice on the animals' care and feeding. The baby turkeys were selling like hot cakes.

There were stacks of handmade, embroidered linens, thousands of pairs of shoes, and many household goods. For the farmers, the market was like the Italian version of a living Sears & Roebuck catalogue. I bought a luncheon tablecloth and some fancy Ball Jar tops -- brass colored, with "Fruits of the Season," written on them in Italian, in script:

CAPSULA QUATTRO STAGIONI ("four seasons top")

PER CONSERVARE SOTTOVUOTO ("for vacuum-pack canning")

The pedestrian words reminded me of our family's original Italian conversations; impressive if you didn't know Italian. In the center of the "four seasons top" was a delightful etching of a beehive, a branch of ripe nectarines, a bunch of grapes, some flowers, a butterfly, and some bees. The tops cost under a dollar for eight, the tablecloth, embroidered with tiny red roses, was $3.00. Annie suggested, "Eight stocking-stuffers and a birthday gift?"

After shopping for over an hour and seeing only a small part of the market, we gave up on shopping all of it. We walked back to the car and drove on to Spello, a medieval hill town a half hour from Spoleto. Tuscany and Umbria are really a series of medieval hilltop towns connected by meandering roads. The towns crown the tops of the tallest hills, and each is more enchanting than the next. It was easy to imagine Rapunzel letting down her hair from one of the steep towers, to conceive of a palace where Sleeping Beauty lay hidden by a thicket of vines.

Henry James wrote excitedly that Venice was "an immense collective apartment." (Today he'd probably pass on commenting.)   The countryside here was the opposite, an eccentric collection of isolated castles.

We drove to the walls of Spello, parked at a lot outside, and entered the pristine, medieval town. How could so much beauty exist in this small country? The locals referred to Spello as the "Town of Flowers." Seemingly, all residents adorned the doors of their prim, stone houses with banks of flowers and suspended vivid flowering baskets from every window shutter. Each May, Spello had a Flower Festival. Using flower petals as their medium, artists created intricate designs -- l'infiorata -- that they "painted" down the middle of every single narrow, twisty, cobblestone street in Spello. I bought some picture postcards of the work, reminiscent of the flower artistry in the Grand Square in Brussels on Assumption Day. I would love to come back to see the Spello's Flower Festa.

The Spello shops were cosmopolitan, the shoppers were well-heeled Italians on Feria from Rome and Florence; city people of discriminating tastes with large bankrolls. The Red Guide recommended three hotels here, one appeared to be rather grand. A suite cost $120 a night. Spello would be a colorful base for exploring Assisi, Perugia, and for shopping at Deruta.

I bought a piece of majolica in one chic shop, a flat bowl painted with sunflowers, with an indentation in the center for olive oil. Dip the bread into the olive oil, wipe the excess on the broad rim, said the proprietor. Apparently, the people of Spello dipped bread into olive oil the way Californians do. The bottom of the piece read, "Fatto a mano, Gubbio." Gubbio was near Spoleto. So many places to see, so little time. The bowl was the most expensive piece of majolica that I bought.

I was getting farfalle; butterflies in my stomach about Crist's performance. We elected to go home and get ready for the evening. Christopher phoned to say that Renee was doing better, that we shouldn't worry. He said they debated about even telling us. I asked when we could talk to her. Tomorrow, he said, and gave me her direct number at the hospital. He said Robert was on his way to New York. We could reach him at Renee's house.

I took a long bath and then a shower while Annie made tuna salad. Both tasks were therapeutic. We dressed up, ate our sandwiches, and headed out. Again, the drive was fantastic, even more spectacular than we remembered from the first time. We arrived in time to watch the sun set over the hills, to hear the final cockadoodledoos of the day, and to hear the dogs tune up for the evening. We sat on a stone wall adjacent to where the performance would be held. The time didn't drag, it fairly flew, as the rich aromas of local dinners being cooked and of newly-cut hay came to our noses, and the hills changed shape and color as far as we could see. Tiny hilltop towns invisible in daylight now blinked into sight. From our perch on top of the world, I counted twinkles from seven towns.

At 9:00 p.m., the performers began to arrive. Crist was in the second wave. She looked beautiful. Her thick, dark hair curled over her shoulders. She wore a long, black, crinkly silk dress and a single strand of gold chain. Her light make-up emphasized her violet eyes, her perfect features, and her full, beautiful lips and amazingly even teeth. The orthodontist was worth every penny. When she smiled at us, she glowed. I gulped and say, "Hi!" as she swept past us.

At 9:10, we three went inside, the first members of the audience. We picked up programs from a wooden stand and sat down. I read my translation. At 9:20, Kate arrived, using a cane but looking very fit. With her was Prof.ssa (abbreviation for Professoressa) Mary Griffiths, Kate's original voice teacher in Scotland, who had come all this way to help Kate. Kate's husband had only driven the group to Montefranco. He returned to San Gim after dropping them off. Mary was the fourth woman in Kate's husband's car, the one I hadn't met at the car in San Jim. Annie and Rolf and I stood to speak to the two women. I asked Kate if the performance would be recorded, as she had originally told me. She said she had brought no equipment. There was no room in the car. That it was a shame but, No, the performance wouldn't be recorded.

Kate told me that the week had been "Splendid, dear," introduced us to Mary, then went off to organize. Mary said she wanted to take photos. Me, too. She asked if I would move up to a front row and sit with her. We moved forward and began to chat as soon as we sat down.

"Cristina is lovely, her voice is thrilling, she is wonderful," she confided in her beautiful Scottish inflection. She went on to say that the week had been difficult for Cristina because the other singers were Italian and didn't speak much English, and what's more, they had all been good friends at the Conservatory in Florence. They were a clique. However, she said, they all got along fine, and the Italians included Crist in their outings. They had cars. They went out at night. I drank in every word.

We laughed and jabbered and realized that the house had filled. Mary told me that the audience was composed mostly of Romans. The men and women looked to be between 30 and 40, slim, attractive, exquisitely dressed. Each component of their clothing and each accessory was beautiful and perfectly coordinated. From coif to sensational shoes and handbags, this was a first-night crowd. Mary confided that we had to wait for the Mayor. No performance in a small Italian town could begin without the Mayor first saying a few words.

Nine forty-five came and went. At 10:15 p.m, Kate stood and welcomed the audience. She explained, in Italian, what was in store. First the set of pieces from Shakespeare plays, then a set of Bellini, Rossini, and finally, Donizetti; it would be the latter's 200th birthday this month. She introduced the director, two piano accompanists, and a flautist. She sat down. The Mayor arrived, wearing a red blazer, just as the first accompanist began to play. The Mayor sat down.

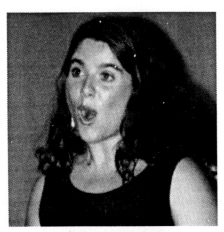

Who is Silvia?

There were two solos before Crist. They were very good, and the audience liked them. Then Crist sang "Who is Silvia." Her voice filled the room, went beyond the ceiling, and is still floating over the hills, I imagine. When she finished, the Roman audience thundered. I looked over my shoulder at Annie and Rolf, who looked stunned. Annie whispered, "They are clapping much more for Cristina!" And so the performance continued. There was an intermission, during which Mary said that Kate had asked her to produce the finale. It was the main reason for Mary's presence, she said. She hoped I would like it, adding with a huge smile and a hug, "Cristina loves it."

But first, Cristina sang a Bellini aria for the Romans. They roared their approval. I remembered back to San Gim, when Kate drilled Crist on her "t's" and "tt's," repeating, "The Italian '-t' is very different from the English, and very, very important, dear!"

When Mary's finale came, Cristina stood in the front row of the group, in the center. The others read from their music, holding large black folios. Cristina did not. She had learned all the music. She sang the finale solos. She looked out, smiling, her face shining, her teeth sparkling, her natural beauty excelling, her voice effortlessly gliding to the uppermost ranges with her new color. It was her night.

At the curtain, the audience insisted on more. "Bis! Bis!" (BEESS!) they shouted. I had to shout in Mary's ear to say that her finale was perfect, that it was the ideal ending to an extraordinary evening. She was thrilled, too. "Bis! Bis!" The audience continued. The group repeated the finale. Electricity ran through the room.

The company bowed through the final applause, again and again. Cristina looked more radiant than I had ever seen. The audience stood and cheered. A dozen Romans quickly shoved forward to surround Cristina. They talked to her all at once. They thought she was Italian. They crushed each other to get closer to her. She had a great career ahead, they agreed. "You touched my soul!" one man dramatized. I wished that the performance had been recorded. Maybe when we got home we could do a recording. But we couldn't record the crowd's enthusiasm and catch the electricity.

I could barely see Crist through the crowd and my tears. I watched her turn from person to person to shake hands. The Romans crushed closer. I saw her smile freeze. She was unprepared for such zeal. She looked scared. Kate broke through the crowd to rescue her. She placed herself between Crist and the fans. She quieted the crowd. She thanked them for coming. She explained that Crist was an American, from San Francisco.

"No, no, no!" they protested. She couldn't be an *American* and sing the Bellini just so! She is our new, Soprano Cecilia! The crowd pushed closer and resumed their high-pitched enthusiasm. Cristina slipped away from behind Kate. We made our way to her. She wanted to go home. A film of perspiration spread over her face. "Now?" she asked. It was one a.m.

She waved "ciao's" to the rest of the company, who stood stranded on the other side of the crowd. Kate squeezed through and made her way back to us again. I thanked her for the world. We said our good-byes, and Crist gave her the antique pin. We left the church quickly. Rolf and Crist went to get her bags while Annie and I got the car. When Cristina returned, people crowded around her again. The word "paparazzi" again popped into my head. Rolf got her into the car with us, and we sped away into the night.

We talked and laughed nonstop all the way home. The windows were open, the crickets were loud, the breeze was warm. The corkscrew driveway was not lighted. My excitement got us up it. Crist explored the palace. After a hard-earned successful performance, she was ready to unwind. She danced across the living room, dipping and whirling. She unpacked and took a bath in the great Roman tub. She had a glass of wine. Then I gave her the earrings. She was elated with the tiny, sparkling jewels. We shared my bedroom, and once settled in, around three in the morning, I told her about her grandmother. She had many questions, the last one being, "Can I talk to her tomorrow?" Yes.

Aaaah --- Arezzo

We pulled to the curb in front of our hotel in Arezzo. I took my eyeglass case containing my VISA card and money, and went to check that our reservations were secure. The manager nodded his head, said he'd be with me in a momento, and returned to his business with two male guests. When it was my turn, the manager handed over the keys to our rooms and asked if I wanted a private parking service. He said someone would come and get the car and park it in a locked garage. It would be very secure. It would cost £18.000.

I said, "Si, grazie." I told him we would bring the bags into the hotel first. As I went out the door, Annie walked in the door. I went to the car. Rolf was already taking the bags from the trunk. I asked Crist to stay with the bags inside the hotel and to watch them carefully. Rolf took the remaining bags inside and the three of them stayed there.

I had work to do at the car. We traveled with our majolica, my niece's silver bowl, the truffles, and other precious goods stowed in bags in the rack above the back seat. I planned to lock all of it in the trunk overnight. I needed both hands. I put my eyeglass case on the front seat of the car, along with my precious Red Guide and Michelin maps, and took the first bag of goods to the trunk. As I was stowing the bags under the open trunk, one of the men who had been asking questions at the front desk came over to me. He asked me, in accented English, "How does the parking work?" I stopped what I was doing and explained my understanding of what the manager had told me. He asked me to repeat what I said. I did.

He left. I finished putting all the bags in the trunk, closed it, and went through the car to see if we had left anything behind. Annie's bag of presents was on the floor of the front seat. I took it out, put it in the trunk, locked it, and went to the driver's side to retrieve my eyeglass case and the book and maps. My case was gone. Annie had probably picked it up, I hoped, though I pictured the two men at the desk staring at the case as I took out my VISA card and now thought that the man who had asked me the parking questions acted suspiciously. I scooped up the maps and book, locked the car, went inside, and asked if anyone had seen my eyeglass case. Annie and Rolf were getting into the elevator to go their room. They hadn't taken it or seen it. Crist stood guarding our bags. She hadn't seen it. They had all been in the hotel the entire time. I searched through everything, but couldn't find it. I clearly remembered leaving it on the seat. I told the manager that the car parking would have to wait, that my wallet had been stolen.

I asked him to phone the Carabinieri; the police. He said, No, I would have to go to the station to file a report. Why? I asked. He repeated: You must go to the station to file a report. He told me how to get there. Crist and I took our bags to our room. I asked her to lock the door, and told her where I was going and that I'd be back as soon as possible. I walked to the police station, several blocks away. I rang a bell and a policewoman buzzed me in. She asked to see my passport. I showed it to her. I explained what had happened. I had to explain in Italian. I did my best. I told her that I thought the two men in the hotel had taken my wallet. While one distracted me behind the open trunk which hid my view of the rest of the car, the other slipped my wallet from the car seat. The policewoman was helpful with the language and sympathetic to my situation.

She conferred with another officer. First he looked at my passport. Then he asked me if one man might have been a South American. I told him yes, or he may have been from the Middle East -- he was short, skinny, middle-aged, had a dark complexion, short black hair, a pock-marked face, heavy accent. The policeman told me that a South American theft ring was operating at the hotels. He asked what was in the wallet. As I told him: half a million lire, a Visa card, an ATM card, all my financial records, my solar calculator, and all my phone numbers, which included Renee's hospital number, I realized my loss. He told me to return to the hotel. Two officers would be there waiting to take my report. I asked if I could make a phone call to cancel my card. I planned to call Robert in New York to ask him to cancel it. "Later," they told me.

I walked back to the hotel. The policemen had driven there, and they were waiting for me at the front desk. I told them what happened, that I believed the two men who had robbed me might be guests at the hotel. The police asked the young man who attended the front desk where the manager was. Gone, he said. He wouldn't be back today. I suggested to the policemen that the hotel manager could be part of this ring. The Carabinieri said dismissively that I had to return to the police station right away to make a written report. Had they understood what I said?

I walked back to the station again, wondering if I was getting the run-around. The same policewoman gave me a form, written in Italian, and a pen, and said I could fill it out using the Xerox machine as a table. I did. I wrote out a description of the thief, of what happened, and my unsolicited appraisal of the situation. In English, of course. I gave it to the policewoman. I asked her if I could make a phone call to New York. She told me to wait. Many minutes later, she returned and asked me to fill out two more identical forms, using exactly the same words as I had on the first form. I could use the Xerox machine again as a table. I pondered whether I should point out the irony of copying these documents by hand on top of the Xerox machine. Why couldn't I use the Xerox machine as a Xerox machine? How do you say "use" in Italian? Would it be stealing to use the machine? I filled out the two forms by hand. I gave them to the policewoman, again asking if I could make a phone call to New York. She asked me to come with her.

She led me to a small, glassed-in room. Two other women sat in the room. They appeared to be street walkers, or worse. They wore tight, colorful clothing and pounds of make-up. Their hair was long and seemed to stand straight out from their heads. They were barefoot. I stared at them. They did not look at me. The policewoman told me I needed to wait for a translator to come and translate my statement into Italian. She left the room and locked the door. I idly wondered if the glass was bullet-proof. I sat as calmly as I could, gathering my thoughts. The hands on my watch moved slowly.

I decided it was useless to translate my statement. It was after 2:00 p.m. The thieves had three hours lead time at that point. If it was a professional ring, by now surely they would have maxed out my VISA card, pocketed the cash, disappeared, and covered their trail.

Crist had been sitting alone in our room for hours. Was she OK? Like a criminal in a TV program, I banged on the heavy glass. Bullet-proof for sure, I thought. I got the policewoman's attention. I shouted that my daughter was alone at the hotel, implying that she was a little girl. I had to leave, I yelled. I desperately hoped she could hear me and would understand what I was saying. The Italian tapes had not prepared me for this situation. I needed a new page in the Italian phrase book, perhaps the page after "At the Barber" entitled: "Locked up At the Police Station."

The policewoman frowned, but unlocked the door and led me to an office where two policemen sat behind a desk. I explained that I needed to use the phone to call New York and to leave. The two men examined my passport. One asked suspiciously why I wanted to call New York when my home was in San Francisco. I explained that my husband was in New

York. Clearly, they didn't believe me. After a long exchange in rapid Italian, the two officers finally said in unison, "Va bene." I could go. They looked relieved to be rid of me.

One officer gave me a copy of my statement, stamped with several official indicia. He signed it with a flourish, and told me to call the American Consulate in Milano as soon as I arrived there, to see if my possessions had been recovered. He also gravely advised me to give my testimony to my local U.S. police when I got home. I tried not to laugh as I imagined the reaction of our small town police if I were to present them with this strange document about a crime committed in an even smaller town in Italy. I asked the officers if there was a chance that the professional ring would be caught, and if so, what were the chances that my money and credit card would be returned? They shrugged their shoulders sheepishly, shuffled their feet, and looked at the floor. I saved the "testimony" for my scrapbook.

I again asked to make a phone call to New York, explaining as best I could that I would call collect. I said "AT & T" maybe five or six times, trying to explain about my phone credit card. They had no idea what I was talking about. I wrote "AT & T" on a card. They shrugged their shoulders. "I will pay," I said. An officer finally handed me the phone. I dialed the AT&T access code, thankful that I remembered it, and made a collect call to Renee's home in New York. It would be around seven in the morning, and Roberto would be there, I hoped, to answer the phone. He was. He was sleepy, but efficient. I asked about his mother. She was better. I skipped the details of my situation, asking only that he give me Renee's hospital phone number and cancel our VISA card.

I thanked the policemen. They smiled affably and said, "Buona giornata!" Have a good day. Have a good day yourselves, I replied. Back at the hotel, the desk clerk told me that Annie and Rolf had gone out to lunch. I went to our room. Crist sat on the bed, dutifully waiting for me in the small, stuffy room. She was fine, she said. So was I, I told her. I didn't bother her with the details of my ordeal, except to tell her that some money had been stolen.

We reviewed our finances. She had £80.000 cash. She had an ATM card with a thousand dollars in the account. I was embarrassed to be happy that she wasn't a big shopper. I had $700.00 in Traveler's Cheques and another $150.00 in American dollars stashed away in my shopping bag. I had another VISA card -- an emergency card that had never been used -- hidden in my suitcase. It was still there. We shoved her lire into our pockets, brushing off "The Incident." We decided to get something to eat. It was after 3:00 p.m. I left a note at the desk for Annie and Rolf, saying we'd meet them at the hotel for dinner around 7:00 p.m.

Crist and I headed out to follow the walk through Arezzo as described in the book, "Day Trips in Italy." These trips all started from a town's train station. Our hotel wasn't right at the train station, so we picked up the walk about a third of the way through the recommended route, beginning at the 13th century Church of San Domenico, around the corner from us. We were alone in the church, quite a contrast from Assisi. Our footsteps echoed. We had only to whisper to each other to be heard. We looked up to Cimambue's crucifix, as the book suggested. Suspended over the high altar, it appeared to hang in space. It was bigger than life. The strong afternoon sun sifted down, endowing the piece with a brilliant light that could only be described as Godly. We walked the length of the church, gaining confidence, beginning to speak in normal tones. I relaxed.

We headed off to the next stop on the tour, the Duomo, on deserted streets. A block later, we began to see clumps of identically dressed young people. Two blocks further, crowds of twin-dressed groups emerged from the side streets. One group wore turquoise robes, another white. Some wore matching jackets, some wore matching suits. They were Asians, French, Italians, dozens and dozens of young people speaking different languages, all heading toward the same locus, similar to a scene in a science fiction movie where brainwashed subjects are drawn to their leader. Ineluctably, we followed. They all entered an auditorium. I asked an official who stood at the door what was going on. It was the International Choral Competition, he explained. Nothing sinister at all. The groups would begin to sing at 4:30 p.m.; very soon. The competition would go for several hours. Crist and I thanked the man and grinned at each other at our luck. We'd be back.

Since all the caffès were closed, we doggedly -- and hungrily -- continued our walk to the Church of San Francesco. In the movie *The English Patient*, this is where Kip hoisted Hana on a rope with a torch, to see the Piero della Francesca frescoes. I loved the movie, and the scene has haunted me since I saw it. I presumed that the frescoes would not be lighted, so I had slipped a flashlight into my shopping bag. I wanted to play the rôle of Hana, to discover the frescoes bit by bit. When we arrived, the domed, frescoed alcove was lighted. As I was getting oriented, the lights went out. An elderly Italian woman who stood next to me fumbled with her change, then went to a machine to the left of the alcove, dropped in some coins, and the lights came back on. I was in two places at once -- behind the lens watching Hana hoisted, and being hoisted myself. Now that I knew the coin trick, we could look as long as we wished. It was not as romantic as the film.

When we had our fill, we continued to the Cathedral to see della Francesca's St. Mary Magdalen, a beauty as delicate and ethereal as Lippi's Assunzione. One chapel was set up for a wedding -- banks of red roses and white lilies adorned both sides of the altar. Bouquets of pouffy white netting decorated each pew. The bride and her family entered. We left discreetly through a side door, to give them privacy. The guests were assembling outside -- an urbane group in Italian couture. A car sped into the square where cars are not normally allowed. The assemblage crowded around the driver, laughing and joking. Leaving the engine running and the car door open, he got out, carrying the bridal bouquet, looking frantic. He dashed into the church, followed by laughter from the guests. We mused, Was he the groom or the florist?

We were tempted to sneak into the church to watch the wedding. But we were very hungry. We pressed on to the park above, a huge expanse of rolling, groomed lawns and important-looking, beautifully manicured parterres. The centerpiece was a giant, pristine, white marble tribute to Arezzo's favorite son, Petrarch. It was the loveliest public park we had seen in Italy. Families strolled the acres, couples smooched on park benches. We spied a gelato stand. We ordered double gelatis and sat on a bench to eat our icy lunch, and to count the well-dressed young couples wheeling their babies. (Nine.) The Italians understood the importance of good public spaces where they could gather informally. Every few blocks of each town offered a piazza or a park: a "buona parte;" a pleasant place to sit with your family and friends, to rest, to stroll, to have a drink of water.

A few blocks later, we happened on a square where a dozen men were setting up for a festa. Several workers unfolded rectangular tables and set them end to end, à la the communist parties. Others laid a smooth, wooden dance floor. A few musicians tuned up. One man counted out tickets and cash and put out a "Cassa" sign. It was the cashier's booth. Crist and I had the same delicious thought: Communists? In Arezzo? I asked the cashier what the scoop was. He said it was the church festa; dinner, music, dancing: £30,000 per person, how many tickets do you want? I asked if we could buy them later, unsure that the church festa would be as festive as the communists'.

"Certo," CHAIR-toh; sure, he answered.

We returned to the Piazza San Francesco. The auditorium was across the piazza from the church. The international choral competition was well underway. We sat on the church steps and listened. The early evening was warm. White umbrella tables filled the piazza. A few people sat sipping espresso and listening to the music. The late day doldrums sank in. We leaned back on the steps, eyes half-closed, sun on our faces, Bach in our ears. Ahh -- Arezzo.

I violated our rule about dining only outdoors, and made a rez at Buca di San Francesco, a 16th century palace just off our new, favorite Piazza. I figured we could make up for the infringement afterwards, by having dessert or coffee in the piazza itself at one of the umbrella'd tables. The Buca resembled a wine cellar; terra-cotta walls with rather low ceilings were punctuated by a series of arches and low, small domes. The walls were fantastically frescoed, the floor was slanty and covered with lumpy oriental carpets. The lighting was dim, monastic. The menu was the same as most other Tuscan ristoranti, porcini pasta, truffle pasta, etc. We ate well, and drank good Tuscan wine.

This was the last large summer weekend, the last Saturday of the Italian summer, the Italian equivalent of our Labor Day weekend. Monday, everyone would go back home and back to work. But on this last balmy evening the Italians were out en masse for the passeggiata, dressed in their best. The women gingerly stepped along the cobblestone streets in designer suits with short, tight skirts, on very high, almost triangular shaped heels or platforms. "This is like Times Square on New Year's!" exclaimed Annie.

The shops were as up-to-the-minute as the people. A kitchen shop window display was devoted to different types of cooking. One window showed only utensils for cooking and serving fish. Another displayed only pasta-cooking utensils. The pasta pot was over a meter in diameter, with a matching giant colander and serving implements. Nothing was for sale. It was merely a demonstration of the store's artistry. A wedding accessory shop specialized in intricate, hand made wedding favors. Baskets containing hundreds of fanciful favors were stacked on shelves, all of them already spoken for. We couldn't buy even one piece. Apparently, in Tuscany, as at home, autumn was a popular time for weddings. A typical favor was a small silk pouch containing either white, sugared almonds or potpourri, decorated with ingenious silk rose petals and dripping with lavish ribbons and lace.

To cap off the evening, we returned to the Piazza San Francesco and ordered some Strega served from an adjacent "Bar" that looked like a movie set of the quintessential Italian trattoria. I went inside and chose one of each kind of cookie that they offered, a heaping plate, a surprise for our party. Annie was delighted. Some officials set up a movie screen in the piazza. A sound man tinkered. The screen filled with the afternoon's choral competition. The sound carried for blocks. The choral groups arrived two and three people at a time to watch, and within half an hour, the Piazza's capacity had reached critical mass. We polished off our diverse dessert and strolled slowly back to the hotel. It was very late.

Pistolieros and Harlequins

I managed to get Renee on the phone from the phone booth in the hotel lobby the next morning. Crist spoke to her and said, "You sound just like you!" We could all hear Renee laughing. We each put in our thousand lire's worth and felt better. We then removed the majolica from the trunk and replaced it with our luggage and drove to the small town of Pistoia, the name derived from the Italian word for "pistol," about an hour and a half from Arezzo. We were minutes from Montecatini Terme, a short hop from Lucca, and 36 k. from Firenze, almost back home to San Gim.

We checked into Michelin's top rated hotel without incident. The group stayed together this time. The hotel was comfortable, but hardly luxurious, unless you counted a hairdryer in the bathroom and gated, on-site parking just outside the door. We did, thankful for both. Crist and I headed out. Mass was in session in most of the churches, so visiting them would have to wait. We walked to the Piazza del Duomo without seeing another person. We picked up some info at the Tourist Office on the way, seemingly the only door open on this Sunday. We sat on the Baptistery steps to map out a walk. The sign next to us informed us that the cats who live in Pistoia are protected by Pistoian law, but oddly enough, we never saw any cats in Pistoia. Perhaps the warning was too late. We went into the Baptistery. The circular baptismal font is the central site within. It didn't look as if it had been used since the time of pistol-slinging.

A middle aged British couple, also feeling the solitude of the town, engaged us in conversation. They had just come from two weeks in Naples. Last evening, they dined in Montecatini Terme, their first dinner in two weeks whose ingredients didn't include tomatoes and sausages. This was their first English conversation in many days. They had had a hard time of it. They told us the details of their car problems -- break-ins, vandalism, a final break-down. They had abandoned their car and were taking buses. How would they get back to England, I asked. They hadn't decided. They had arrived in Pistoia an hour ago. They didn't have a place to stay. They didn't have much money. They were rumpled and carried all their belongings in backpacks.

If a trip goes too smoothly, there's not much to talk about. Crist and I decided we wouldn't share the details of our robbery with them. We wished them luck and excused ourselves. We walked through the dreary town in the baking heat to a piazza and found the only caffè in town that was aperto. There were two tables outside. We took one. We sat under an umbrella and watched heat mirages appear and disappear all around us. We ordered some white wine and a slice of pizza. We downed the cold wine like water.

A group of young gypsy men filed past us, the only other souls within our view on the big piazza. They were skinny as skeletons and wore only skimpy lavender batik tights and sandals, no shirts; a troupe of troubadours reminiscent of down and out Picasso Harlequins. The forlorn gypsies sat in the shade to the side of the caffè passing a bottle of wine between them and smoking dissolutely. One of them suddenly stood and moved slowly into the sun. He had bruises on his chest and scars scattered over his back and arms. He carried a medieval toy: a faded pink plastic disk and two sticks connected by a string. The gypsy held the sticks in his hands. He tossed the disk into the air, caught it on the string that connected the sticks, and manipulated the disk in a series of tosses and catches. He spun the disk under his spindly legs, behind him, and tossed it high into the air again, catching it on the string each time.

His friends, who ignored their compadre, occasionally broke into drunken choruses of Italian songs. The entertainer worked hard. Sweat ran down the protruding bones of his hollow chest. When we left, I handed him £1.000, and asked his name. He smiled with his whole face, exposing a mouth of black stumps. "Bruno!" he roared. We guessed he was no older than Crist.

We saw "public gardens" on our tourist map, and thinking they might be as lovely as those in Arezzo, we walked through vacant streets to the park. The grass was yellow, and the entire area appeared to be the hang-out for poorly and only partially-dressed young men on Vespas. We returned to the hotel. I thought we should drive to Montecatini Terme for the afternoon. But a sad lethargy sank in. We sat on our beds, read, recapped Cristina's performance, made small talk, did nothing.

Crist and I went back out around 5:00 p.m., hoping that things had picked up. We were alone again. We visited the churches. I am not so spiritual that being alone in a cathedral would make my religious juices simmer. I thought it was creepy -- tombs, paintings and frescoes of the dead and dying, so many dispirited monuments to death and so few celebrating life and birth.

Pistoia appeared to be having a "Savonarola Slept Here" summer commemoration, or at least the Dominicans were. I gathered from reading the info on posters placed near various works of art in the Dominican churches that

Savonarola, who originally preached in San Gim, made a special pilgrimage to Pistoia around 1485, when France's Charles VIII marched on Italy -- some 500 years ago. The info came from the diary of the artist Paolo and was posted in front of a painting of Paolo's entitled "Christ on the Cross." I didn't understand the significance, except to link a famous name with a town for tourist purposes or maybe to demonstrate that the Dominican monks still believed that Savonarola was a Christ-like figure. It all happened so long ago.

Back at the hotel, I re-read the slim paragraph on Pistoia from the *Insight* Guide, wishing to heck I had my green Michelin Guides from the box. *"When dusk falls, the lamp-lit shadowy streets of Pistoia still have an authentic medieval atmosphere. Franciscan monks stride along in their brown habits and rope belts, and the stone slabs outside the shops are laid out with goods for sale just as they were in the Middle Ages."*

I phoned Annie's room and read her the paragraph. "Sounds good!" she enthused. I was starting to phone around for dinner reservations when we heard distant chanting. It became louder and closer. We went to our window and looked down at the street. The Pistoia soccer team and their fans were parading with a full police escort. They had been victorious. The team wore their colors tied to their right wrists, and waved them as they chanted their victory song, which sounded like "Pistoia über alles." Dozens of cars followed the paraders. Several of these warriors looked up to our window, cheered, raising their bannered arms high in a salute. We waved back. No wonder the town was deserted this afternoon. We dressed and hoped for a festive celebratory evening.

We must have had dinner somewhere, but I made no note of it, nor do I recall the experience. We walked for a time after dinner, searching for a victory celebration, but nothing was open. No goods were laid out. No Franciscan monks appeared. The town was deserted. We went to bed early. When I think "Pistoia," I see young, muscled men stripped to the waist, driving mopeds at high speeds -- pistolieros -- and their shadowy gypsy counterparts.

The Grand Spa and the Lucca Market

The hotels of the past nights blurred together. I looked for my toothbrush where I had put it in a previous hotel. I thought I had everything packed, then found clothing in a closet. Being on the road is hollow traveling. The hotel personnel are cordial, but not friendly. I felt the loss of no longer being an insider, of not having our own place. We were vagabonds, common tourists. I didn't feel crisp and clean any more, only rushed and wrinkled.

At breakfast, I shared with Annie and Rolf the description of Montecatini Terme that I found in the *Insight* Guide:

"Montecatini Terme is by far the most splendid of all spas, famed throughout Europe along with Marienbad or Baden-Baden, and frequented since the 18th century by the grand and leisured, from European royalty to Hollywood stars. It comprises whole avenues of huge spa buildings dispensing waters to drink and treatments from baths and inhalation to the famous mudbaths.

238

"The Leopoldina pavilion is the most magnificent, a baroque 1920's edifice of rose marble, with fountains gushing the healing waters and an orchestra playing. Glamorous women sip coffee and eat pastries served by formally attired waiters, and romantically pale Death in Venice types waft through the marble columns, glass in hand."

I found the description utterly irresistible. I asked if anyone minded a brief detour. "Andiamo!" Let's go! was the response. From the car, I saw a sign to Montecatini Terme almost immediately and took the road indicated. Within a few minutes, we were driving down the main street of Montecatini Terme. Sprawling, posh, pink hotels with large verandas, verdant lawns and lush gardens, beautiful shops, ristoranti, and bustling caffès lined the streets. Enormous, leafy trees filtered sunshine onto the broad promenades where a glamorous crowd made their way to their spa appointments -- a stunning contrast to dreary Pistoia.

I stopped at the "bigliette;" ticket office, to inquire about the Leopoldina Pavilion we had read about. The woman said we would need appointments for everything, and handed me several brochures. Treatments ranged from "Mud with needle baths" for £50.000, to a complete facial-body with mudpack for £100.000. There were 34 Treatment Offerings in the Leopoldina brochure, two "Crenorheo-therapy Treatments," plus a number of Drinking Water Cures, Fangotherapies, Inhalation Treatments, and Whirlpool Baths. The latter included an "underwater massage in the whirlpool." The woman told us that we couldn't get into any of the spas without first booking treatments.

I handed the brochures to Annie to review and asked if we should enroll in a brief treatment so we could get inside one of the spas. While she read and tried to pronounce "crenorheo," I drove around and found the pavilion that was pictured in the guide, the photo that looked like Cleopatra's bath in the movie *Cleopatra*, the one with Liz Taylor. It was the Tettucio Pavilion, not the Leopoldina. We parked the car and went to the Pavilion to have a look. A sign told us that we could pay an entrance fee of £10.000 each and stay as long as we liked. We liked. We paid our lire and I bought four plastic spa cups embossed with the Tettucio's logo for a couple dollars more. The cup booth also sold cut glass spa cups which later on I would wish I had bought instead. Later on, we wished we had bought more of everything everywhere.

We filled our plastic cups from a huge central marble fountain at the edge of a pool encircled by flowers. The water tasted salty, and it was warm. We sipped and strolled over to the Countess Borghese shop. This was where the exotic ads were shot. It was real. Beautiful shop girls offered samples of scents. We let them spray us.

The photo in the travel book did not compare to the Tettucio's true grandeur. A full orchestra in tuxedoes played Viennese waltzes. Sophisticates sat at tables sipping and listening. Unbelievably, all this was going on at 10:00 a.m. We wondered what the poor people were doing today. We wafted through the pavilion, sedately, like the others, gliding on floors of inlaid marble. The Tettucio was the movie set's movie set. The 30' ceilings were supported by mammoth pink marble columns. The experience was heady; similar to promenading on a ship -- the QE-2, first class deck.

We were royalty in a royal palace. Cristina said she felt like a princess. For sound effects, there was only the soft murmur of water and subdued conversation and a subtly sumptuous swishing of dresses. Fashionable men and women, singly and in couples, moved as romantic dancers through the gigantic pavilions. The air smelled of the soft perfumes drifting from Countess Borghese's shop mixed with complex scents worn by the expensively dressed nonchalants.

The orchestra played on one side of a marble floored pavilion half the size of a football field. On the other side of the pavilion were a half dozen magnificent white marble sinks, inlaid with what looked like jade. Each elaborate sink had four basins and two large, gold water dispensers, each with two spigots. This was Shirl Wagner times 10. The water ran constantly. The types of water dispensed were labeled. Some spigots were "caldo," hot. Men and women moved from the orchestra side of the pavilion to the sinks, to ever-so-slowly rinse their cups in the caldo, refill them with the spa water of their choice, and saunter on. Starting several feet above each sink were 12' x 12' paintings on tile, depicting spa-goers from Roman times, drinking and lounging. The more things change, the more they are the same.

We walked into the garden. A garden clock fashioned of flowers read:

1
Settembre
Lunedi

(September 1, Monday)

The flower clock was replanted daily. We walked on through the parterres and to the second pavilion of the Tettucio, where people stood at bars sipping coffees. We gaped at the fountains in this pavilion, strolled the gardens, then undulated back to the main Pavilion.

I hadn't brought my camera; what a mistake. I went to the Tettucio souvenir shop and chose some picture postcards to substitute for photos. They didn't sell the one-use cameras. The pictures couldn't capture the portentous proportions of the pavilion or the spectacular -- bordering on preposterous -- ambiance. Regrettably, we wouldn't take home photos of us four sophisticates "taking the waters." As I was paying for the cards, I glanced at the newspaper headlines. At most newsstands, the front page of each Italian paper is mounted on poster board, and placed out front of the stand. Today's newspapers all had the same headline:

La Principessa Diana e morta in Parigi

I looked in vain for a newspaper written in English, then whispered to the vendor, asking if the Italian paper actually said that Princess Diana was dead? Yes, he told me gravely, and gave me the details. I didn't understand all he said, but I gathered that there was a car crash in Parigi; Paris, and that it happened the day before. I told Annie and Rolf and Cristina, and we stood there quietly, staring at the central fountain. It was a princess's setting. It all seemed unreal. We agreed that we should leave. We walked for a while, looking for a newspaper printed in English. All newspapers in every language were sold out.

We walked a while longer in this lavish F. Scott Fitz-Palm Beach resort town, reading posters advertising dances that night and various luxurious entertainments and diversions. But our day was diminished. We returned to the car, without a plan. The first road sign I saw on the way out was to Lucca. I took the road without asking permission. It was only minutes away.

There are six gates into Lucca. Foremost, I wanted to see the Lucca Market, without having to walk a kilometer there and back. Annie wouldn't be up to it. We drove the perimeter, and found the gate that led to Piazza San Francesco, the gate that the Guide indicated was nearest the market. We arrived around 1:00 p.m., and meandered through the back streets, the medieval maze of residential neighborhoods.

Tempting aromas drifted to our noses. Preparations for lunch were underway. In the back alleys, we saw only locals riding their bikes or walking home for lunch; shopgirls, businessmen and businesswomen. Asking for directions, we found the famous Lucca market. At this late hour, the vendors were packing up, closing shop. I felt an urgency. After drinking all the spa water, we needed a bathroom. I asked a shopkeeper where there might be a rest room. She walked us down the street past a few shops, to the left side of the market, and pointed through an archway. We found the rest room, which was spotlessly clean, with "real toilets," but without toilet tissue. I went to the nearest Alimentari, bought a four-pack, and distributed the rolls. It's not a bad idea to carry a wad of tissue along on day trips. The Italian toilet tissue was as good the American.

The outdoor market, which sold fresh fruits and vegetables and flowers, was interior, entered through an archway from the street. Inside, the produce market was open to the sky. The market was about a city block square, rimmed by exterior specialty shops that opened both to the market and to the street. So when the central, interior produce market was closed, shoppers still had access to the shops on the street. The small specialty shops included poultry butchers, beef butchers, a cavallo butcher who sold only horsemeat; ground, steaks, chops, roasts. A putridly sweet smell came to us as we passed the open door.

There were cheese shops, delicatessens specializing in preserved meats and salamis, in olives and peppers in oil, eggplants, and artichokes in oil. Dozens of fragrant, whole prosciuttos hung from the salami shops' ceilings. The many rich smells mixed together. The sight of all the specialized foods was dizzying and we were hungry.

I stopped briefly at a coffee shop to buy an etto of "superiore" beans, the most expensive they had, at £24.000 ($13.00) a pound. It was a token present for Amy, who was house-and-cat-sitting for us. Amy was the manager of the deli "Ultra Lucca" at home. She wanted a souvenir that said "Lucca." I bought the coffee for the bag it came in, a fancy one with "Lucca" printed all over it.

Several shop windows displayed various Lucca olive oils, the extra-vergine first presses, "naturale," unfiltered. The date the oil was pressed was hand written on each bottle. The first press looked cloudy and tasted sharp and peppery on the back of the throat. The bottles were all too large to consider buying and carrying home. We walked on to Lucca's famous San Michele Church, squeezed into the space where the Roman forum once stood, and difficult to truly admire because the buildings surrounding it pressed close, and because it was immense. San Michele reminded me of the Spoleto Duomo, but it was much more elaborate, taller, and architecturally detailed. Four stories of arcades -- arches -- were supported by dozens of columns. Almost every column had its own unique carving. San Michele must have been cleaned recently, because it gleamed white as bone in the midday sun.

Being at San Michele was like being in Assisi again. Japanese tour groups clumped around their guides. An Austrian group's leader stridently and repeatedly told his followers to stay together, STAY TO-GE-THER! I wondered where he thought they could go in this small square. We side-stepped the groups, and walked down a tangent to the Puccini for lunch. In the square next to the ristorante sat a statue of Giacomo Puccini. He wore a suit and tie, fingered a cigarette in his right hand, casually rested his left ankle on his right knee. The sculpture was arresting, life-like. Sig. Puccini was a dead-ringer for the actor Donald Sutherland.

We sat on the terrazza at the Puccini, though the indoor restaurant was one of the most chic in Italy. The Italians were dining inside, and the tourists outside, similar to the Café Marly crowd in Paris. We had "seafood salads," which turned out to be large bowls heaped with steamed clams and mussels in a pungent tomato sauce that we dipped our bread into, stretching the salad into a soup course, too. We relaxed, enjoying being in Lucca, a town I thought we'd miss on this trip. The few hours spent there were among the most memorable and satisfying of our trip. We regretted not buying the olive oil.

As I jot this down, I understand the importance of making notes at the end of a day. I look back at previous notes and I am able to remember the details and the tastes and smells and textures and conversations and moods -- especially the smell of the horsemeat.

We walked with the locals away from the tourist area, back through the neighborhoods and to our car, asking directions only once from two attractive Lucchese, women on bicycles, wearing silver and amber jewelry that was almost identical to mine. The women were charming and beautiful. We chatted a while. I complimented their amber, they examined mine. When I told them I had bought mine at Sak's Fifth Avenue, they were delighted. They thought amber was an "Italian thing." I told them I thought it was an "American thing." The Italians we met were fascinated with Americans. These women hadn't met an American woman before. I had never met a Lucchese. We are all so much the same. I could easily imagine hopping on a bicycle and toodling off through the streets of Lucca to my apartamente.

Modena
MOE-de-nah

Our next adventure would be among the summer's most remarkable. We followed what appeared on the Michelin map to be the most direct route from Lucca to our next stop, Modena.

ASIDE: I interrupt myself to say that the squiggly green roads on the Michelin map are the slow, country roads. The squigglier they are, the slower you will drive, and the more hairpin turns you will make.

We took S66, then S12, an Alpine drive of switchbacks and blind, hairpin turns that tested all my driving skills and made me grateful for the experience I had under my belt driving our old Porsche 356 on the famous twists of California's coastal highway, U.S. 1. I wondered how many Americans had experience driving a stick shift car.

When we had been on the road for an hour, I thought we were almost to Modena. I relaxed and asked how the back seat passengers were doing. Crist thought the drive was "cool." Annie was asleep. My co-pilot Rolf was having a great time. He said it was the best scenery of the trip. Then we saw a sign: "Modena 110 k." My peak speed had been about 30 k. I was glad my passengers were enthusiastic. I decided to stop counting the "k's" and to enjoy the drive along with Crist and Rolf. It was a sleigh ride as long as I kept the reins tight.

We continued on, following signs for the "Abetone Pass." So far, we had seen no other cars on the road. "Not one," said Rolf, shaking his head. Visions of the Donner Party danced in my head, but I stayed calm. We came to the ski resort with the same name as the pass -- Abetone, elevation 4,660 feet. Abetone was a popular central Italian ski resort, and no wonder -- the runs were steep and the grouping of hotels looked exactly like a charming, Swiss village. We didn't stop. Nothing was open. We continued on up and through the pass.

We drove through pine forests, along steep cliffs that pitched to deep valleys and looked across to immense, green mountains rising above the valleys. No houses. No other cars. I couldn't sightsee. The road demanded all my attention. There were no straight-aways, only curves. When we reached the peak and began our descent, I began to feel like a mechanical man: clutch in, turn the corner, brake, shift up, turn the corner, brake, downshift, turn the wheel. At no point did I simply sit and drive.

Three hours later, the sun began to cower behind the mountains. It turned cold. I was driving slower and slower and working harder as the road became more and more challenging. After a total of four and half hours, we made a final series of sharp turns and came out on the flat, in farm country. A sign read, "Modena 2 k." The sun returned from the other side of the mountains.

My shoulders ached, my clutch foot was worn out. Probably the clutch was, too. We entered Modena at rush hour. Bicycles and motor bikes and people coming from work filled the streets. I missed the Red Guide's indicated turn to the hotel and we found ourselves in the center of town, at the Duomo. The sun shone brightly downtown. The air was hot. I woke up Annie. We rolled down our windows and wove in and out of laughing people, intermingled with bicycles, threaded between landmarks, cars and mopeds, enjoying the sights, the liveliness, the shops, the warmth, the wonderful crush of humanity at leisure on a level playing field in Pavarotti's home town.

I circled the square and then found our hotel easily. It was a couple blocks from the Doge Palace and seemed a cut above the last two hotels. I asked everyone to please wait in the car while I checked our rez. No problem. Annie and Rolf and Crist went inside. A bellman took our bags inside and up to our rooms while I parked the car in a secure, gated lot behind the hotel.

I had chosen the hotel because it was somewhat outside of "Centro." The Red Guide indicated many one-way streets in Modena and I was afraid I wouldn't be able to navigate them. Now that I had proved myself to be Master Driver of the World, I was sorry we were out of the mainstream. The hotel had no ristorante. The Red Guide showed the best restaurants across town. I began phoning around for a dinner rez, one ristorante after another. They were all booked. I looked through the free City Guide I picked up in the lobby and called their suggestions, which were alphabetized. I got a reservation for 8:00 at a place called Zelmira, across town, the last ristorante listed. I phoned Annie and Rolf's room to tell them the good news, and to suggest that we take a taxi. Yes. Good idea. They were extremely tired. I took a long shower. I felt fabulous, as if I had won a grueling singles tennis match.

We met in the lobby at 7:45, and the taxi arrived subito. The driver dropped us at the address I gave him and drove away. We walked back and forth, up and down the block, but couldn't find the ristorante known as Zelmira. The storefronts were dark. Nothing was open. There were no passers-by. We were equally far from our hotel and from Centro. We wouldn't be strolling the streets after dinner.

Crist spotted a small sign. "Zelmira!" she exclaimed. "The arrow points down this street. Viena qui!" We went down the street, half way down another, and into a courtyard. The ristorante owner waited at the entrance; a gate in a clipped privet hedge that trimmed the ristorante terrazza. She led us to a table. Roses and camellias and floating candles filled large, crystal bowls on a table heaped with platters of elegant antipasti.

Zelmira was full of attractive people who appeared to be locked in witty conversations. Laughter and rose scent washed through the ristorante. The owner showed us to the last available table. It was set with peach colored linens, a vase of roses, a bowl with flickering, floating candles. She brought our menus along with shrimp grilled on rosemary sticks, compliments of the chef; a promising beginning.

The aches of the day melted away. We each ordered an entrée that had a Balsamic component and shared yummy bites. Mine was a pasta dish, Rolf's a veal dish deglazed with Balsamic. We drank a dreamy bottle of Montalcino Rosso. We lingered over dolce and espresso. Fickle tourists that we were, we decided that this was our favorite ristorante of the entire Italian experience.

The owner obliged us by phoning a taxi to return us to our hotel. When we were back, I was at loose-ends. No terrazza to sit on, no veranda, piazza, passeggiata, Sambuca, biscotti, gelati. As I said the words out loud, Crist said, "Your Italian sounds great." This was high praise. I repeated the words again, with attitude. Si!

Wait 10 Minutes

I awoke early in Modena. Lying in bed, I watched the sun turn a dark gold building across the way into a pale yellow one in 10 minutes. Birds fluttered from the red tiled rooftops to the pale yellow building's chimney and back. I was going to miss this leisure of looking. Tomorrow we would leave for home. But we still had an unstructured day ahead. Anything could happen, I thought with excitement.

We packed and went downstairs for a simple Continental breakfast. Crist and Annie and I walked a couple blocks to the Ducal Palace, now the Military Academy. We hoped we could tour it. A young Italian officer was leaving as we were entering. He opened the door for us, saluted us, and smiled broadly at Crist. We asked him if we could walk through the Palace. He explained in clipped Oxford University English that one could tour the Accademia only on a Sunday. The Doge Palace was now an Italian officer's training school, he explained. He asked where we were from and we in turn asked him. He told us he was originally from Modena. His home was in the countryside outside town. He was anxious to return to his home. He didn't like living in the city, although now that it was fall, he said, Modena was better, less crowded. Seventeen days and six hours remained before he could return from his inscription. The officer was tall, handsome, aggressive, and smart. He bowed to us when he left.

We walked to Via Emilia, the great Modena shopping street. Gucci, Prada, MaxMara, Coach (yes, Coach) and other designers paraded their goods in the windows, but were "Chiuso" at that hour. Prices for all window components were neatly written on white cards near the outfits and accessories, as they are in most Italian shops. A typical window featured a mannequin wearing a dress, jacket, scarf, shoes, and carrying a bag. The small, printed cards informed the shopper of the price of each piece.

As the almost-officer had told us, fall is dead in Modena, and elsewhere in Umbria and Tuscany. We visited the Duomo, wandered some, and visited the public park behind the hotel. The park was populated by children not yet of school age, who rode the merry-go-round. We watched the Koi in the pond that rambles through the park. University students sat on mounds of grass, scribbling in their notebooks, their texts at their sides. The young men wore tailored, dark suits with trousers cut tight below the knees, a look that seemed to be the start of a trend. The thin young women who accompanied them wore long, flowery dresses and long, flowing hair. The students reminded me of the early 60's; the Beatles and their girls.

When we returned to the hotel, workmen were noisily hammering scaffolding in place all around the building. Another restoration was underway. Annie said the scaffolding covered her window. We sandwiched our bags into the car. We intended to drive the two or three k's to Maranella, to maybe see some Ferraris. As we left town, we became hopelessly locked in a colossal traffic jam. I saw a sign to Milano and without taking a vote, I got onto the Super Strada. We flew along, and around one o'clock, the sign to Parma beckoned. "Anyone for lunch in Parma?" I asked my prisoners.

When we got into town, I stopped at a curb to take a look at the Red Guide. It described numerous delightful Parman culinary opportunities. I drove to the area that looked nearest a recommended ristoranti in Centro, and we parked. We walked through the town. The lively medieval streets were lined with shops and gelato parlors. Near the Duomo, an alfresco ristorante invited us. We sat. The waiter had no menus. He said there was pasta and pizza and wine. We ordered the pasta and some house white.

The outdoor service was linked to a caffè, so after lunch I walked over to investigate. A long zinc bar ran up the right side of the ristorante. Local businessmen tailored by Saville Row stood drinking Campari, smoking cigars, and nibbling from small bowls of pistachios and olives. The menu was displayed in the back dining room via plates in a glass case -- arrangements of vitello tonnato, chicken scallops, pastas, salads, lovely slices of Parma ham.

None of these piatti was offered on the outdoor menu. I had already eaten some wonderful ziti tossed with succulent bits of eggplant, onion, and olive oil, but the display made me covetous. The locals dined inside, as usual. I returned to our table, ordered un cappuccino, and recommended the caffè tour to the group. When Rolf came back from taking a look, he was smiling and smoking a cigar.

We could have stayed in Parma for a few days. At the start of our trip, we had thought we'd have time to stay wherever we wanted for as long as we wished and to do whatever we wished in that time. I had been too optimistic, too ambitious, too greedy, too ignorant. Over our capp's, Crist reminded me that we had also talked about going back to Verona for a few days, and that we could always return to Italy another time.

After lunch, we went to a gelato shop. I asked for a cone with two kinds of gelati; pesca; peach, apparently pronouncing it correctly, and "frutte di bosco," forest fruits, the color of blackberries. The young woman behind the bar skillfully scooped and sculpted an exquisite rose with the gelati, fashioning the center with blackberry petals, filling it with petals of pale peach. Annie and Rolf and Crist each ordered two kinds, too. We walked a bit more, tasting and marveling at the beauty of our multi-colored and flavored rose treats and the grandness of Parma, living in the moment. Reluctantly, we decided to press on.

Leaving Parma, the signs to Milano were confusing, pointing in two directions. I pulled to the curb when I saw two motorcycle Carabinieri. I asked for directions to the Autostrada going to Milano. One officer walked to the car. He smiled agreeably and began to explain. Then he stopped talking, shook his head, and excused himself. He conferred with the other officer. After several minutes, the two of them shouted back at us and indicated that we should follow them. They pulled out in front of us.

"We have a police escort!" Rolf exclaimed, delighted.

The Carabinieri parted the traffic for us. When we came to red lights, one stopped the traffic and waved us on while the other led us through the intersection. We followed our escort over a circuitous route for several k's. When we reached the Autostrada, the two pulled to the side of the road, pointed to the on-ramp, and saluted as we passed them. We waved like maniacs, shouting "Grazie! Molto grazie!! Grazie mille!!!"

<u>ASIDE:</u> When the Italians point, they use their entire hand, never one finger. When they count, they begin with their thumbs. If you use your index finger to indicate "one," you will get two.

And so our final afternoon in Italy began. We felt good. We were ready to make our final passage. I got the loaded-down Fix It Again Tony up to 125 k and Rolf was calling me "Queen of the Road" and asking me, "What's next?" when a red Ferrari 540 shot past us. Soon a black Testarossa zoomed by. Then another red 540. Annie and Crist snapped to attention. Rolf laughed. We counted 10 Ferraris in a stretch of about 25 k's.

The car rental contract was clear that the gas tank had to be 3/4 full when we returned the car, so I pulled off the Autostrada to a Benzina. Three of the Ferraris that had passed us were also filling up. The owners, three slim, 20-something men with Armani model looks, dressed in jeans, Polo shirts and loafers, no socks, chatted with a beautiful young blonde woman who wore hip huggers and a short top, no shoes. The woman owned the red 540, the men's cars were two black Testarossas. Annie shrugged a "What did you expect?"

While I made the benzina arrangements, Rolf went over to take a closer look at the cars -- and the woman. He asked the young Italians if they were having a Ferrari rally. They laughed and answered in perfect English, "No, we're just buzzing up to Milano for a snack." Why not.

The Italians who speak English fluently have learned it in England, where their parents sent them to study during the summers. The combination of the British accent on an Italian palate neutralized the British accent, and the language came out more American than British. I paid for the gas, more expensive now that we were closer to Milano, and we said "ciao's" to our new hot rod friends. They soon passed us again. We all waved.

In the late afternoon, we arrived at our four star hotel near the Malpensa Airport for our last night in Italy. Sitting on our elevated terrazza overlooking the Lombardy countryside, Crist and I did our final sightseeing: a huge farm, now in ruins, lay in a fallow field. There was nothing else to see.

The hotel grounds were grand and manicured. There was a swimming pool -- we had planned to swim. But as we sat on the terrazza, the sky clouded over, and a few drops fell. The air quickly turned cold. The wind picked up. It felt more like football weather than summer vacation. We went indoors.

Crist and I shared what we were casually told was once Hitler's suite. To us, it was rather extravagant digs, with hand painted walls contrasting with furnishings that Philippe Stark might have designed. It gave us a chill to think that Hitler might have actually inhabited our rooms and it disturbed us more that the man who revealed this unwelcome information to us did so because he thought it would add a frisson -- a shiver -- that it would be a selling point.

Church bells rang, telling us it was 5:00 p.m.; 8:00 a.m. at home. Crist and I made several phone calls. We checked on Renee, who sounded good, and checked in with Roberto and Jensen, both of whom had stayed at this hotel before flying home.

Between sips of his breakfast coffee, which he didn't hesitate to tell me tasted exceptionally good, Roberto said he'd pick us up tomorrow at the airport in San Francisco. He gave me Jensen's new phone number at school. He said that San Francisco was in Indian summer. All my roses were all in blossom. Chablis, a Tea Rose the color of crème fraîche and the size of a dinner plate when it blossoms, which is rarely, was especially lovely. Chablis is my favorite rose, as a stray cat would be my favorite animal. He said he would bring Romeo home tonight when he got home from work. He said the cats were sleeping on his side of the bed and he'd be glad when they moved back over to my side. He sneezed. I couldn't think of a thing to say but thank you.

I phoned Jensen. She was studying for a quiz. She seemed surprised that I was still in Italy. After a few minutes, she locked into the conversation and advised me not to eat at the hotel, except for breakfast. "Great breakfast, mom, but for dinner, walk down the lane next to the hotel to the Osteria. It's really cool. Osteria? I can't believe I just said Os-tay-REE-ah. Seems like a year ago! Gotta go. Love you!"

Va bene, I guess, and ciao. I phoned to confirm our airline reservations. They told me that Crist and I had been upgraded to First Class for the trip home. Cool.

I phoned the Concierge to ask if he could arrange a rez at the Osteria for us, an early rez, if possible. He phoned back to say we could dine as early as seven-thirty if we wished. I asked him if we could have some clothing pressed and ready by eight in the morning. Si. Since we had the first class upgrade, we thought we should try to look the part. In fact, we looked more like Contadini than first class passengers. Our perfect July haircuts had grown out ragged. We were deeply tanned. We had gained a few cups of custard around our middles. I hadn't worn make-up during the day for weeks.

We showered and flipped on the TV while we dressed for dinner. The BBC broadcast all the intricacies of the aftermath of Diana's death and previewed the preparations for Saturday's funeral. A million people were expected. The Americans were concerned that the Princess would not have a State Funeral. We saw the footage of the smashed car for the first time. We began our jarring re-entry to the real world, to the commonplace and to the extraordinary legerdemain.

But first, our last supper. We walked through a mist, down the lane to the Osteria. The owner greeted us and seated us. He gave me the wine list. It was extensive, inexpensive, intensely interesting. I ordered a beautiful bottle of Barolo. The owner uncorked it, decanted it, and told us that for such a fine wine as this, he would prepare something special to accompany it.

Molto grazie. Crist requested a vegetarian dinner. He bowed solemnly and said, "Subito, Signorina."

The raw materials for our very special dinner were mainly horsemeat. After sharing Cristina's penne with tomato and basil sauce with her and surreptitiously shoving the meat on my plate onto Annie's and Rolf's, we ambled back to our rooms in light rain. Crist and I turned on the TV and watched part of *Return of the Jedi* , on the French station, in French. Though my French is normally fluent, it seemed the characters were speaking Esperanto. I had begun to think in Italian. Quel timing.

Homeward Bound

At 8:00 a.m., we squeezed into our freshly pressed, first class clothing, ate a first class breakfast, stuffed our stuff into the car, and departed. Malpensa airport was a 10 minute drive. Crist and I took Annie and Rolf and their luggage to their airline. I got them carts and when I was sure that all was secure with them, I drove to where we had picked up the rental car so long ago. The car had to be returned by 9:00 a.m., or we would be charged a per-hour rate that could amount to as much as another full day's rental. I found the rental car parking lots. Though it was early in the morning, 8:30, the lots were full. Signs showing the rental car companies' names were tacked to posts. I found AutoEurope, but I couldn't find a place to park. I didn't see an office or a shuttle bus. A man was getting out of a new Mercedes. I stopped the Fix it Again Tony, noting that it was filthy and shabby. I asked the well dressed man tentatively, in Italian, Please, sir, could you tell me how this parking thing works? He answered, "No parlo Italiano." I asked, "English?" Ya. He was German. He explained that you park the car, then take your rental car agreement into the main terminal, along with the keys. "Where do you get the shuttle bus?" There was no shuttle bus. "Taxi?" No taxi. You walk.

I drove back to the terminal and off-loaded Crist with our bags. She would wait at the curb while I took the car back to the lot. Annie and Rolf were nowhere in sight. I drove off, leaving

Crist standing alone with the bags amid the crowds. There were no parking spaces in the lot, nor any people. I parked behind two cars, locked up for the last time and without looking back, I ran to the main terminal. The woman at the information booth told me the rental car offices were in the next terminal over. I jogged there, and at two minutes to nine, I handed off the rental agreement and keys to the AutoEurope agent. She took the keys and paperwork and smiled, "Buon viaggio." Have a good trip. "E tutti?" That's all? I panted. "Si. Buona giornata." Have a nice day.

Crist was where I had left her. She was fine. The bags were fine. She was glad to see me. I was glad to see her. I was sweaty, wrinkled, disheveled. My hair hung in sticky shreds. I looked more like steerage than first class. Cristina was pristine. Perhaps I could pretend I was her maid. I got two luggage carts, free at Italian airports, and we loaded up. I realized that soon I'd have to come up with a dollar and two quarters to rent a cart in San Francisco.

Annie and Rolf's departure to New York was from the same area as ours. They were serenely sitting in the waiting area. We had two hours to kill before boarding. We all checked in and shopped the duty-free mall, a veritable village of stores with cheeses, salamis, wine and grappa, Gucci ties and scarves, Italian designer clothing, tailors to fit the clothes for you, perfumes, colognes, and Cuban cigars. I bought a bottle of Badia a Coltibuono olive oil and tucked it into my carry-on bag, which was already full. Annie's carry-on bag, which was my shopping bag from Castellina, held her cleverly concealed geranium cuttings and majolica. She couldn't squeeze in another thing. I had exactly enough Italian change left to buy Cristina a Coke. It cost the same at the airport machine as it did at the machines at home. We all said *arrivederci* and went to our airplanes, but we had already gone our separate ways.

Crist and I boarded. We sipped orange juice until take-off. As we rose into the Italian autumn sky, we shared a piece of American chewing gum that I had put in my carry-on bag two months and an age before. We quietly watched the peaks of the Alps poke holes through whipped cream skies.

So it was over. The planning, the learning, the packing, the organizing. How would my garden look? How was Romeo? Live in the moment, I scolded myself. Just a little while longer. And when you're home, festiva tarde, or you have learned nothing.

Crist and I didn't talk much. Mostly, we just dozed and smiled dazedly at each other. Her earrings sparkled. She sighed. I wondered what she was thinking.

Much later, she nudged me, indicating that I should look out the window. The serrated edges of the Rockies glowed orange-red in the sunset. I hadn't expected tangerine Rockies. I was dazzled.

In the semi darkness of dusk, I whispered hopefully, "Are you glad we went?" Without hesitating, she squeezed my hand and said softly, "It was the best." I could tell she was smiling.

Printed in the United States
1218600001B/94